Heroes

Heroes

What They Do & Why We Need Them

SCOTT T. ALLISON

GEORGE R. GOETHALS

OXFORD
UNIVERSITY PRESS
2011

OXFORD
UNIVERSITY PRESS

Oxford University Press, Inc., publishes works that further
Oxford University's objective of excellence
in research, scholarship, and education.

Oxford New York
Auckland   Cape Town   Dar es Salaam   Hong Kong   Karachi
Kuala Lumpur   Madrid   Melbourne   Mexico City   Nairobi
New Delhi   Shanghai   Taipei   Toronto

With offices in
Argentina   Austria   Brazil   Chile   Czech Republic   France   Greece
Guatemala   Hungary   Italy   Japan   Poland   Portugal   Singapore
South Korea   Switzerland   Thailand   Turkey   Ukraine   Vietnam

Copyright © 2011 by Oxford University Press, Inc.

Published by Oxford University Press, Inc.
198 Madison Avenue, New York, New York 10016

www.oup.com

Oxford is a registered trademark of Oxford University Press, Inc.

Library of Congress Cataloging-in-Publication Data

Allison, Scott T.
Heroes: what they do & why we need them / by Scott T. Allison and George R. Goethals.
p. cm.
Includes bibliographical references and index.
ISBN: 978-0-19-973974-5
1. Heroes. 2. Heroes in literature. 3. Courage. 4. Altruism. 5. Conduct of life.
I. Goethals, George R. II. Title.
BF575.C8.A45 2011
179'.9–dc22
2010009519

To Two Heroic Grandmothers

Claire Lawrence Bergvall
and
Priscilla Howes Goethals

Acknowledgements

When the two of us first contemplated tackling a book on heroes, we asked a number of colleagues: Is this a good idea? If so, where might be the best place to publish such a book? Two years later, we are looking at pages proofs. The project evolved very quickly. Along the way, we have benefitted greatly from the good advice of our fellow social psychologists, other professional colleagues, and from the support of key people at Oxford University Press. Just as important, our families and friends have been unfailing in their encouragement and counsel.

In the early going, several colleagues at the Jepson School of Leadership Studies helped shape our overall approach to heroism, and guided our thinking toward eventual publication. We are grateful to Joanne Ciulla, Don Forsyth, Doug Hicks, Crystal Hoyt, Terry Price, and Tom Wren. We have also benefitted from the wisdom of the faculty at Richmond's Department of Psychology: Catherine Bagwell, Jane Berry, Cindy Bukach, Jeni Burnette, Beth Crawford, Craig Kinsley, David Landy, Peter LeViness, and Andy Newcomb. We also wish to thank University of Richmond colleagues David Leary and Jack Mountcastle.

It is not really possible to convey how much we owe to Lori Handelman, our editor at Oxford. Lori's good sense, hard work, and unwavering support were crucial to the creation and completion of this book. We were sustained by her remarkable sense of humor. It was really needed at crucial moments. We are very grateful. We also thank Aaron van Dorn, Aravind Kannankara, and Rachel Mayer at OUP for their help in overseeing the marvelous transformation from manuscript to book.

Special thanks go to Sue DeMarsh and the support systems of Raquette Lake, New York. Tacker and Tricia LeCarpentier offered valuable support and advice. Thank you. Our children, Heather, Jefferson and Andrew have been wonderful sources of wisdom and goodwill. We thank you as well. Finally, our wives, Connie and Marion, have put up with us and loved us. They have both been heroic. Our warmest of thanks to them.

Contents

Heroes

Introduction

At the end of the movie *Casablanca*, one of Hollywood's most memorable love triangles is resolved. The setting is a fog-bound airport in North Africa during World War II. Quick decisions have to be made before Nazi villains arrive to arrest all three characters. The three are the leading man, Rick Blaine (played by the charismatic Humphrey Bogart), the love of his life, Ilsa Lund (portrayed luminously by Ingrid Bergman), and Ilsa's husband, the suave and heroic Victor Laszlo. We've learned that Rick and Ilsa had an affair in Paris at the beginning of the war, and that they had planned to escape together. Unknown to Rick, Ilsa had recently married Victor Laszlo, a courageous resistance leader, but she had been told that he had been killed in a German concentration camp. Just before she and Rick are to leave Paris, Ilsa learns that Laszlo is alive. Waiting in the rain for their departing train, a distraught Rick receives a hurried note: "I cannot go with you or ever see you again. You must not ask why. Just believe that I love you. Go, my darling, and God bless you. Ilsa." It is one of cinema's most wrenching moments.[1]

How do these three characters get to the final scene at the airport, fleeing from the Nazis? Early in the film, Rick and Ilsa encounter each other again, by accident. Not knowing that Rick is the owner, Ilsa and Victor walk into his nightclub in Casablanca. Ilsa and Rick tensely greet each other, and Victor soon learns that they had had a relationship while Ilsa believed that Victor was dead. As the plot unfolds, Ilsa decides to stay with Rick in Casablanca while Victor flies to the United States to continue his fight against the Nazis. However, at the critical moment, instead of telling Victor that Ilsa is not going with him, Rick tells Ilsa that she must. There is a lump in our throats as Rick explains: "Ilsa, I'm no good at being noble, but it doesn't take much to see that the problems of three little people don't amount to a hill of beans in this crazy world." With that, Rick sends the love of his life off with another man for the good of the cause that is bigger than he is. Victor welcomes Rick "back to the fight": "This time I know our side will win." Ilsa looks to both men for guidance. Both signal that she should go with Victor. She turns and says: "Goodbye, Rick. God bless you." Rick painfully deadpans: "You better hurry, or you'll miss that plane."

At this moment, Rick Blaine's character has finally met all the tests on our mental lists that define heroes. This book explores these mental lists and the ways people perceive men and women whose lives do or do not match them. Let's start by saying more about the film. Then we'll return to the lists. *Casablanca* won the Academy Award for Best Picture in 1942. It is always ranked at or near the top of any list of great movies. Made in the midst of World War II, its three main characters—Rick, Ilsa, and Victor—are caught in the web of Nazi domination in North Africa.

The film opens with the shooting of Nazi officials carrying two letters of transit allowing their holders to escape Casablanca and fly to America. The letters are of great value and of intense interest to two other characters, a German officer, Major Strasser, and the local French police chief, Captain Louis Renault. Louis bends to the power of the Nazis, but it is clear he doesn't really like them. He will work to help Major Strasser find the murderers who stole the letters, but without much vigor.

We soon encounter Rick Blaine. Rick runs a successful nightclub and is widely admired for his cool, quick wit, and his smooth, commanding presence. Louis envies his sex appeal. He describes Rick as "the kind of a man that, well, if I were a woman ... I should be in love with Rick." Louis also suspects that, somehow, the stolen letters have come into Rick's possession. He is right about that, but Rick keeps his own counsel.

At this point a beautiful woman, Ilsa, and the man escorting her, Victor, enter the night club. When Rick first sees Ilsa, he looks stunned. They greet each other awkwardly, but act correctly. Late that night, Rick complains, "Of all the gin joints in all the towns in all the world, she walks into mine." Shortly thereafter, Ilsa returns to the club and tries to explain to Rick why she jilted him in Paris. But he is drunk, quite rude, and won't listen.

The main dramatic tension of the film then turns on the fact that Rick has indeed acquired the stolen letters of transit, and that Victor and Ilsa need them to escape to America. They both plead for the letters, but Rick, still hurting from being deserted by Ilsa in Paris, won't let them go. As events unfold, Ilsa tells Rick that she has always been in love with him and can no longer live without him. She will stay with him in Casablanca if he helps Victor get to America. They agree on that plan. After several plot twists, Rick, Ilsa, and Victor end up at the airport where the plane for America is about to take off. That's when Rick explains to Ilsa that she is to go with Victor, so that she can support his resistance work. "The problems of three little people" are not as important as the Allies' struggle against totalitarianism.

The characters of Victor Laszlo and the Nazi Major Strasser are prototypes of the personalities we often encounter in studying heroes and villains. Victor is tall, good-looking, and virtuous in manner, appearance, and behavior. At one point, he has to explain to Rick that he is not carved from stone. Pleading on Ilsa's behalf, he asks Rick "as a favor to use the letters to take her away from Casablanca." Rick replies, "You love her that much?" and Victor explains, "Apparently you think of me only as the leader of a cause. Well, I am also a human being." The way Victor's character is portrayed, this needs saying, since his nearly saintly persona seems somewhat bloodless. In contrast to Victor's heroic character, fighting the good fight for the good cause, Major Strasser is the unequivocal villain. He is formal and precise, cold and calculating—an unapologetic and ruthless agent of the Third Reich.

Rick Blaine is much more complicated than either Victor or Major Strasser. He initially comes off as impressive and likeable, but distinctly nonheroic. As we will see throughout our exploration of heroism, one of the defining traits of heroes is that they put the common good, and we emphasize *good*, ahead of their personal concerns. And yet, early in the film, we hear Rick claim more than once, when he might have put himself out to help someone else, "I stick my neck out for nobody." We also see him behave callously toward a woman he's been dating. When she asks where he was the night before, he claims that was too long ago to remember. When she asks "Will I see you tonight?," he replies coldly "I never make plans that far ahead." And in a discussion of the war with Major Strasser and Louis, he says indifferently that he hasn't "the slightest idea" who will win. He claims to see both the Nazi perspective and Victor Laszlo's. He says that he has no particular sympathy for the efforts of Laszlo, "the fox," to escape: "I understand the point of view of the hound too." Then he excuses himself saying, "Gentlemen, your business is politics. Mine is running a saloon."

Yet, there is another side. Part of it is shrouded in mystery. Louis asks Rick why he can't go back to America: "Did you abscond with the church funds? Did you run off with a senator's wife? I'd like to think you killed a man. It's the romantic in me." Rick enigmatically replies, "It was a combination of all three." Later, Louis presses his questions, and states, "my dear Ricky, I suspect that under that cynical shell you're at heart a sentimentalist" and mentions that Rick smuggled guns to Ethiopia and fought against the fascists in Spain. We too suspect that Rick cares more than he admits. When we first see him, he is cold, but he refuses to let a German banker push his way into a card game:

"Your cash is good at the bar."

"What! Do you know who I am?"

"I do. You're lucky the bar's open to you."

It's obvious that a large part of Rick's harsh attitude results from having been deeply hurt when Ilsa abandoned him in Paris. In one scene, he recounts to Ilsa his feelings when he received the note saying that she couldn't leave with him. Ilsa says that she didn't count the days they had together in Paris. Rick replies: "Well, I did. Every one of them. Especially the last one. A wow finish. A guy standing on a station platform in the rain with a comical look on his face, because his insides had been kicked out." Ilsa pleads with Rick "to put your feelings aside for something more important." Rick responds: "I'm not fighting for anything anymore, except myself. I'm the only cause I'm interested in."

But shortly thereafter, the hurt is removed. Ilsa declares her love for Rick and her willingness to stay with him while Victor goes to

America. She seems overwhelmed with emotion and confusion and asks Rick "to think for both of us, for all of us." Of course, Rick does, and he surprisingly tells Ilsa at the end to join Victor. She can help Victor in the Allies' struggle, Rick says, but she can't help him. He will fight the Nazis on his own. Thus, the film concludes with the three principal characters—Victor, Ilsa, and Rick—planning to leave Casablanca, each in their own way to aid in the good fight.

HEROES AND VILLAINS

We noted that Humphrey Bogart's character in *Casablanca*, Rick Blaine, met the tests "on our mental lists that define heroes." One of the central ideas in this book is that human beings do have mental lists or models, or images, of heroes, and also of villains. In psychology, these mental models or images are called schemas or sometimes archetypes. The basic idea is that we have general images or conceptions of many kinds of people, including heroes. We also have mental images of dancers, politicians, shortstops and U.S. marines. And we have schemas or images of nonhuman entities such as cars, birds, and tables and even images of events, called scripts, such as what happens when we walk into a restaurant.[2] In a nutshell, this book is about these images. We try to tell the story of where our images of heroes, and also villains, come from, how they develop, and how they shape and are shaped by our perceptions of either real or fictional individuals whom we think of as heroes or villains.

More broadly, our book addresses two overarching questions. The first is, How do people perceive heroes and villains? What do such terms mean to perceivers? Are there general conceptions of heroism? If so, how do they differ from one person to another, or from one time or place to another? Our second question is, how does heroism happen? What are the paths that people take to become heroes, or villains? What are the capacities, traits, circumstances, decisions, and actions that lead individuals to behave heroically, or just take a pass? Why and when do people become villains? These are our central concerns.

Let's begin addressing them by noting how Rick Blaine illustrates several key aspects of common notions of heroism. Most important, perhaps, is the fact that Rick makes a moral choice. In the end, he decides to do the right thing. We sense that Rick has made moral choices in the past, and that he is a good man, but he seems calloused and unfeeling. He also declares himself to be selfish—"I'm the only cause I'm interested in"—and in some ways, we support his selfish wish for Ilsa and him to live together, happily ever after. But he sacrifices his completely understandable self-centered love interests for the moral good. Moral choices are typical of heroes. For example, U.S. President Lyndon Johnson, despite his Southern background, made what most people view as the moral choice, casting all of his enormous power and political savvy behind civil rights and voting rights legislation in the 1960s. Such choices are almost universally considered heroic. Fictional superheroes such as Wonder Woman and Spiderman are defined by doing the right thing. The opening of every episode of the 1950s television series *Superman* reminds us that he fought for "truth, justice, and the American way." (There was no doubt in viewers' mind that the American way was as moral as truth and justice.) So, Rick meets the common standard of making the moral choice.

But Rick, like many heroes, has more going for him than virtue. He is also highly competent and in complete control of himself and his environment. He is handsome, and attractive to both men and women. He is tough, clever, and successful. In one scene, Victor and Ilsa return to Rick's nightclub and ask for a table "as far away from Major Strasser as possible." Rick looks around saying, "Well, the geography may be a little difficult to arrange" but immediately snaps his fingers for the headwaiter and orders "Paul! Table thirty!" His command is seamless. In these ways, Rick fits common images of heroes as talented individuals who look good and do good. Many other heroes are also defined by competence, and generally by extremely high levels of skill or ability in an important domain. Real-life examples include Einstein in science, Tiger Woods and Michael Jordan in sports, and actress Meryl Streep. Other fictional examples include ballet dancer Billy Elliot and detective Sherlock Holmes. In mentioning individuals such as Meryl Streep and Billy Elliot, we underline the fact that some people are seen as heroes by large, broad audiences, while others are heroes to a much smaller group. For example, it has been clear from recent Academy Award ceremonies that Meryl Streep is a hero to most other movie actresses, but she may not be a hero to most moviegoers or to the general public.

As we will see, many heroes are also leaders. The relationship between leadership and heroism will be one of our overarching concerns. Sometimes heroes, and villains, intentionally exert leadership, and sometimes their examples are followed, whether they intend to lead or not. Rick Blaine is a leader on a small scale within his business, and also as he orchestrates Ilsa and Victor's airplane departure from Casablanca. When Ilsa asks him to think "for all of us," he takes command and makes things happen. Martin Luther King and Nelson Mandela are heroes to many precisely because of their exercise of leadership. Antarctic explorer Ernest Shackleton's rescue of the stranded crew of the ship *Endurance* provides a vivid example of heroic leadership. For many, former British Prime Minister Margaret Thatcher achieved hero status on the basis of her firm leadership during the Falklands War in 1982. In the novel *One Flew over the Cuckoo's Nest*, the protagonist Randle Patrick McMurphy is a hero by virtue of his uplifting leadership of mental patients on a locked hospital ward. In the chapters that follow, we will explore the multiple and complex relationships between heroism and leadership.

Many heroes are defined by doing the right thing at a critical moment even when their lives until that point have not been heroic. In *Casablanca*, Rick Blaine is not initially heroic. He has many characteristics of heroes, such as attractiveness and competence, but his actions in the early parts of the film are not entirely praiseworthy. As we have seen, it is hinted that while he may have behaved admirably on occasion, such as fighting for the virtuous underdogs in the Spanish civil war, he may also have killed someone or stolen money. Interestingly, Victor Laszlo argues that Rick is actually suppressing or denying his own virtuous tendencies. When Rick asks him whether what he is fighting for is really worth it, Victor tells Rick that he sounds "like a man who's trying to convince himself of something he doesn't believe in his heart" and "I wonder if you know that you're trying to escape from yourself and that you'll never succeed." When Rick takes heroic action at the end, our hopeful sense that he is fundamentally noble is confirmed, as are the varying hopes and expectations of Ilsa and Victor. The idea that nonheroic people often decide in the end to do good provides the theme of redemption that we explore fully in Chapter 3.

There are numerous other examples of individuals who surprisingly but gratifyingly act heroically at the decisive moment. McMurphy in *One Flew over the Cuckoo's Nest* decides to stay and fight the Big Nurse when he could easily have escaped in the climactic passage in the novel. The outlaw Ben Wade in Elmore Leonard's *3:10 to Yuma* spares the life of the sympathetic and law-abiding Dan Evans at the end of the story, and he shoots a more vicious villain to protect Evans. In both cases, the characters' decisions are heroic, and they represent a decisive commitment to act morally at a critical juncture.

In some cases, redemption is not a matter of a moral choice by an ethically questionable character but rather of a highly effective action by a person who hasn't previously been seen as being especially competent. A fictional example of redemption based on competence comes from the film *The Karate Kid*, where an overmatched young boy becomes a sympathetic martial arts champion. The recent U.S. President George W. Bush illustrates this sequence in a particularly interesting way. Polls show that Bush was not seen as especially competent, and certainly not charismatic, at either the beginning or end of his presidency. During the 2000 election campaign he was once described as looking like "a small mammal in distress."[3] He often seemed overwhelmed by the challenges and complexities of governing. And at the end of his term, in the fall of 2008, he seemed completely overmatched by impending economic collapse. He became president having lost the popular vote and left office with extremely low approval ratings. However, he was viewed as charismatic and heroic when he rose to the occasion and exercised what most people perceived as effective and even heroic leadership following the September 11 terrorist attacks in 2001. And his confidence and swagger were notable during the early stages of the war in Iraq. They reached a pinnacle when Bush landed on the deck of an aircraft carrier wearing a flight suit, with a huge Mission Accomplished banner prominently displayed for television in the background. In those early years of his presidency, his decisive leadership had redeemed him. But as his competence became increasingly doubtful, and his approval ratings fell, the flight suit moment became a target of Comedy Central's late night television humorists. Sometimes heroic action cements a person's image as a hero. In that case, the appraisal doesn't change. But heroes can also fall from popular grace.

In many instances, particularly compelling stories of heroism involve both moral choice and competence. This was true of Rick and also Victor Laszlo in *Casablanca*. Readers who know of Jimmy Dean Sausages sold at many supermarkets, particularly in the South, might not know that Dean also had a career as an actor, television variety show host, and country singer. In 1961, he had a number-one hit called "Big Bad John." The song tells the story of a large, somewhat mysterious man with a violent past. Early in the song we are told the following: "He stood six foot six and weighed two-forty five"; "Nobody knew where John called home" and "he didn't say much, kinda quiet and shy." And later: "Somebody said he came from New Orleans, where he got in a fight over a Cajun Queen, and a crashing blow from a big right hand sent a Louisiana man to the promised land." John and his fellow workers are miners. One day the mine caves in, but John uses his size and strength to hold up sagging timbers. The lyrics tell us "twenty men scrambled from a would-be grave and now there's only one left down there to save—Big John." Of course, the mine collapses, John is killed, and later a marble stand is placed in front of the now abandoned shaft: "At the bottom of this mine lies a big, big man, Big John." Typical of many hero narratives, John is impressive and skilled but uncommunicative and dangerous. But in the end he uses his capacity to save others. The song declares him a hero, and there's no quarrel with that assessment.[4]

Rick Blaine has many of the same qualities as Big Bad John. He had a mysterious and perhaps violent background, he is competent but distant, and he ultimately decides to help others at some sacrifice to himself. The qualities that Big John and Rick share put some of the essential features of heroism into focus.

As these examples suggest, many instances of heroism involve overcoming challenging obstacles. In Big John's case, the challenge is an external, physical one that calls on his competencies, in this instance his great strength. In the case of Ernest Shackleton and *Endurance*, the crew's struggle is against the elements. For Rick Blaine the challenge is an internal, psychological one. He has to put aside his pain and his anger at Ilsa for having deserted him in Paris, and then his long sought-after chance to have her love in his life. He has to shed his cynical protective armor in order to see the importance of the world's raging war and then contribute to that important struggle. He also has to overcome Major Strasser, but the bigger challenge is his own internal mix of pain and longing.

Examples of people overcoming obstacles heroically abound in actual human history and in fiction. Heroes from the military are frequently defined by overcoming long odds and winning important fights. In U.S. history, George Washington is a vivid example. His struggles, and those of his troops, against freezing weather, inadequate shelter and supplies, and a superior British army, enshrine Washington as a military hero. His actual fighting record wasn't very good, but he did what he had to do to win: keep the army together and avoid decisive defeat.[5] He persevered and eventually prevailed. World War II hero George Patton is an example of a bold and dashing military leader who fought extremely skillfully to win difficult, decisive battles. Patton is well known for having to overcome internal obstacles as well as the wartime enemy. His blunt, uncensored comments often caused political turmoil and nearly got him removed from command. But when it mattered most, he fought brilliantly and saved Allied armies.[6] In a different domain, pilot Amelia Earhart overcame daunting obstacles to achieve record-breaking success. She became the first woman to win the Distinguished Flying Cross, and she became a much-admired hero in her time. In Great Britain, Prime Minister Winston Churchill became an invincible charismatic hero by rallying the English people to battle Adolph Hitler.

In fiction, the Greek mythic war hero Odysseus was acclaimed for overcoming numerous obstacles on his return from Troy to his home in Ithaca. He attained such heroic status that long and difficult journeys are now called odysseys, in recognition of Odysseus' adventures. For many fictional heroes, and some real-life ones as well, obstacles come in the form of villains. Superman battles Lex Luthor while Batman battles The Joker, and so forth. In the Sherlock Holmes stories, the arch villain is Professor Moriarty. Holmes tells Dr. Watson that Moriarty is "the Napoleon of crime," and in one story he apparently kills Holmes.

Overcoming obstacles creates surprisingly different heroes. Some heroes—some real and some fictional—are not even human. The underdog racehorse Seabiscuit won the hearts of millions during the depression, beating the Triple Crown winner War Admiral by four lengths in an epic 1938 match race. A beloved animal hero, Seabiscuit's story naturally became grist for the film industry. A highly successful 2003 movie featuring actor Toby McGuire was a huge hit. The child's tale *The Little Engine That Could* shows that even inanimate objects, endowed with admirable human qualities, can become heroes. The train's mantra—"I think I can, I think I can"—defines one of the most enduring qualities of the lone hero, the uncompromising struggle against difficult obstacles when others refuse to help.[7]

Hero status is often achieved by making a great personal sacrifice for a cause. We saw that with Rick Blaine, giving up his long lost and newly found love. The boxer Muhammad Ali gave up the best years of his career, and risked going to jail, to fight for his political and religious beliefs. In the end, he didn't serve time because the Supreme Court of the United States ruled unanimously in his favor in his Conscientious Objector claim. Other people are not so lucky. They give their lives for their cause. While they are unfortunate in life, they achieve heroic immortality that honors them in death. Many soldiers who die in battle are given awards for heroism posthumously. During the Civil War, Stonewall Jackson's heroic stature was only enhanced when he died from friendly fire after the battle of Chancellorsville. No one knows exactly what happened to Amelia Earhart. It is presumed that her aircraft crashed in an attempt to reach the air base at Howland Island during her flight around the globe. Both her death and the mysteries surrounding it fixed her reputation as a hero.

Two assassinated U.S. Presidents provide vivid examples of death cementing, and preserving, heroic status. Both Abraham Lincoln and John F. Kennedy achieved almost immediate recognition as heroes after their murders. Kennedy's case is particularly interesting. He served less than 3 years, and his record of accomplishment was mixed. But his wife Jacqueline's comment that his presidency was reminiscent of the mythical kingdom of Camelot crystallized a heroic myth that endures nearly 50 years after his death. Distinguished scholar Samuel Eliot Morison published his classic *Oxford History of the*

American People just 2 years after Kennedy's assassination. The book ends with moving lyrics from the musical *Camelot*.[8] In 2009, a C-SPAN survey of historians ranked Kennedy as the sixth greatest president. We'll see later that his assassination still plays a crucial role in his place in history. Although examples of real-life dead heroes abound, there are fewer fictional ones. True, some do die at the end. Herman Melville's Billy Budd, "the handsome sailor," is one example. Another is Larry McMurtry's cowboy icon Augustus McCrae from *Lonesome Dove*. But fiction more often provides happy endings. Handsome heroes live happily ever after with beautiful women.

There is one further aspect of heroism that we will see throughout our study. In *Casablanca*, Rick and Louis enjoy a friendship that is often seen in hero narratives. The main protagonist or hero frequently has what we can call a buddy or sidekick aiding in his or her heroic efforts. Heroes sometimes seem too good to be true—a little wooden and perhaps overly idealistic—and sidekicks provide doses of hard-nosed pragmatism, common sense, and comic relief. *Don Quixote*, sometimes thought of as the first novel in the Western tradition, offers the squat, hapless Sancho Panza. He takes on the role of squire, striving humorously but vainly to cue the knight errant Don Quixote toward seeing windmills, for example, for what they are. More recent fictional sidekicks include the Lone Ranger's "faithful Indian companion Tonto," Robin in the Batman comics, and Barbara Havers in Elizabeth George's Inspector Lynley mystery novels. They all help and humanize their heroes. There are sidekick examples from real life, although they might better be described as collaborative relationships. Sometimes in the middle of the night Abraham Lincoln would wake up his young secretary, John Hay (later Secretary of State), to try out ideas, express anxieties, or often just relate barnyard-type jokes and stories. The president generally found these yarns more amusing than his young aid. But it helped Lincoln to tell them. Heavyweight boxing champ Muhammad Ali, regarded as a hero all over the world both for his athletic skill and his commitment to political, social, and religious justice, relied on Bundini Brown, a member of his training entourage. Brown laughed, released tension, and offered Ali cogent advice on matters inside and outside the ring.

In the Casablanca story, while Rick and Louis have a congenial relationship, for most of the film they are independent agents who deal with each other in a good-natured but business-like fashion. At one point Rick derails one of Louis' attempts to extract sexual favors from a young bride who needs money to escape to America. He rigs the roulette game so that the woman's husband can win the needed funds at the gambling table. Louis cheerfully accepts being checked on this occasion but makes clear that he expects Rick to stop interfering: "Well, I forgive you this time. But I'll be in tomorrow night with a breathtaking blonde, and it will make me very happy if she loses." Similarly, Louis has no hesitation in obeying Major Strasser's command to close down Rick's nightclub in the wake of a spontaneous anti-Nazi demonstration, led by Victor Laszlo. Rick asks: "How can you close me up? On what grounds?" In one of the film's most appealing scenes, Louis exclaims, "I'm shocked, shocked to find that gambling is going on in here." Just then Rick's croupier walks by and hands Louis a roll of bills, saying, "Your winnings, sir." Without being embarrassed in the slightest by his patent hypocrisy, Louis offhandedly replies, "Oh. Thank you very much."

At the end of the film, however, after Rick makes the pivotal decision to send Ilsa away with Victor, Louis makes his own pivotal decision. Endangering himself, he diverts the police officers trying to find Rick. Thus, both Rick and Louis decide to forgo personal advantage and to put themselves at considerable risk, in order to collaborate in the struggle against the Third Reich. Louis comments, "Well, Rick, you're not only a sentimentalist, but you've become a patriot." Rick says, "It seemed like a good place to start" and Louis agrees, "I think perhaps you're right." At this point the typical sidekick relationship comes into focus, as both characters acknowledge "the beginning of a beautiful friendship."

When we explore the many facets of heroism, we often see that our heroes are defined in relation to villains. The drama of *Casablanca* requires the evil Major Strasser. It's chilling when he tells Ilsa that while it is not safe for Victor to leave Casablanca, it is also not safe for him to stay. He makes the likely resolution clear: "My dear Mademoiselle, perhaps you have already observed that in Casablanca, human life is cheap." Our story is as much about the defining characteristics of villains as the nature of heroism. Beginning with Major Strasser, what are some of the central elements? Perhaps the clearest is that villains represent evil. They fight for selfish, immoral interests. Jealousy or envy is one motive that drives evil. In Grimm's classic *Snow White*, jealousy is the reason the queen wants to kill her young stepdaughter. When the queen implores, "Mirror, mirror on the wall, who is fairest of them all," she gets the wrong answer. As a result, she tries repeatedly to kill Snow White. In Shakespeare's *Othello* the villain Iago, himself driven by envy, takes advantage of Othello's vulnerability to jealousy to manipulate him into killing Desdemona. Power is another powerful motive leading to evil behavior. Major Strasser, a proxy for Hitler, wants power. He asks Rick: "Can you imagine us in New York?" The desire for power impels a number of Shakespearean characters, including Macbeth, and the king Claudius in *Hamlet*. Russian dictator Stalin and Cambodian despot Pol Pot are twentieth-century figures widely regarded as villains for their ruthless, power-hungry, and murderous rule.

And of course plain old greed, one of the seven deadly sins along with envy, is a frequent source of villainy. Many of us are brought up learning that money is the root of all evil. One novelty song from the early days of rock 'n roll provides a perfect narrative of greed producing villainy. The Coasters sing of Salty Sam repeatedly threatening Sweet Sue, "if you don't give me the deed to your ranch." Sam tries to cut her in half, blow her to bits with dynamite, and throw her on the railroad tracks. In each case he ties her up and leaves her to her fate. But of course all three times the song's hero saves the day: "and then along came Jones."[9]

It's worth noting that the evil of many fictional villains needs no explanation. We are all aware that evil exists, and so it isn't surprising that some villains don't seem to have any particular motive for turning to the dark side. The villain Jack Belmont in the novel *The Hot Kid* robs and kills for no apparent reason, except to become the FBI's Public Enemy Number One. Why Jack thinks that way is unfathomable, but it's seldom hard to believe that some individuals do.

Villains are the antithesis to heroes in terms of morality, but they are similar to heroes in their talent and competence. Iago, for example, is a master of manipulation. In John Milton's epic poem *Paradise Lost*, Satan is a master of rhetoric, both in organizing his partners to oppose God, and in tempting Adam and Eve. Professor Moriarty nearly matches Sherlock Holmes' brilliance. In real life, villains from Hitler to Bernie Madoff of 2009's ruinous Ponzi schemes are consequential because of their talent and their capacity to wreak havoc of one kind or another. Our consideration of villains will illustrate a range of evil inclinations and a spectrum of talents toward realizing them.

In contrasting heroes and villains we quickly see that there is often a fine line between them.[10] And this is true in two important ways. First, in many cases whether an individual ultimately acts for good or evil is by no means certain. In *Casablanca*, Rick ultimately does the right thing. But that outcome isn't obvious. At one point it seems that Rick plans to take Ilsa to America and abandon Victor Laszlo to the Nazis. And his friend Louis is only to happy to arrest Victor and gain credit with Major Strasser for detaining him. So when Louis ultimately protects Rick we are pleasantly, but not totally, surprised. In the Peter Jackson films based on Tolkein's *Lord of the Rings* trilogy, Frodo nearly succumbs to the temptations of evil in the climactic scene. The New Testament of the Bible likewise tells of the evil temptations that Jesus had to resist.

Many historical figures ultimately opted for good late in their careers. German industrialist Oskar Schindler, immortalized in the Stephen Spielberg film *Schindler's List*, only began to protect Jewish workers from certain death after years of exploiting their labor. President Lyndon Johnson's famous "We Shall Overcome" speech on behalf of the 1965 voting rights bill was the culmination of a long political odyssey from young racist to mature defender of African American aspirations and basic human decency. But individuals also get turned the other way. Adolph Hitler may not have become the monster he was had he not been frustrated in his early career as an artist. American traitor Benedict Arnold might not have betrayed the American colonies in their fight for independence had he not been consumed by greed and envy.

There is a fine line between heroes and villains in another sense. Some people's actions often represent combinations of good and bad, not just unalloyed virtue or vice. Leadership scholar Barbara Kellerman in her book *Bad Leadership* paints U.S. President Bill Clinton as a villain for not intervening in the Rwanda genocide of 1994.[11] There's no way Clinton's actions, or nonactions, can be described as heroic. But they did reflect his conscientious judgment about what the United States and the United Nations could usefully do at that time. Clint Eastwood's antagonist in his 2008 film *Gran Torino* is heroic, but just barely. His character ultimately does the right thing, but the usual toxic elements of Eastwood cynicism and violence find their way into the mix.

There is a fine line also in that who is a hero and who is a villain is in the eye of the beholder. There's no better example than Islamist militant Osama bin Laden. He is the ultimate villain to most Americans of the twenty-first century. Yet he is a hero to those who cast their lot with Al Qaeda. Some U.S. Presidents are seen as both heroes or villains, depending on who you ask and when you ask. Andrew Jackson is seen as a hero to many who applaud his efforts to elevate the common man. But he is vilified by just as many for his Indian removal policies. Early in the twentieth century, historical consensus defined President Ulysses S. Grant as a villain for fostering Reconstruction in the South after the Civil War. Later he was seen as a villain, but somewhat less so, for not pushing hard enough. Now many historians think he got it just about right. Of course, that appraisal may change, too.

In short, what makes heroes and villains, and what makes us perceive various people as heroes and villains, is enormously complex. Their stories form the basis for our study of heroism and villainy. Next we preview our plan to explore those stories.

THE ORGANIZATION OF THIS BOOK

What follows are six chapters exploring the issues touched on earlier and a concluding discussion of our findings from the research pertaining to those questions. We begin each chapter with a case study that illuminates its central themes, and we discuss where pertinent the relevant scholarship. Please note that the first letters in the title of each of the six chapters are, in order, H-E-R-O-E-S. That is, heroes. We hope this arrangement helps readers track and remember our central themes.

Chapter 1 is called, simply, Heroes. It considers who heroes are and what they do. We will see that people identify numerous heroes and numerous kinds of heroes, and that each kind presents a compelling array of personal qualities. We try to isolate the most important variables that differentiate the many kinds of heroes. Our opening case for this chapter is the Polish woman Irena Sendler, a relative unknown. We bet that our readers will admire her tremendously as we relate her story.

Chapter 2 is called Exemplars, and it considers how human beings think and feel about heroes. We begin with the fascinating fictional character Randle Patrick McMurphy from Ken Kesey's *One Flew over the Cuckoo's Nest.* Our goal in this chapter is to explore the basic human thought processes, as understood through research on social cognition, that guide our perceptions of heroes, and also villains. One of the most intriguing questions is whether a human collective unconscious provides us with inborn latent images of heroes and villains, images that are activated when we encounter people who seem to fit them.

Chapter 3 is called Redemption. It considers Princess Diana's transformation from an attractive but lightly regarded young woman into one of the most frequently mentioned heroes of modern times. We'll also explore Abraham Lincoln's struggle with issues of emancipation and abolition, and how he has become perhaps the ultimate American hero for the decisive steps he took to free slaves. Lincoln's struggle was not a simple one. But we'll see that many other heroes, Martin Luther King Jr., for example, also struggled mightily before ultimately deciding to commit themselves fully to doing the right thing.

Chapter 4 is called Obstacles. We noted earlier that heroes frequently have to overcome one kind of obstacle or another. We explore Babe Zaharias's struggle to overcome gender prejudices and establish her credibility as an athlete in a range of male-dominated sports. We'll consider the research that shows how difficult it can be for people to do the right thing, especially in the face of common social pressures that would lead them in a different direction. We'll also see how ready people are to admire those who struggle to do good.

Chapter 5 is called Evil. Here we explore both how people become villains and how we perceive villains. We open with the character of

Brutus from *Julius Caesar*. In many ways, he is Shakespeare's most complex villain. Marc Antony turns an angry crowd against Brutus but finally calls him the "noblest Roman of them all." And Hitler figures prominently in this discussion. Both their examples, and many more, alert us to how resourcefully human beings can rationalize or justify evil behavior.

Chapter 6 is called Shaping. We consider how heroes and villains, both real and fictional, shape our lives, and also how complex life events shape them. We focus particularly on the role that heroes, but also villains, play as leaders. How do they move us, their followers, toward good or evil?

Finally, in our Conclusion, we hope to pull together in a clear and coherent fashion, the central implications of our study. We hope you enjoy the ride.

1

HEROES

Who They Are and
What They Do

The task facing Irena Sendler was gut wrenching and yet, in her mind, it was absolutely necessary. She wasn't even sure how to go about it. How do you ask parents to give up their children? Sendler knew that these children would die at the hands of the Nazis if they stayed in their homes. She knew that the parents knew it, too, but that didn't matter. Most parents would be very reluctant to hand their children over to a complete stranger, especially one who could make no promises. Giving the children up meant the very real possibility of never seeing them again.

Sendler began knocking on the doors of the crammed residences of the Warsaw Jewish Ghetto. It was 1942 and these people, hundreds of thousands of them, were doomed to be shipped to the death camps. Sendler introduced herself to parents and described her plan. She would take the children, give them new Christian identities, and place them in the homes of Polish citizens outside the ghetto who were willing to risk their own lives to harbor the Jews. "Can you guarantee they will live?'" distraught parents asked her. Sendler could only guarantee they would die if they stayed. "When will we see them again?" they inquired. Sender again made no promises. Possibly never again. But she did give them a code name and promised to try to reunite the families if the war should end favorably.

Who was Irena Sendler?[1] And what inspired her to help save the lives of complete strangers during World War II? Born in Otwock, Poland in 1910, Sendler's values and worldview were shaped significantly by her father, a physician who directed a local hospital. Sendler often repeated what her father taught her: People make choices to be either good or bad. Their race, religion, and nationality don't matter.

Sendler witnessed the German invasion of Poland in 1939 and was appalled at the Nazis' treatment of Polish Jews, who were stripped of their basic civil rights. She began to risk her life by becoming an underground supporter of Jews. When the war began, Sendler was a senior administrator in the *Warsaw Social Welfare Department*, which provided meals and financial assistance for orphans, the elderly, and the poor. Sendler surreptitiously arranged for her department to provide clothing, medicine, and money for the Jews. She registered Jews under fictitious Christian names and, to discourage Nazi inspections, Jews were reported by her agency as having infectious diseases such as typhus and tuberculosis.

In 1942, the Nazis packed hundreds of thousands of Polish Jews into a 16-block area known as the Warsaw Ghetto, where Jewish families lived while awaiting certain death. When Sendler learned of the horrid conditions in the Ghetto—5,000 people were dying each month from starvation and disease—she became determined to help Jewish children escape from it. Sendler faced several challenges. First, she and her colleague Irena Schultz had to find a way to enter the Ghetto without arousing German suspicion. They managed to obtain official passes from doctors in Warsaw's Epidemic Control Department. Second, she faced the daunting task of persuading Jewish residents of the Ghetto to part with their children. For Sendler, a young mother herself, convincing parents to part with their children was in itself unbearable. Another challenge facing Sendler was outside the Ghetto, where she had to recruit families willing to shelter the Jewish children. These families, of course, knew that they risked being executed by the Germans if they were caught harboring Jews.

Sendler visited the Ghetto daily and used both legal and illegal methods to bring in food, medicines, money, and clothing. With people dying daily of starvation and disease, Sendler made the decision to help children escape the Ghetto. This was no easy task. And the task became more challenging as time went on as the Germans sealed the various avenues—underground passages, holes in the Ghetto wall, and so on—that were used to sneak people out. Some guards could be bribed, and children could and sometimes were thrown over the Ghetto wall. One of Sendler's favorite methods of smuggling children out of the Ghetto was to use an ambulance. Other children were taken out in gunnysacks, body bags, toolboxes, potato sacks, or coffins.

With the help of others in the underground movement, she issued hundreds of false documents allowing almost 2,500 Jewish children to escape the Ghetto safely. The children were first placed in a temporary shelter to help them recover from their period of destitution in the Ghetto. This shelter also provided time for them to receive false identity papers from members of the Polish underground. These papers had to be excellent forgeries, good enough to pass German inspection. Each child had to be provided with a fictitious birth, baptismal certificate, and family history. The children then had to commit this information to memory.

Using her coding scheme, Sendler carefully kept track of each child's original name and new identity. She placed these records in jars and buried them under an apple tree in a neighbor's backyard, across the street from German barracks, hoping that someday she would be able to retrieve the information and return the children to their original families.

Unfortunately, the Nazis discovered Sendler's underground work and arrested her on October 20, 1943. She was imprisoned and tortured by the Gestapo, who broke her feet and legs. Sendler would never again walk without crutches. She bravely withstood the torture, refusing to betray her friends or any of the Jewish children she had placed in different families. The Polish underground saved her by bribing German guards on the way to her execution. She was left in the woods, unconscious and with broken arms and legs. She was listed on public bulletin boards as among those executed.

For the remainder of the war, Sendler lived in hiding, but she continued her work for the Jewish children. After the war she dug up the jars and used the notes to track down the 2,500 children she had placed with adoptive families. Although Sendler tried to reunite them with relatives scattered across Europe, she found that most had lost their families during the Holocaust in Nazi death camps.

In the years following the war, Sendler lived in obscurity, her heroism remaining largely unnoticed. Then in the year 2000, students at Uniontown High School in Kansas became aware of Sendler's story and wrote a play based on her heroic achievements. The play was called *Life in a Jar*, and it won the 2000 Kansas state National History Day competition. Thanks in part to the publicity generated by *Life in a Jar*, Sendler began to receive many honors late in life. In 2003 Pope John Paul II sent Sendler a personal letter praising her wartime efforts. That same year she received Poland's highest civilian decoration, the Order of the White Eagle, and the Jan Karski Award "For Courage and Heart" from the American Center of Polish Culture. Unable to leave her nursing home at age 97 to receive an honor from Poland's Senate, she sent a statement through Elżbieta Ficowska, whom Sendler had saved as an infant. Sendler wrote: "Every child saved with my help is the justification of my existence on this Earth, and not a title to glory." Sendler was nominated for the Nobel Peace Prize in 2007 but lost to Al Gore.

After she was recognized for her heroism, Sendler's picture appeared in a newspaper. "A man, a painter, telephoned me," said Sendler, "'I remember your face,' he said. 'It was you who took me out of the ghetto.' I had many calls like that!" Irena Sendler did not think of herself as a hero. She wrote, "Heroes do extraordinary things. What I did was not an extraordinary thing. It was normal." Sendler claimed no credit for her actions. "I could have done more," she said. "This regret will follow me to my death." Sendler died in 2008 at the age of 98.

IDENTIFYING PEOPLE'S HEROES

Who are your heroes? Surely, Irena Sendler is now one of them. If you're anything like the 450 people we've interviewed for this book—average Americans of all ages and from all walks of life—you can easily list several heroic people. You probably have at least a few fictional heroes from the pages of books, television, or movies. You also likely have a number of real-life heroes who have made their mark in sports, politics, business, or philanthropy. Moreover, if you're like most people, you can easily explain why these individuals are your heroes and why their accomplishments are meaningful to you.

Of the hundreds of people we sampled, over 95% were able to list at least two heroes, and about two-thirds of our respondents needed only a few minutes to list a half dozen or more heroes. On average, participants in our study listed over five heroes each, a fact that may come as a surprise to anyone who believes that people today are either too jaded or too sophisticated to believe in heroes. We do appear more than willing to place at least several people up on a pedestal. Even if we acknowledge that our heroes have some flaws, we readily admit that we know of at least several people who have achieved greatness, either by performing extraordinary actions or by displaying strong virtues.

It may even be more surprising to see the names and types of people considered to be heroes. One surprise is that roughly one-third of all the heroes listed were family members. Parents, grandparents, siblings, aunts, and uncles were frequently assigned the label of hero. Explanations for their heroism focused on their inspirational sacrifice: "My parents went through rough times to raise six kids successfully," "My father did without to give to us," "My mother courageously weathered many storms," "My grandmother's great strength and unshakeable faith held the family together," "My brother, for overcoming cancer," "My mother, for teaching me to never give up."

Another possibly surprising finding is that another third of the heroes generated by our sample of participants were simply the product of someone else's imagination. Fictional heroes were mentioned about 600 times by our sample. Some of these imagined heroes are classic superheroes such as Batman and Spiderman; some are science fiction stars such as James Kirk and Han Solo; some are spirited adventurers such as Indiana Jones and Huckleberry Finn; some are sports legends such as Roy Hobbs and Rocky Balboa; still others are flawed and ordinary blokes such as Lester Burnham, Napoleon Dynamite, and, yes, our friend Rick Blaine from Casablanca. It doesn't seem to matter to us that these heroes are a total fiction. The themes they illustrate, the values they embody, the emotions they evoke, all seem to resonate to people at a deep level.

The remaining third of the heroes listed by our sample were nonfictional, nonfamily members. Not surprisingly, these heroes were teachers, pastors, statesmen and women, athletes, artists, explorers,

Table 1.1 Examples of Heroes Generated by Our Sample of 450 People, Sorted by Category (Percentage of Our Sample Generating Each Type of Hero in Parentheses)

Fictional Heroes (34% of the total)

Science Fiction (9%): Han Solo, James Kirk, Fox Mulder, Xena
Everymen (8%): Napoleon Dynamite, George Bailey, Andy Taylor, Rick Blaine
Superheroes (6%): Superman, Wonder Woman, Batman, Spiderman, Ironman
Sports Legends (6%): Rocky Balboa, Roy Hobbs, Karate Kid
Adventurers (5%): Robin Hood, Indiana Jones, Huckleberry Finn, Tarzan

Nonfictional Heroes (66% of the total)

Family Members (32%): Mother, Father, Grandparents, Brother, Sister, Uncle, Cousin
Underdogs (10%): 1980 U.S. Olympic Hockey Team, 1969 New York Mets
Sports Stars (7%): Roger Federer, Babe Ruth, Babe Zaharias, Michael Jordan
Humanitarians (6%): Gandhi, Mother Teresa, firefighters, Martin Luther King Jr.
Entertainers (4%): Oprah Winfrey, Mel Gibson, Miley Cyrus
Everymen (4%): Frank Champi, Anne Frank, Rosa Parks
Heads of State (3%): George Washington, Nelson Mandela, Margaret Thatcher

and survivors of tragedy. In Table 1.1 we list a representative subset of the heroes, sorted by category, that our sample of respondents generated. Note the variety of people in this table. Heroes are judged to come from all corners of human existence, from royalty to paupers, from real flesh and blood to the imagined, from the elderly to children, and from close family to complete strangers.

How do the results of our survey compare to other studies of contemporary heroes? In the year 2000, the editors of *Time* rolled out their list of the top-20 heroes of the twentieth century.[2] These heroes were all nonfictional, but there was considerable overlap with our survey results. As with our respondents, *Time*'s list included a grouping of athletic heroes (e.g., Pelé), humanitarians (e.g., Mother Teresa), rulers (e.g., the Kennedys), entertainers (e.g., Marilyn Monroe), and everyday people with courage (e.g., Rosa Parks). Then in 2006, *Time Europe* presented its list of top heroes from the past 60 years.[3] These nonfictional heroes from Europe included rulers (e.g., Juan Carlos), political heroes (e.g., Shirin Ebadi), agents of social change (e.g., Simone de Beauvoir), and software giants (e.g., Linus Torvalds).

Other surveys of fictional and nonfictional heroes include the American Film Institute's 2003 list of the best all-time movie heroes.[4] The AFI's top-20 list featured nine names that overlapped with our survey results: Rocky Balboa, Indiana Jones, James Bond, Rick Blaine, George Bailey, Oskar Schindler, Han Solo, Robin Hood, and Shane. The remaining 11 from the AFI list were Atticus Finch, Will Kane, Clarice Starling, Ellen Ripley, T. E. Lawrence, Jefferson Smith, Tom Joad, Norma Rae Webster, Harry Callahan, Virgil Tibbs, and Butch Cassidy and the Sundance Kid. Another survey of top fictional heroes was conducted recently by Lucy Pollard-Gott, an expert in the literary arts.[5] Her top-10 list included Hamlet, Odysseus, Don Quixote, Eve, Genji, Oedipus, Don Juan, Chia Pao-yu, Sherlock Holmes, and Arjuna. Interestingly, of these 10 individuals, only Sherlock Holmes was mentioned by our respondents.

As psychologists, we are more interested in laypeople's perceptions of heroes than in experts' opinions. Especially fascinating to us are the reasons given for people's choices of heroes. Consider the following heroes and the explanations given by our participants:

- Martin Luther King Jr.—he used peaceful tactics to rally a good and necessary change.
- Sue Stokes—a family friend who fought cancer for years with the most positive and happy-go-lucky outlook on life, before eventually passing away.
- Abraham Lincoln—he went against what others thought he should do to create something better than what was there before.
- Joan of Arc—she went against societal constructs to do what she wanted to, even though she was killed.
- Uncle Jeff—a man of extreme strength, both physically and mentally. He was a wild youth, but he grew to be an amazingly responsible adult, husband, and father.
- Robin Hood—he selflessly stole from the rich to give to people in need.
- Mr. Melican—my 12th grade science teacher whose wife passed away and still managed to teach, take care of his young children, and have a smile on his face every day in class.
- My coach—he believed in me from a very young age and gave lots of his personal time so that my dreams would come true.

- Barack Obama—anyone who can overcome a country's racial barriers and become the most powerful person in the country deserves respect.
- Superman—he helps people.
- Franklin Roosevelt—he served the country in a truly tough time.
- God—He has blessed me.
- Jesus—from a nonreligious perspective, he was a poor carpenter who influenced billions of people for the past 2,000 years by courageously challenging the established order.
- George Washington—one of the few people in history who insisted that he give up his position of power even when he was so popular.
- Aung Sun Suu Kyi—would-be president of Myanmar who is held in house arrest by militant corrupt government. She's an international symbol of freedom and struggle.
- Military personnel—because I admire their sacrifice and lifestyle.
- My mom—she manages to accomplish everything and is very selfless.
- Mr. Spock—he successfully carries out his mission to explore the universe while balancing the challenges of being half-Vulcan, half-human.
- Rocky Marciano—one of the greatest boxers of all time, one of the few athletes clever enough to step out on top.
- Sully Sullenberger—(the guy who landed the plane on the Hudson River) I can't think of anything more typically heroic than making an emergency landing on a river and staying on the plane until every person got off safely.

Our participants' explanations for their choices of heroes follow a clear pattern. Whether they are rulers, parents, deities, or teachers, heroes are described as courageous, selfless, and skillful. Fame is not a requirement for heroism. We recognize unsung heroes who toil in obscurity and whose actions, often behind the scenes, make a positive and enduring impact on others. We also see heroism in people who obviously did not set out to become heroes. Interestingly, while heroes do uncommon things such as land planes safely on rivers, they also do things familiar to every human, such as dealing with illness or death. But they earn heroic status by handling these common challenges with uncommon courage and grace, setting them apart from most others.

As noted earlier, we found that about a third of the heroes listed by our sample of average Americans were family members, another third were fictional characters, and the remaining third were real-world individuals. Let's look at these three groupings of heroes in a bit more detail.

FAMILY MEMBERS AS HEROES

Many highly successful people are often quick to credit their families for their triumphs. Irena Sendler admitted that her goodness, courage, and willingness to do the right thing, even at great peril to herself, came from her father. The first significant relationship we have is with our parents. It is therefore not surprising that good, loving parents can become heroes in their children's eyes.

Michelle Obama often speaks of the two "strong women" who paved the way for her husband Barack's success: "The two women who really raised him, his mom and grandma, are both strong, and they've struggled in the course of their lives and overcome great obstacles."[6] President Obama has echoed these sentiments, particularly in reflecting about his grandmother, Madelyn Dunham, who raised him during his teenage years.[7] "She's the one who taught me about hard work," Obama said in his speech at the Democratic National Convention in Denver. "She's the one who put off buying a new car or a new dress for herself so that I could have a better life. She poured everything she had into me." Later Obama added that his grandmother "was the cornerstone of our family, and a woman of extraordinary accomplishment, strength, and humility," and that "she was one of those quiet heroes that we have all across America."

Tiger Woods has spoken similarly of his father's influence on him. Many times Woods has referred to his dad as a hero and ideal role model. Shortly after his dad passed away in 2006, Tiger noted that his dad "was my best friend and greatest role model, and I will miss him deeply. I'm overwhelmed when I think of all of the great things he accomplished in his life. He was an amazing dad, coach, mentor, soldier, husband, and friend …. I wouldn't be where I am today without him, and I'm honored to continue his legacy of sharing and caring."[8]

In a similar vein, seven-time Tour de France champion Lance Armstrong has called his mother a hero: "How do you articulate all that you feel for and owe to a parent? My mother had given me more than any teacher or father figure ever had, and she had done it over some long hard years, years that must have looked as empty to her at times as those brown Texas fields. When it came to never quitting, to not caring how it looked, to gritting your teeth and pushing to the finish, I could only hope to have the stamina and fortitude of my mother, a single woman with a young son and a small salary—there was no reward for her at the end of the day, either, no trophy or first-place check."[9]

The most common reason our respondents gave to explain why a family member was a hero centers around the idea of giving, or sacrifice. In our survey we found three major types of sacrifice among family heroes: *emotional, financial,* and *temporal.* The emotional support that our families give us is very easy to understand, especially during difficult times. Here are a few examples of statements written by our respondents about the emotional generosity and sacrifice shown by heroic family members:

- "My mom always gave me comfort and support when I needed it the most."
- "My dad was always there for me to cry on his shoulder."
- "It didn't matter if I screwed up. I was always unconditionally loved by my mom."

The financial sacrifice made by heroic family members was also mentioned many times by our respondents. Children, of course, rely almost completely on their parents for food and shelter, and kids recognize when family members must go to heroic lengths to provide these basic necessities. Here are examples of statements about family heroes whose sacrificial deeds were described as financial in nature:

- "My mother held two jobs to raise us kids."
- "My dad saved all his money to send us to college."
- "My aunt and uncle took us in when my parents lost their job."

Heroic family members don't just love us and put food on the table. They also give us the gift of time. Our survey respondents strongly emphasized the importance of being generous with time even when it is inconvenient or burdensome. Here are some examples of families making significant temporal sacrifices:

- "For years, my parents attended every one of my marathon-length swim meets."
- "I had major health problems growing up, and my grandmother cheerfully took me to every one of my many doctor appointments."
- "My brother was my constant companion and mentor during difficult times."

One reason family members often serve as heroes for each other can be found in the idea of *kin selection*.[10] According to evolutionary theory, all living things are driven by the goals of self-preservation and reproduction. Given these two goals, one might think that selfless behavior should be rare or nonexistent. One might also assume that selfish acts designed to promote one's own well-being should dominate our behavior.

But as we know, selfless sacrificial acts among family members are commonplace. In fact, we see heroic acts directed toward family relatives throughout much of the animal kingdom. Alarm calls in ground squirrels are a classic example. One squirrel will alert other squirrels to danger, drawing attention to the caller and exposing it to increased risk of being eaten. Most importantly, these alarm calls occur most frequently when the caller has relatives nearby. Similarly, male prairie dogs heighten their rate of calling when closer to kin. The greatest self-sacrifice is directed toward close relatives, and this pattern is seen in many other animals such as honeybees, scrub jays, and wild turkeys.

Kin selection can explain self-sacrifice in a world where self-preservation is the overriding goal. Because family members share many of the same genes, any selfless act directed toward a family member indirectly serves one's own goal of sending one's genes into the next generation. Thus, animals and people tend to perform actions that favor the reproductive success of their relatives, even at a cost to their own individual survival and reproduction.

For these reasons, we suspect that family members who make heroic sacrifices for their children don't view their actions as a loss, but as a gain. Indeed, one particular respondent to our survey, a 20-year-old young man, noted that his father was his hero because of one particularly large sacrifice that the father made. The young man wrote that his father gave up his kidney, and that this generosity saved our respondent's life. The father might say that his was an act of love, and while that explanation is no doubt true, evolutionary biologists might cynically add that the father was merely looking out for his own genetic fitness.

FICTIONAL HEROES

When there are so many real-world heroes to choose from for inspiration, why do so many of our heroes come from television, books, and movies? One reason is that the creators of fiction purposely construct characters who perfectly embody classic heroic stories or narratives. Fiction writers know we will be drawn to such characters. These make-believe individuals are thus crafted to be *hero prototypes*—individuals possessing powerful heroic qualities that we easily recognize and admire. Superman is a classic example. Heroes should be strong, and of course no one can match Superman's superhuman strength. Moreover, heroes should be virtuous, and no one saves the world from being destroyed better than Superman. Other fictional heroes have these same prototypically heroic traits, albeit to a lesser extent. Consider Rick Blaine of Casablanca: He is attractive, suave, courageous, and self-confident. When faced with a challenging situation, he does the right thing. The same can be said for dozens of classic fictional heroes: Captain James T. Kirk of the popular Star Trek franchise, Lara Croft, James Bond, Wonder Woman, and scores of other heroes of fiction.

In constructing heroic tales, fiction writers are no doubt trying to entertain us, but we believe that hero stories also serve at least two additional purposes: to educate and to inspire. Consider the ubiquitous nature of children's fairy tales. Vivid fables about heroes and villains, intended for a child audience, are found in almost all human cultures. What is the point of these stories? For one thing, they teach us valuable lessons for living. The story of the *Three Little Pigs* teaches us to plan ahead, to take effective precautions against danger. The third little pig is clearly the hero of the story in thwarting the wolf attack and protecting his siblings. *Little Red Riding Hood* teaches us the dangers of talking to strangers, and the woodcutter is the hero for rescuing Red Riding Hood's grandmother from the belly of the wolf. In *Hansel and Gretel*, we learn that appearances can be deceiving and that cleverness is often required to defeat the villain.

Hansel and Gretel is particularly interesting because Gretel's heroism—she tricks the witch and pushes her into the oven—defies the male hero bias that permeates most fairy tales. In many tales, such as *Cinderella, Snow White*, and *Beauty and the Beast*, a Prince Charming–like character often emerges as the hero who rescues a woman in distress. To counter these ancient ideas of female dependence on males, modern tales of strong women heroes have emerged in abundance. Disney has released feature-length animated movies featuring female heroes such as *Pocahontas, The Little Mermaid*, and *Mulan*. On television, *Xena the Warrior Princess, Buffy the Vampire Slayer*, and *Lara Croft the Tomb Raider* are all examples of recent and more enlightened portrayals of fierce and intelligent female heroes.

Many children's tales of fiction provide inspiration as well as education. We are inspired to witness Bambi's triumph over adversity. We are thrilled that the *Little Engine That Could* is successful in its struggle up the steep hill. Hans Christian Andersen's *The Ugly Duckling* inspires us to have faith in a better future. Fairy tales are rife with themes of overcoming poverty, villains, and dysfunctional families. The message from these stories is clear: With hard work, perseverance, and the help of friends, deities, and sometimes magic, anyone can better his or her situation, no matter how difficult it may seem.

Because fictional stories often contain classic themes and images, fictional heroes and villains tend to be portrayed in extreme terms. That is, make-believe heroes tend to be extremely virtuous and make-believe villains tend to be extremely evil. Consider the fact that in many Hollywood movies set in the early American West, the good guys wore white hats and the bad guys wore black, and very few characters showed any shades of gray. Is the world of fictional heroes and villains more black and white than the world of nonfictional heroes and villains?

Because we are social scientists, we couldn't resist conducting a study to answer this question. First, we used our survey results to randomly select the names of 10 fictional heroes, 10 fictional villains, 10 nonfictional heroes, and 10 nonfictional villains. Table 1.2 shows the names of these 40 individuals.

In the next phase of our study, we asked 75 participants to rate how good or bad each of these 40 heroes and villains was on a 10-point scale. The highest end of the scale—the number 10—was labeled "extremely good"; the lowest end of the scale—the number 0—was labeled "extremely bad"; and the midpoint, 5, was labeled "equally

Table 1.2 The Names of 40 Heroes and Villains from Fiction and Nonfiction, Drawn Randomly from Lists Generated from Our Studies

	Heroes	Villains
Fiction	Indiana Jones	The Joker
	Hercules	Professor Moriarty
	Spiderman	Captain Hook
	King Arthur	Lex Luther
	Jack Sparrow	Shark from Jaws
	Robin Hood	Mr. Hyde
	Luke Skywalker	Satan
	Paul Bunyan	Wyatt Earp
	Harry Potter	Frau Farbissina
	Fox Mulder	Hannibal Lecter
Nonfiction	Barrack Obama	Joseph Mengele
	Muhammad Ali	Alexander the Great
	Princess Diana	Bernie Madoff
	Parents	Osama Bin Laden
	Eleanor Roosevelt	Richard Nixon
	Harry Houdini	Nancy Pelosi
	Ronald Reagan	Bill Buckner
	Anne Frank	Adolf Hitler
	Harrison Ford	Mao
	Michael Jordan	Lee Harvey Oswald

good and bad." The results confirmed our suspicion about fictional heroes and villains being portrayed more extremely than nonfictional heroes and villains. Our participants gave our fictional heroes an average rating of 8.7, whereas they rated the nonfictional heroes an average of 7.8. A statistical test showed that the difference between these two averages was not due to chance or random variation. We also found that our participants gave our fictional villains an average rating of 2.2, whereas they rated nonfictional villains an average of 3.9. Again, this average difference was unlikely to be due to chance or random variation. These average ratings appear in Figure 1.1.

The results of our study are very suggestive that fictional heroes and villains are viewed as more heroic and villainous than their non-fictional counterparts. We suspect that creators of fiction draw from classic prototypes of good and evil when constructing their characters. While elements of these prototypes can surely be found in real-world heroes and villains, fictional prototypes are more cleanly drawn with their essential features accentuated. As consumers of fictional stories, we cannot help but be drawn to the heightened prototypical qualities that fictional characters embody. We resonate to powerful archetypal heroes, as they represent the best of humanity, and curiously enough we are also drawn to villains who represent the antithesis of our values. Fictional accounts of heroes and villains don't just entertain us; they educate us and prepare for us for encounters with good and evil.

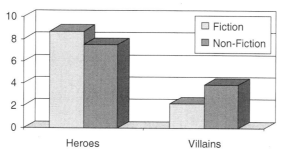

Figure 1.1 Average ratings of fictional and nonfictional heroes and villains. The higher the average rating, the greater the perceived goodness of the individual.

REAL-WORLD HEROES

Our respondents generated many nonfictional heroes, and it's not surprising. After all, the world we live in is set up to guarantee a constant flow of newly minted real-world heroes. Consider the following:

1. *The proliferation of athletic competitions.* Many respondents to our survey listed sports heroes, and just consider the number of opportunities for heroes of this type to emerge. There are Olympic games, world championships, national championships, as well as local and regional championships for dozens of different athletic events. These levels of competition exist in almost every country. In the United States, there are dozens of formal sporting activities, including professional and amateur football, soccer, baseball, basketball, hockey, auto racing, swimming, horse racing, golf, tennis, and the martial arts. In the sports world, heroes abound, and more are guaranteed to emerge on the scene every day.

2. *Increasing leadership opportunities.* All organizations and collective movements have either explicit or implicit opportunities for leadership. Moreover, the higher the stakes, the more likely that leaders of groups can become heroes, which may explain why the leader of a nation is more likely to become a hero than the leader of the local stamp-collecting club. As the population of humans increases, the number of human groups increases, breeding even more leadership opportunities and thus more heroes.

3. *The inevitability of disaster.* Disastrous events are an inevitable part of human existence, and almost all accidents, emergencies, wars, and atrocities are fertile ground for heroes to surface. On April 16, 2007, Seung-Hui Cho shot and killed 32 people on the campus of Virginia Tech University before taking his own life.[11] A horrible event, to be sure, but it did provide several opportunities for genuine heroism to materialize. Consider the following:

   • Professor Liviu Librescu held the door of his classroom shut when Cho attempted to enter. Thanks to Librescu, most of his students escaped through windows, but Librescu died after being shot multiple times through the door.

- Professor Couture-Nowak saved students in her French classroom by ordering them to the back of the class. She was also killed attempting to barricade the door.
- A student, Henry Lee, was also killed while helping Professor Couture-Nowak barricade the door.
- Another student, Partahi Mamora Halomoan Lumban-toruan, protected a classmate, Guillermo Colman, by diving on top of him. Cho killed Lumbantoruan, but Colman was protected by Lumbantoruan's body.
- Student Zach Petkewicz barricaded his classroom door to protect others from Cho.
- Cho attacked the classroom of students Katelyn Carney, Derek O'Dell, Trey Perkins, and Erin Sheehan, a few of whom were injured yet managed to barricade the door and successfully prevented Cho's attempted reentry.

Tragedy begets heroism. The worst in human nature brings out the best in human nature. Cho, a clear villain, created circumstance in which great heroism could arise. Other notable tragedies have similarly produced heroes. During the sinking of the *Titanic*, a number of passengers were willing to drown to allow others safe passage on lifeboats. On September 11, 2001, the passengers of United Airlines flight 93 heroically overpowered terrorists intent on crashing the plane into the White House or the U.S. Capitol building. Even if all evil is erased from the world, there will always be accidents, and these accidents will spawn heroes who show uncommon valor to save lives.

4. *Increasing role of media coverage.* None of the aforementioned hero-generating mechanisms—sports, leadership, and tragedies—could succeed in hero creation without significant assistance of the media. Many athletic contests enjoy significant media coverage, ensuring high visibility to those individuals who shine heroically in competition. The leaders of nations and other important groups use the media to promote

their policies and their popularity. And the media especially prey on tragedies and their aftermath, especially human interest stories focusing on unsung heroes who go far out of their way to mitigate the tragedy.

Several scholars have concluded that heroes only exist to the extent that society recognizes their heroism, usually through media coverage. If no one is around to witness a woman save an infant from drowning, and she takes the incident to her grave, is she a hero? While many marginally heroic people are propelled to heroism by the media, a great number of legitimate heroes go unnoticed. A classic example of the "unsung hero" is Irena Sendler. Until the past decade, very few people were aware of her extraordinary feat of saving thousands of Jewish lives during the World War II. Thanks in part to media coverage, including this book, the world is being made aware of Sendler's remarkably heroic actions.

It may be true that the media crave heroes more than anyone. Appealing heroic tales most definitely increase newspaper and magazine circulations, digital viewership, television ratings, and Internet site visits. For this reason, the media are motivated to turn ordinary people into heroes. The popularity of the television show *American Idol* attests to this fact. One moment a person may be toiling in obscurity, and the next moment her face may don the cover of *People* magazine. But the media don't stop there. They are aware of the phenomenon of *schadenfreude*—the tendency of people to enjoy the misfortune of successful others. And so the beneficiary of media-generated heroism one day may be the victim of media-generated schadenfreude the next. The media ensure that what goes up must come down. And we, the audience, love it.

The story of Britney Spears is a classic example of the media's love affair with the rise and fall of heroes.[12] First receiving national attention for her performance on *Star Search* in 1992, Spears captured the hearts of millions of young people with her wholesome image of the squeaky-clean girl next door. She performed on the Disney channel's *The New Mickey Mouse Club* show, and her early music recordings projected an air of innocence that endeared her to teens and parents alike.

Spears enjoyed unparalleled success as a solo recording artist in the late 1990s and early 2000s, but gradually her song lyrics began to reflect more mature themes. The same media that built her stardom was now spotlighting the steady decline in her "wholesomeness." At the 2000 MTV Video Music Awards, she surprised fans by wearing a sexually provocative outfit. Her clothes were described as both wild and weird, and the media devoted significant attention to this departure from her clean-cut image. Spears' behavior, such as her long-time relationship with Justin Timberlake, also began to cast doubts on her earlier claim that she would remain a virgin until marriage. When she did marry in 2004, the marriage lasted just two days, and media coverage of her every move became intensified. Her live concert tour that year attracted huge media attention for its sexually charged choreography, which was thought to be inappropriate for the many young children in the audience.

With much media fanfare, Spears' image began to sink to new lows. She posed nude on a magazine cover, was married and divorced again, was photographed by paparazzi driving in a car with her baby on her lap without seatbelts, was admitted to a drug rehabilitation center, and was accused of being an unfit mother and emotionally unstable person. Clearly, the one-time hero to millions was now vilified and demonized on the pages of magazines, on the Internet, and on television.

Susan Boyle is another person who was knocked off the pedestal by the same media that propelled her to fame. Boyle appeared on *Britain's Got Talent* as a rather frumpy, unkempt, middle-aged woman in 2009. She then thrilled the world with her soaring voice that won over the hearts of millions of viewers and earned her great critical acclaim. But shortly after her remarkable performance, Boyle was criticized in the media for altering her appearance. The media reported that she had colored her hair, improved her wardrobe, and put on makeup. Her vanity, eccentricities, nerves, and inability to handle the spotlight were highlighted on newscasts and entertainment shows. Clearly, Boyle's success made her a media target.

Michael Jackson is yet another example of media-created schadenfreude. An immense talent, Jackson was catapulted into the spotlight by his music, MTV, and the press. Soon the media began to devote significant attention to changes in his appearance, and his numerous facial surgeries began to attract more media attention than his music.

A huge media blitz emerged over Jackson's legal problems stemming from accusations of child molestation. Interestingly, when he died in 2009, the same media that built him up and tore him down was more than willing to place him on the hero pedestal once again. This same roller-coaster ride characterizes the media's treatment of Princess Diana. She was first portrayed as a fairy-tale princess, then as a disrespectful anorexic, and then finally, upon her death, as a great humanitarian hero. We'll discuss the role of death in cementing the heroic status of celebrities later in Chapter 6 of this book.

We don't claim that the media are entirely responsible for the construction and deconstruction of heroes. Behavior often speaks for itself, independent of biased or overzealous press coverage, and the media are often just doing their job in reporting good and bad behaviors. But the media are far from objective and often have hidden, as well as not-so-hidden, agendas. Evan Thomas, a writer for *Newsweek*, best described the media's appetite for heroes. He recently wrote that the media are mostly "looking for narratives that reveal something of character. It is the human drama that most compels our attention."[13] There can be no greater drama than the rise and fall of heroes. The transition between heroism and villainy is captivating and engrossing. We know it, and the media know that we know it.

WHAT HEROES DO

Our images of heroes appear to follow a systematic pattern. Indeed, to be perceived as a hero, a person needs to follow a particular path. We all have a script in mind for what must be done to qualify as heroic. Interestingly, one of the earliest and most important studies of people's scripts for heroes was conducted not by a psychologist, but by a Professor of English at Sarah Lawrence College named Joseph Campbell. A comparative mythologist, Campbell published a remarkably influential book in 1949 called *The Hero with a Thousand Faces*, in which he argued that myths and epic tales of heroes throughout the ages have tended to follow a predictable pattern. According to Campbell, "a hero ventures forth from the world of common day into a region of supernatural wonder: fabulous forces are there encountered and a decisive victory is won: the hero comes back from this mysterious adventure with the power to bestow boons on his fellow man."[14]

In his book, Campbell describes in considerable detail the three major components of the hero's story or narrative. He calls the first part of the classic hero story *departure*, which describes the forces that set the hero's journey in motion. The second part of the story, *initiation*, refers to the obstacles that heroes must overcome to complete their task. Finally, there is the hero's *return* to the world in which he or she started. Let's briefly examine each of these phases of the hero's journey.

Departure

The first stage of the hero narrative, called the *departure*, focuses on how the hero's adventure begins. Sometimes the hero decides voluntarily to undertake something great, as when Bruce Wayne chooses to adopt the persona of Batman to rid Gotham City of crime. At other times the hero first refuses to undertake the journey but then grows to understand his or her destiny as a hero. Examples of this kind of reluctant hero include Moses from the Bible, Frodo in the *Lord of the Rings*, and John McClane from the *Die Hard* movies. Sometimes a situation beyond the hero's control sweeps him or her onto a heroic path. A classic instance is found in Homer's *Odyssey*, where the angered god Poseidon creates fierce winds that cast Odysseus off to distant lands.

The hero's departure also includes her initial steps into the unknown and out of the safety and comfort of her own familiar world. When Rosa Parks refused to move to the back of the Montgomery, Alabama, bus in 1955, she knew that her defiance was going to upset the status quo and change her world. According to Campbell, the hero's departure from the known world into the unknown is like being in "the belly of the whale," a different place that the hero is born into and comes to accept. Often a guide or helper appears to assist the hero with this transition. Rick Blaine in *Casablanca* has Sam; Luke Skywalker in *Star Wars* has Yoda; Barack Obama has his wife Michele; John F. Kennedy had his brother Robert. As for Rosa Parks, she had Edgar Nixon and Clifford Durr, who bailed her out of jail on the night of her bold defiance, and later a young unknown reverend named Martin Luther King, Jr., helped represent her cause on a larger scale.

Initiation

This second major phase of the hero's journey refers to the series of tests and challenges the hero must overcome to succeed. According to Campbell[14]:

> ... this is a favorite phase of the myth-adventure. It has produced a world literature of miraculous tests and ordeals. The hero is covertly aided by the advice, amulets, and secret agents of the supernatural helper whom he met before his entrance into this region. Or it may be that he here discovers for the first time that there is a benign power everywhere supporting him in his superhuman passage. The original departure into the land of trials represented only the beginning of the long and really perilous path of initiatory conquests and moments of illumination. Dragons have now to be slain and surprising barriers passed—again, again, and again. Meanwhile there will be a multitude of preliminary victories, unretainable ecstasies and momentary glimpses of the wonderful land. (p. 90)

A common test faced by heroes is the temptation of the flesh. As most ancient societies were patriarchal, the heroes Campbell studied were primarily males who were often seduced by women. According to Campbell, the lure of women and romance diverts the hero from the journey to which he is called. A classic example is Odysseus's temptation by the sirens, but we see many modern-day examples. Indiana Jones is distracted by his former love Marion; Captain Kirk's many love interests sidetrack him from his mission; Bill Clinton had his Monica Lewinski; and television evangelist Jim Bakker was brought down by his affair with Jessica Hahn.

The ultimate challenge faced by a hero is what Campbell calls the "atonement with the father," usually a male figure who has life-and-death power over the hero. Luke Skywalker's confrontation with

Darth Vadar is a classic example, and in fact George Lucas, creator of Star Wars, admits to being influenced by Campbell's work. The father represents the ultimate power over the hero, and the hero can become seemingly omnipotent if he can wrest this power from the father. In defeating the father figure, the hero assumes the head of the table and thus becomes the new patriarch. Here it is clear how Campbell was influenced by Freud's psychodynamic theory, which proposes that all human males experience inevitable conflicts with their fathers and other father figures.

Return

According to Campbell, the hero returns to his or her original world with a great reward, or boon. George Washington returned from war bringing independence from Britain to the U.S. colonies. Charles Lindberg returned with great fanfare to the United States with the first transatlantic flight under his belt. Xuanzang returned to China with Buddhist sutras after a 17-year journey to India. Sundiata, founder of the Mali Empire in Africa, returned from exile with the Kouroukan Fouga, the groundwork of the Mali constitution. Sometimes the hero's return is fraught with danger, with the hero facing as many tough trials as he or she faced during the initiation phase. During their decent from the summit of Mt. Everest, Sir Edmund Hillary and Tenzing Norgay encountered difficulties retracing their steps because swirling winds had covered their tracks. Soldiers returning from war often experience great challenges rebuilding their lives and adjusting emotionally to a non-war setting.

Campbell notes that the hero often needs assistance with the return[14]: "The hero may have to be brought back from his supernatural adventure by assistance from without. That is to say, the world may have to come and get him." (p. 178). Superheroes may defeat their archenemies, but they often must rely on help from mere mortals and sidekicks to completely seal the deal. It is not unusual for Superman, at the last moment, to get a little assistance from Lois Lane or Jimmy Olsen. Clarice Starling in Silence of the Lambs receives help from an unlikely source, Hannibal Lecter, to nab the villain. Animal heroes on television, such as Lassie and Flipper, usually need human assistance for their heroic acts to come to full fruition. Campbell also notes that upon returning, many heroes are forever changed. Initially they may experience adjustment challenges, but eventually heroes may undergo a spiritual awakening or a feeling of freedom from material concerns. They may even no longer fear death.

Campbell based his script of the hero's journey on his examination of hero myths across time, culture, and geography. He suggested that myths reflect basic truths about the human condition. An inescapable part of being human is to confront challenges and to figure out ways to overcome them. Campbell believed that the basic hero myth has many commonalities with our nighttime dreams. Just as the hero myth describes a set of problems and overt ways of solving them, our dreams often contain conflicts and suggested solutions, often draped in symbols. "Myths are public dreams," he said, "and dreams are private myths." (http://www.mythsdreamssymbols.com/mythanddreams.html).

IMPORTANT DISTINCTIONS AMONG HEROES

We can define three important ways that people separate one kind of hero from another. Or, as psychologists say, our perceptions of heroes vary along three dimensions. First, we view heroes as being either moral or competent or, very often, both at once. Second, we believe that heroes are either born or made. That is, they either tend to have stable heroic traits, or they became heroes because they were thrust into circumstances that gave rise to heroism. Third, heroes inspire or show great leadership, and they do this either directly, through our interactions with them, or indirectly, through their deeds and works. Let's look at these three distinctions more carefully.

Morality versus Competence

Let's first examine the distinction between a hero's morality and competence. Heroes are individuals who perform remarkable moral actions, display significant intellectual or physical competencies, or accomplish tasks that require a high degree of both morality and competency. Some heroes are clearly known for their supreme morality; Irena Sendler and Mother Teresa's unparalleled humanitarian work are classic examples. Other heroes are known more for their prowess than for their morals. Tiger Woods' domination of the game of golf makes him a hero to some, despite his moral failings off the golf course. Still other heroes are revered for commitments and achievements that require both high morals and high competence. In fiction, superheroes such as Batman and Superman embody both morality and competence, while real-life heroes such as Abraham Lincoln and Nelson Mandela achieved their greatness with both skill and morality.

Moral heroes evoke powerful emotions from us. Irena Sendler was motivated by the desire to save innocent lives. Obviously the vast majority of us believe in the principle of preserving life, but few of us risk our own lives to save the lives of strangers. As noted earlier, it often takes a disaster to bring out such selflessness. On January 13, 1982, Air Florida flight 90 took off from Washington National Airport in a blizzard and crashed into the icy waters of the Potomac River.[15] All but six of the 84 passengers perished in the crash, and these six needed rescuing quickly before either drowning or succumbing to hypothermia. Within minutes several heroes appeared on the scene. Helicopter pilot Donald Usher and paramedic Gene Windsor arrived, and at great risk to themselves they first lowered their aircraft to the surface of the ice and water. Then they dropped rescue ropes to the six survivors who were trapped in the fuselage of the plane. One survivor was too weak to grab the line, and so Lenny Skutnik, a bystander standing on the bank of the river, jumped in the frozen water to help her to safety. One of the survivors, Arland Williams, could have pulled himself to safety, but instead he repeatedly handed the lines to others. He died before he could pull himself to safety.

From the story of Arland Williams and Air Florida flight 90, we can see that extreme selflessness is not the only defining characteristic of being a hero. Heroes also show complete and utter selflessness *at great personal cost*. Irena Sendler underwent torture and suffered permanent crippling injuries to keep her secret jars safe from the Nazis. Rick Blaine loses his café and his reputation, and possibly his freedom and his life, by staying in Casablanca so that Ilsa can leave with Victor. The best heroes don't just perform remarkably moral acts; they are willing to pay the ultimate price to do so.

Consider the story of Welles Crowther, age 24, who was working as an equities trader in the World Trade Center when it was struck by an airplane flown by terrorists. Crowther became known as "the man in the red bandanna," a label given to him by survivors of the ordeal whom he saved.[16] High up on the South Tower, Crowther assisted numerous injured people, carrying them to safety on his back at times and directing others to stairwells. Rather than going down the stairwells to save himself, Crowther climbed to higher floors to find others to help. "He was the cowboy coming in to save the town," said Judy Wein, whose life Crowther saved. "In this day and age when we have no real heroes, here was a young man who basically gave his life," she said.

After saving as many people as he could, Crowther finally made it down to the ground level of the South Tower. The tower then collapsed on top of him. His body was found on March 19, 2002, among a group of firefighters who died there. "I think he felt totally fulfilled," said Crowther's father, who called his son his best friend. "I don't think for a moment he was thinking about his own safety. He was thinking about the lives of all these people. His last hour was his legacy."

Think about that last line. *His last hour was his legacy.* Do people judge us by the last actions we perform in life? Once again, as social scientists, we couldn't resist conducting a study to answer this question. We had participants read about someone who was predominantly bad as a young man but became a kind and generous person at the end of his life. This was the sinner-to-saint condition. We then asked other participants to read the opposite; the man was kind and generous early in life but was bad at the end. This was the saint-to-sinner condition. Whom did participants rate more highly as a person? By far, it was the man who went from sinner to saint. Crowther's father was right about his son. His willingness to sacrifice his own life to save others most definitely sealed his legacy as a hero.

While we may place moral heroes on a higher pedestal than competent ones, we shouldn't underestimate the great awe that competence alone can inspire. Tiger Woods is a notable example. Before Tiger's arrival on the professional golf scene in 1996, it was considered common knowledge that no player would be able to dominate pro golf the way Jack Nicklaus, Arnold Palmer, Ben Hogan, and a few others had previously. Throughout the 1980s and 90s, before Tiger's appearance on the PGA tour, the prevailing view was that there were far too many excellent players on the tour for any one player to dominate. The era of superstar golfers in the mold of Nicklaus and Palmer was over. Or so it was thought.

When Tiger Woods turned pro at age 20, he brought with him an unparalleled record of success as an amateur, having won three U.S. junior amateur championships and three U.S. amateur championships. Despite this impressive resume, skeptics questioned Tiger's chances to compete successfully at the professional level. While the young Tiger Woods himself spoke of doing nothing less than winning every time he teed up his ball, knowledgeable golf fans snickered at this notion. In a famous 1996 television interview with Tiger during his rookie year, Curtis Strange—himself a two-time U.S Open winner and popular golf announcer—smirked as Tiger confidently proclaimed that winning every tournament was his intention, that finishing second "sucks," and that finishing third "is worse." Strange listened and then simply said, "You'll learn."[17]

But it was the world that learned. Competing in his first major championship as a professional in early 1997, Tiger Woods dominated the Masters Tournament as no one ever had before, shooting a record-low score and crushing the second-place finisher by a record 12 shots. The golf world took notice; what was thought to be impossible now seemed very possible. A dominating player, perhaps like no other, had arrived and forever changed what we believe is possible in the game of golf. Curtis Strange had to admit in 1997 that he had significantly underestimated Tiger's ability. What was once perceived as naïve brashness was now viewed as the type of supreme confidence necessary to win consistently.

Tiger Woods' heroic status became especially crystallized at the 2008 U.S. Open, where he competed despite being hobbled by a torn ACL and broken bone in his leg. During the championship no one knew the extent of Tiger's injuries, and cynically a few of Tiger's competitors witnessed his limp and accused him of exaggerating his injuries. Wincing in pain after nearly every tee shot and at times crumpling in pain, Tiger played with distinction. He birdied the 72nd and final hole in dramatic fashion to force an 18-hole playoff, and then birdied the 90th hole to force a one-hole playoff. He then won this final sudden-death hole to win the championship. Tiger played 91 holes on one leg and in extreme pain, yet still won. None of Tiger's previous victories better underscored his greatness as an athlete and competitor. Immediately after the tournament he underwent surgery to repair his broken leg. He then spent the next 10 months rehabilitating his leg before competing again and dominating the competition as he had before.

Thus, we see that great skill alone can engender heroism—even a skill as trivial as hitting a ball into a hole better than anyone else. In Tiger's case, the greatness of the skill was enhanced by the exhibition of the skill despite great injury. The perceived greatness of his skills may also have been heightened by our recognition that Tiger has overcome racial barriers in the game of golf. Overall, Tiger's heroic status is clouded by his marital infidelities. But there is no denying his unsurpassed golf ability nor his grit in overcoming obstacles.

Born or Made to Be a Hero

The second dimension of heroism is the degree to which heroic individuals are *born* to be heroes or are *made* to be heroes. In *Twelfth Night* Shakespeare wrote: "Some are born great, some achieve greatness, some have greatness thrust upon them." (Act II, Scene V, Line 74). That is, heroism may be innate or acquired. It may reflect the hero's basic personality, or it may develop steadily over the course of a person's life, or it may emerge from the circumstances that person faces in a defining moment, or perhaps a surprising combination of all of these.

Examples of born heroes include Superman, who was born with super powers, and Jesus of Nazareth, whom Christians believe was born through immaculate conception and was thus half man, half God. Although it seems unlikely that many born heroes walk the earth, there is a growing body of research in psychology and biology suggesting that people are born with a rudimentary moral center. Harvard professor Marc Hauser has recently argued that humans have evolved a universal moral instinct and that our life experiences shape the way our innate sense of morality expresses itself.[18] Could born heroes therefore exist? Possibly, but not without great assistance from parents, society, and our educational system.

So while heroes can be born with the right stuff, they must still be molded into heroes by environmental forces. Acquiring heroic status is neither easy nor common. Even with the right stuff, one must acquire greatness through either hard work or by being in the right place at the right time. Hard work doesn't just mean difficult work; it means putting in the hours. Ten thousand hours, to be exact, according to Malcolm Gladwell in his book *Outliers*.[19] Gladwell reports that great achievers such as Mozart, the Beatles, and Bill Gates all practiced and honed their skills for at least 10,000 hours before their greatness began to emerge. Examples of greatness achieved through hard work are Isaac Asimov, one of the most prolific writers in human history; Napoleon Dynamite, who works tirelessly to learn a difficult dance routine that helps his friend Pedro win his high school election; and Tom Kite, an accomplished professional golfer whose extraordinary work ethic, perhaps more than ability, propelled him to greatness.

There are also instances of heroism acquired by being in a unique situation Consider the story of Rosa Parks, whose refusal to sit at the back of a Montgomery, Alabama, bus helped fuel the civil rights movement; Arland Williams, one of the heroes of Air Florida flight 90; and Rick Blaine, who found himself in the unique position of being able to help Victor Lazlo. These individuals typically don't set out with the intention of being heroes. In fact, the situations they find themselves in are usually unpleasant, requiring a difficult choice that has painful consequences. The choice, however, is the correct one from a moral perspective.

Psychologists have made a distinction between how much a person's behavior is caused by *traits*, defined as stable and enduring features of one's personality, versus *states*, defined as temporary and fleeting conditions.[20] From this perspective, a hero who performs heroic actions over time and in many different situations can be said to have the trait of heroism. This heroic trait, or set of traits, is a long-term and permanent part of the person's makeup. In contrast, a hero who performs a single heroic action stemming from an unusual situation can be said to have been in a state favorable for heroism to occur. The heroic state of this person is short term and unlikely to appear under more ordinary circumstances.

When we talk about the trait of heroism, we are most likely referring to a cluster of traits, such as courage, hard work, and selflessness. The presence of these traits in an individual does not guarantee that he or she will become a hero. They only increase the chances of heroism emerging if this person finds him or herself in an environment where these traits can manifest themselves in behavior. A brave selfless person seeking a career as a firefighter, for example, is more likely to become a hero than that same person seeking a career as an accountant. When we say that someone's heroism was state based, then it is likely that extraordinary circumstances gave rise to the heroic act. In state-based heroism, a person need not possess all the traits associated with heroism. Extraordinary circumstances tend to produce extraordinary behavior. We don't mean to minimize the accomplishments of one-time heroes who respond to states of emergencies. State-based heroes clearly have the right stuff. It just takes an extraordinary situation for that stuff to see the light of day.

Direct versus Indirect Leadership

Heroes are very frequently leaders, and they are leaders in one of two ways, or in some cases, both ways. Psychologist Howard Gardner distinguishes the two kinds of leaders.[21] First, a hero may be a direct leader. This is the more familiar kind, where the leader interacts directly with potential followers, and by his or her words or deeds, attempts to persuade or mobilize an audience to believe something or to do something. When President Franklin Roosevelt in his first inaugural address reassured the country that "the only thing we have to fear is, fear itself," he was exercising direct leadership. Roosevelt was attempting to convince people that the nation's present problems could be solved just as those in the past had been.

In contrast, a hero may be an indirect leader, one whose works and deeds provide an example or model. When Albert Einstein wrote his papers on relativity theory in the early 1900s, he was exercising indirect leadership. His ideas influenced other physicists and directed their theoretical thinking. Einstein's leadership was indirect because it had nothing to do with a formal leadership role or with his relationships with other scholars. The products of his ideas led others. In the same way, we can see comedian Steven Colbert, dancer Martha Graham, or fictional detective Sherlock Holmes as leading by their products and performances. Unlike direct leaders, indirect leaders probably never view themselves as leaders. But they can exert as powerful an influence on others as direct leaders can.

In examining the relationship between heroism and leadership, we see that there is certainly some overlap. The lists of heroes given in Table 1.1 include many who were leaders, but it would appear to be true that not all heroes are leaders and not all leaders are heroes. For example, while almost everyone would agree that Adolf Hitler was the leader of Germany, no one with any sense of decency would dare call him a hero. Only a very few of the 44 U.S. Presidents are considered heroes. Both of us, as authors of this book, have served as chairs of academic departments, and we can say with complete confidence no one who has served under us would ever associate us with the word *hero*. Leaders, it seems, can be heroes, villains, or neither.

Heroes, on the other hand, are usually leaders. If they are direct leaders, they achieved their greatness by benefiting people directly, in face-to-face interactions. The leadership shown by direct leaders is usually intentional and, as such, their heroic acts are also intentional. Indirect leaders typically do not have physical face-to-face contact with those whom they benefit. They lead by example, and if they are deemed to be heroes, their heroism is usually unintentional. Irena Sendler never set out to be a hero. In fact, she rejected that label her entire life. When Elizabeth Barrett Browning created her inspired poetry and Claude Monet his great artwork, they didn't have leadership in mind. Yet their bodies of work led countless poets and artists who followed them.

Direct leaders who become heroes usually enjoy a great deal of success in exerting influence over those whom they lead. Social scientists who study the art of persuasion know that there are two routes to persuasion: a central route and a peripheral route.[22] The central route to persuasion is the most direct route. If I am running for mayor and I want to convince you to vote for me, I will give you some strong arguments for why I am the best candidate. That kind of direct approach reflects the central route to persuasion. It assumes you have a brain and will use it wisely. The peripheral route to persuasion is a bit sneakier because it relies on your heart more than your brain. If I use the peripheral route to get you to vote for me, I might pay Irena Sendler or Mother Teresa, if they were alive, to sing my praises on TV ads. The peripheral route often invokes emotion to persuade.

Direct leaders who evolve into heroes seem to know intuitively that effective persuasion relies on a combination of both central and peripheral routes. An effective leader can influence her followers by providing strong factual evidence in support of a particular course of action (the central route) and by being likeable and charismatic (the peripheral route). These central and peripheral processes can feed off each other and become entangled. In short, the heart can affect the brain, and vice versa. For example, studies have shown that the viewpoints expressed by a likeable and charismatic leader are judged as more credible than those same viewpoints expressed by a less likeable and charismatic person.

Heroes are thus able to tap successfully into both central and peripheral processes in their interactions with others. By definition, heroes are loved and admired, and this affection we have for them colors our interpretations of their actions. Their words and works stir us emotionally, deepening not just our admiration but also our beliefs about how much they fit the ideal heroic image. John F. Kennedy comes to mind as an example. His speeches were not just intelligently crafted. They moved Americans. "Ask not what your country can do for you; ask what you can do for your country," he said, using the central route to persuasion to exercise direct leadership. But what made Kennedy a hero was largely the peripheral sphere of his influence. He was young, handsome, and likeable. More importantly, he died at a young age, forever freezing that appealing image of him in our minds. His assassination, still tugging at our heartstrings today, forever sealed his legacy as a hero.

2

EXEMPLARS

Our Images of Heroes

Near the end of the novel *One Flew over the Cuckoo's Nest*, the hero, Randle Patrick McMurphy, is lobotomized. The villain, Big Nurse, has prevailed. She ordered the surgery, rendering McMurphy brain dead. Many heroes die in their struggles. The outcome for this hero—essentially being turned into a vegetable—feels much worse. But the novel's narrator, Chief Bromden, doesn't let the story end that way. The Chief is one of the patients in the mental hospital who has been most helped by McMurphy. He has become the typical "sidekick" in a far from typical hero narrative. He describes what he does next, lying close to McMurphy in the hospital ward at night:

> I moved to pick up the pillow, and the eyes fastened on the movement and followed me as I stood up and crossed the few feet between the beds. The big, hard body had a tough grip on life. It fought a long time against having it taken away, flailing and thrashing around so much I finally had to lie full length on top of it and scissor the kicking legs with mine while I mashed the pillow into the face. I lay there on top of the body for what felt like days. Until the thrashing stopped. Until it was still a while and had shuddered once and was still again. Then I rolled off. I lifted the pillow, and in the moonlight I saw the expression hadn't changed from the blank, dead-end look the least bit, even under suffocation.

I took my thumbs and pushed the lids down and held them
till they stayed. Then I lay back on my bed.[1]

After smothering McMurphy so that his living but lifeless body
doesn't remain in the ward as a reminder of Big Nurse's power, Chief
Bromden awaits his own punishment. Then he is reminded that
McMurphy had shown him a way to escape, if he can believe in his
own power. He goes into the tub-room, looks at the huge control
panel, and struggles to lift it. Using all his strength, he rips the panel
from its moorings on the floor, staggers to the nearest window, and
throws it through the glass and the screen. Then he leaps through the
opening and flees. "I remember I was taking huge strides as I ran....
I felt like I was flying. Free." (pp. 270–271). At the very end, he thinks
of all the places from his youth on the Columbia River he'll visit on
his escape to Canada. "Mostly, I'd just like to look over the country
around the gorge again, just to bring some of it clear in my mind
again. I been away a long time." (ibid p. 272).

Like many other heroes, R. P. McMurphy has sacrificed himself to
help others. He didn't start with the intention of being a hero or putting himself in harm's way. But when he saw Nurse Ratched humiliating patients and undermining their steps toward autonomy and
psychological health, he allowed himself to be pulled into a struggle
for their sanity. As a result, the central drama of *One Flew over the
Cuckoo's Nest* is the power struggle between McMurphy and the Big
Nurse, Miss Ratched. At stake is the well-being of the patients under
her sway.

When McMurphy arrives, Nurse Ratched's mental hospital ward
in a rural section of Oregon is a well-oiled machine. It runs smoothly
because the patients are kept in their place—dependent on medica-
tion and the whims of Big Nurse. Electroshock therapy and even
lobotomy are used often to maintain calm and control. The psychiatrists nominally in charge see patients infrequently. Day to day,
the nurses on the ground control every aspect of patients' lives.
The patients are reasonably comfortable, and reasonably looked
after, as long as they keep their place. For Nurse Ratched, that place

is under her thumb. All that begins to change when McMurphy arrives.

The story's unfolding events are conveyed through the thoughts of Chief Bromden, the son of a former Columbia Indian chief and a white woman. He isn't really a chief himself, but everyone at the hospital, somewhat mockingly, calls him Chief. He is six feet seven inches tall and extremely strong, but he experiences himself as small and weak. Part of his paranoid delusion is misperceiving how big he is and how big and powerful others are. He is not really deaf and dumb, but he has convinced the hospital staff and other patients that he is. He spends most of his time standing in the halls sweeping, for hours on end. He is ridiculed by many as Chief Broom. Because no one thinks that he can hear, he fades into the background and goes unnoticed. But he is vigilant and observant, and knows exactly what is going on.

When Randle Patrick McMurphy arrives on the scene, the Chief realizes that he is "no ordinary Admission." "He sounds big" and his voice, "loud and full of hell," reminds the Chief of his Papa. Right away McMurphy "commences to laugh. ... It's free and loud and it comes out of his wide grinning mouth and spreads in rings bigger and bigger till its lapping against the walls all over the ward. ... This sounds real. I realize all of a sudden it's the first laugh I've heard in years." McMurphy is large and boisterous. He makes an immediate impact. He asks the patients, "Who's the bull goose loony here?" and declares his intention to be that person, the craziest one, himself. He has been "bull goose catskinner" in logging operations, "bull goose gambler" in Korea, and "bull goose pea weeder" in prison (pp. 15–24).

As the Chief observes McMurphy during the first few days, he notes that "he looks like he's enjoying himself, like he's the sort of guy who gets a laugh out of people" (p. 26). The Chief also notes how perceptive McMurphy is about others, and fears that McMurphy senses right away that his deafness is just an act. When he gets around to shaking the Chief's hand, the Chief immediately senses his charisma and power: "the fingers were thick and strong closing over mine, and my hand commenced to feel peculiar and went to swelling up out there on my stick of an arm, like he was transmitting his own blood into it. It rang with blood and power. It blowed up near as big as his." (p. 26).

Most of the other patients are immediately taken with McMurphy, but some are jealous of his power and cynical about the obvious fact that he faked being crazy to get released from a prison work farm and placed in a cushy mental hospital. To them he seems only to want to dominate, and to win money and cigarettes in different card games and gambling contests. But it is clear that he likes his fellow patients and that he is disgusted by their servile attitude toward Big Nurse.

Right away McMurphy challenges many of Nurse Ratched's rules. The nurse attempts to turn others, including the hospital doctor, against him by reading from his file that he has "a history of street brawls and barroom fights and a series of arrests for Drunkenness, Assault and Battery, Disturbing the Peace, repeated gambling and one arrest" for Statutory Rape. McMurphy winks at the doctor and says that he thought the 15-year-old girl was "seventeen, Doc, and she was *plenty* willin'." (p. 44). McMurphy willingly points out that his record also says that he is a likely psychopath, and that he is "*over-zealous*" in his sexual relations. He asks: "Doctor, is that real serious?" (p. 46). This attempt by Nurse Ratched to alienate the others from McMurphy clearly backfires.

But the struggle goes on. McMurphy realizes that the patients are not really "crazy" and that the whole mental health system, as represented by Nurse Ratched, actually enables and enforces withdrawal, submissiveness, and lifelessness. The Chief sees that system as part of the larger "Combine" that enforces conformity and mediocrity throughout society. McMurphy sees how the nurse turns the patients against each other in group therapy meetings, humiliating them one by one by focusing on their inadequacies. One patient explains that they have to act like rabbits and "recognize the wolf as the strong." McMurphy protests, "You're no damned rabbit," (pp. 60–61) but he sees that the Nurse has persuaded the patients to act like one. From then on his struggle against the Big Nurse is toward getting the patients to stand up for themselves and find ways to return to the world outside the walls of the hospital.

One pivotal moment comes when McMurphy causes the nurse to let the men vote on whether the time for watching television can be changed so that they can see the World Series. Not many of the men dare to vote against the nurse's wishes, and she is able to rig the election to thwart McMurphy. He responds by sitting in front of the dark television as if the game were on. Many of the patients sit down beside him and join in the fantasy of watching, thereby enraging Big Nurse. The Chief thinks: "If somebody'd of come in and took a look, men watching a blank TV, a fifty-year-old woman hollering and squealing at the back of their heads about discipline and order and recriminations, they'd of thought the whole bunch was crazy as loons." (p. 128).

McMurphy commits himself more and more to the struggle against Big Nurse on the patients' behalf—even when he knows that he is committed to the hospital, and that she controls his destiny, even when she orders one electric shock treatment for him after another. At one point McMurphy persuades the doctor to let the men take an outing on a deep sea fishing boat. Interestingly, once on board he assists them in fishing only up to a point. Increasingly he turns control over to them. He lets them experience their various competencies. When a storm comes up and the boat is three life jackets short, three patients volunteer to go without. Everyone "is surprised that McMurphy hadn't insisted that he be one of the heroes; all during the fuss he'd stood back against the cabin, bracing against the pitch of the boat, watching the guys without saying a word. Just grinning and watching." (p. 214). The effect is transforming. When the boat returns and the patients proudly walk off with their catch, men who heckled them when they set off "could sense the change that most of us were only suspecting; these weren't the same bunch of weak-knees from a nuthouse that they'd watch take their insults on the dock this morning." (p. 215).

McMurphy's fight to empower the men is working, but it is taking its toll. The Chief notices on the bus trip back to the hospital that McMurphy's "face reflected an expression," usually hidden, that was "dreadfully tired and strained and *frantic*, like there wasn't enough time left for something he had to do ..." (p. 218).

The struggle climaxes when the nurse terrorizes Billy, one of the younger, least confident patients by saying she will tell his mother that he spent the night with a prostitute that McMurphy sneaked into the ward. When Billy is taken to an office to await his fate, he slashes his wrist and kills himself. During the ensuing moments of confusion, McMurphy could easily have escaped. Instead, he lunges at the nurse and nearly strangles her before he is pulled away by several aides. Then the "treatment" McMurphy receives to control his outbursts is the lobotomy that effectively kills him.

Even though the nurse destroys McMurphy, he has succeeded in empowering and liberating most of the patients. Including, at the end, the Chief. Nearly all of them have checked out of the hospital or transferred to other wards. Hers is a Pyrrhic victory: McMurphy has ultimately defeated her and "the Combine" that she represents. (Since many readers may be more familiar with the 1975 movie starring Jack Nicholson than the 1962 novel, it is worth noting that the film ends differently than the book. In the film, the nurse has regained complete control. The patients have again submitted, except for the Chief. Perhaps director Milos Forman took a darker view of heroic possibilities than author Ken Kesey.)[2]

EXEMPLARS: THE SOCIAL COGNITION OF HEROISM

There is little doubt that McMurphy is perceived as a hero by readers. He is also viewed as a hero by other characters in the novel, as Nurse Ratched realizes, to her dismay. During a staff meeting about his treatment, the nurse argues forcefully for leaving him in the ward so that she can break both him and his hold on the others. She will make him pay for his rebellion with shock treatments, permanent incarceration, and, if necessary, a lobotomy. Then McMurphy will cave in: "If we keep him on the ward I am certain his brashness will subside, his self-made rebellion will dwindle to nothing, and that our redheaded hero will cut himself down to something the patients will all recognize and lose respect for: a braggart and a blowhard." (p. 136).

Both readers of the book and patients in the hospital view McMurphy as a hero for a simple but important reason. Our psychological development and our culture provide us with mental models or templates for heroes, and McMurphy fits the model. Or, as many social psychologists would say, we have hero schemas and McMurphy is an exemplar of that schema.[3] That is, he is a very good example of our general idea of a hero. To understand this more fully we need to consider what we know about how human beings think about each other and themselves.

Schemas

For some time, psychologists have used the concept of schema to understand social thinking. Roughly speaking, a schema is an image or a mental model, a general idea of something. The term *schema* comes from the Greek word for "shape" and thus refers to the rough outline of what we know about certain individuals or kinds of individuals. More formally, psychologists define a schema as a mental representation that contains our general knowledge about something, whether that something is an individual, a group, an object, or even an event. Most relevant here, we have schemas about categories of people such as fathers, nurses, bullies, cheerleaders, and, yes, heroes. For starters, we can say that our schemas define heroes as moral, self-sacrificing, concerned with the common good, highly skilled, competent, and generally attractive and admirable. As the patients in the ward get to know McMurphy in *One Flew over the Cuckoo's Nest,* they attribute all these qualities to him.

Let's see just how this works. If a person has characteristics that bring a particular schema to mind, we then see many of the person's traits and behaviors through the lens of that schema. The schema creates expectations of what the person is like, and we tend to see what we expect. For example, we have schemas about people from different social backgrounds, different occupations, and different countries. These schemas about groups are, of course, stereotypes. They create expectations, and we interpret the behavior of people from those groups according to these stereotypic expectations.[4] Our stereotypes are so powerful that even when we try to put them aside, they exert a powerful effect on what we see and what we remember.[5]

Just this kind of power is shown in an important study in which college students were given information about a little girl in middle school. Some students were given biographical summaries and pictures showing that the girl came from a relatively wealthy background. Other students were led to believe that she came from a much less affluent working-class background. Many people in America have stereotypes of upper- and middle-class children as being more academically successful, and basically brighter, than working-class children. How would these stereotypes affect impressions of the little girl? Somewhat surprisingly, when the students judging the girl were simply asked to predict how she would do in school, they made the same judgments regardless of her background. Social class stereotypes didn't govern the predictions. Yet when other students watched a videotape of the girl taking tests in school, those who were told that she came from a working-class background perceived her as struggling and doing poorly. Students watching the same videotape who believed that she came from a privileged background thought that she was working steadily and successfully. Resistance to stereotypes stopped students from simply assuming that the poorer girl was less intelligent. But when they had to interpret her test-taking performance, the stereotypes wormed their way into their perceptions.[6]

Schemas not only cause us to interpret information about people in ways that fit our expectations, they also blind us to information that doesn't fit the schema. Baseball expert Bill James describes how images of home-run hitters affected sportswriters' assessment of Chicago Cubs Hall of Fame shortstop Ernie Banks. Basically, Banks was dismissed as a poor fielder compared to other shortstops. His 512 home runs led writers to see him only as a slugger. James wrote, "People have trouble reconciling the image of the power hitter—the slow, strong muscleman—with the image of the shortstop, who is lithe, quick, and agile." Statistics show that Banks was actually an excellent fielder. But expectations, derived from schemas, swamped the data. Writers didn't see what didn't fit their schemas.[7]

There is a poignant example of schemas leading people to ignore what doesn't fit their expectations near the end of *One Flew over the Cuckoo's Nest*. The patients have a schema or an image of McMurphy. When he is wheeled into the ward after his lobotomy, they refuse to believe that it's him. The chart on the gurney reads, "McMurphy, Randle P. Postoperative, Lobotomy." But one patient says, "Aaah, what's the old bitch tryin' to put over on us anyhow? That ain't him." "*Nothing like him*" one of the others confirms. "How stupid she think we are?" (p. 269). It's only when the Chief sees in the clear moonlight that the lifeless form really is McMurphy that he smothers him and escapes.

Schemas not only lead us to ignore things that are there but also to see things that aren't. In a classic study of expectations, first-grade teachers were told that several pupils in their classes had been identified by a reliable measure, the "Harvard Test of Inflected Acquisition," as "spurters," or late bloomers, who would excel in their classrooms. The teachers in fact saw those students as more intelligent, even though there was no such test and the students named were randomly chosen.[8] In his book *Blink,* Malcolm Gladwell provides another example in his chapter called "The Warren Harding Effect." Ohio politician Harry Daugherty took notice of small-town newspaper publisher Warren Harding. Harding caught Daugherty's attention because of his good looks. He had chiseled, masculine features, a large but graceful figure, a dynamic manner of moving and speaking, and a clear, resonant voice. Daugherty thought that Harding just "looked like a Senator."[9] He fit the image, the schema, or the model, whatever we might call it. Once the schema was activated, other senatorial and leadership qualities, such as intelligence, seemed detectable to observers. Harding was not only elected Senator, he quickly became a national figure. In 1920, he became the first incumbent U.S. Senator elected President of the United States. (There have been only two others: John F. Kennedy and Barack Obama). In fact, Harding lacked both the self-confidence and intelligence that good political leadership requires. It should have come as no surprise to Harry Daugherty, who was intimately familiar with Harding's deficits, that he is typically rated as the worst or one of the worst presidents in U.S. history.

The case of Warren Harding suggests that in addition to rich leader schemas there may also be rich hero schemas. We have already discussed how Rick Blaine, Irena Sendler, and R. P. McMurphy fit the image. But we can say more about the elements of that image. Our own studies actually allow us to be much more specific about those elements, or what we might call the colors in the hero portrait. Here's what we did. We asked 75 college students to list the traits that they believed described heroes. Then another group of 50 participants sorted cards listing the resulting traits into piles based on how similar or different they thought the traits were to each other. A statistical analysis of the sortings showed eight different trait clusters, which we've called the Great Eight. These are the traits our students think of as heroic: Smart, Strong, and Selfless, Caring and Charismatic, Resilient and Reliable, and finally, Inspiring. Following is a list of the great eight traits, as well as a number of closely related traits in each cluster.

Smart: intelligent, smart, wise
Strong: strong, leader, dominating, courageous, gallant
Selfless: moral, honest, selfless, humble, altruistic
Caring: compassionate, empathetic, caring, kind
Charismatic: eloquent, charismatic, dedicated, passionate
Resilient: determined, persevering, resilient, accomplished
Reliable: loyal, true, reliable
Inspiring: admirable, amazing, great, inspirational

It's interesting to see how these personal characteristics relate to some classic studies on how human beings make sense of the people, objects, and events in their worlds. These studies essentially ask, How do people make meaning? How do they construct interpretations of their experience? Conducted in the 1950s by psychologists Charles Osgood, George Suci, and Percy Tannenbaum, this research identified three basic dimensions of judgment.[10] First, people make good-bad judgments. These constitute what we call the Evaluative dimension. Whatever people observe or encounter they evaluate positively or negatively. And we can say two other things about these good-bad judgments. First, it's likely that they are people's very first reactions. Also, they are often affective or emotional. In short, we quickly experience what we encounter as good or bad, and react with positive or negative emotion. Sometimes we may thoughtfully appraise what we encounter before we evaluate it. But usually our initial response is a good versus bad emotional judgment.

Osgood and his colleagues also described the Potency and Activity dimensions. We not only judge things as good or bad but also as strong or weak, and active or passive. How do the Evaluative, Potency, and Activity dimensions coincide with the Great Eight traits? Selfless, Inspiring, and Caring are clearly Evaluative judgments. Smart and Strong are clearly Potency judgments. Reliable sounds both strong and good, so it is both an Evaluative and a Potency judgment. Similarly, Resilient reflects both Potency and Activity dimensions.

Charismatic may reflect judgments of all three dimensions. Charisma is usually seen as good, strong, and active.

Finally, we should remember that we initially identified morality and competence as the two basic dimensions of heroism. So, we can say that heroes are moral, that is, good, by being Caring, Selfless, and Inspiring. The competence dimension signals that they are also strong and active, and those traits, as noted earlier, are represented by the other five of the great eight: Resilient, Reliable, Charismatic, Smart, and Strong. We hope not to confuse you, the reader, by peppering you with lots of labels. What we are presenting is how people, including you readers of course, construe heroes. Think about which template best captures how you think about heroes. That they are moral and competent? That they are strong, active, and good? Or that they have most or all of the Great Eight? All of these are good ways to describe how we think about heroes.

Our Heroes Thus Far

Perhaps we can most easily get used to thinking about the Great Eight by considering how some of the heroes we've discussed so far rate on those traits. Rick Blaine in our Introduction is clearly Smart, Strong, and Charismatic from the outset. We also think he's probably Resilient. He is potentially Inspiring, but there are grave doubts about whether he is Caring, Selfless, and Reliable. Those doubts create the dramatic tension of the story. Given that Rick is an exemplar of the hero schema, that is, given that he fits the model, we'd like to see him as moral (Caring, Selfless, Reliable) as well as competent (Smart, Strong, Charismatic). We have hints that underneath the hard shell, he is, as Victor Laszlo says, someone willing to fight for the right cause. But at one point near the end of the film, it looks like he's going to sell out Victor to the Nazis. Then, of course, he does the right thing. The ending is bittersweet because our hopes for Rick to be the complete hero are gratified, but he has to pay the price of giving up the love of his life for another man. He makes us feel a little better when Ilsa asks, "But what about us?" and he answers, "We'll always have Paris. We didn't have, we'd lost it, until you came to Casablanca. We got it back last night." So there's some consolation, but the lump in our throats doesn't go away. Rick underlines the idea that there are costs to being a hero.

What about Irena Sendler? When she makes the crucial decision to smuggle children out of the Warsaw Ghetto, we see that she is Selfless, Caring, and Inspiring. Then she shows that she is Smart. And when we learn of her capture and torture, we are impressed with how remarkably Strong, Reliable, and Resilient she is. Maybe she's not Charismatic, but she is an excellent exemplar of seven of the eight traits of the hero schema.

In *One Flew over the Cuckoo's Nest*, McMurphy becomes heroic fairly early. Right away he is Strong, Smart, and Charismatic. The others come quickly to admire him for his courage to act as he truly is. By that point in the story he is also Inspiring—especially to The Chief, who feels that he has been worn down by the Combine since childhood. He is in awe of McMurphy's uncompromising courage: "I was just being ... the way people wanted. How can McMurphy be who he is?" (p. 140). We saw earlier that Nurse Ratched tries to makes the patients see McMurphy in terms of another schema, that of "a braggart and a blowhard," but McMurphy does not "back down" as she predicts. Toward the end the nurse tries to shake the hero schemas by raising doubts about whether McMurphy is Caring, Selfless, and Reliable. She plants the idea that McMurphy only cares about winning money from bets with the patients. Even the Chief is momentarily doubtful. But McMurphy continually fights for himself, and through himself for the others.

The only question then becomes whether McMurphy is sufficiently Resilient. He keeps challenging the nurse, and she keeps sending him to "Building One" for additional shock treatments. He tries to make the Chief believe that it's no big deal: "all they was doin' was chargin' his battery for him, free for nothing." He says, "When I get out of here the first woman who takes on ol' Red McMurphy the ten-thousand-watt psychopath, she's gonna light up like a pinball machine and pay off in silver dollars. No, I ain't scared of their little battery charger." (p. 242–243). But the Chief isn't so easily fooled. He noticed McMurphy's "tired and strained" look coming back from the fishing trip. Now he notices that at announcements of further electroshock treatments "the muscles in his jaw went taut and his whole face drained of color, looking thin and scared—the face I had seen reflected in the windshield on the trip back from the coast" (p. 243). But in the end, McMurphy is Resilient enough to inspire most of the patients back to health and independence.

Charisma

One of the Great Eight traits reveals an especially interesting aspect of the way we perceive heroes. That trait is Charismatic. Charisma is often seen as part of heroism and even more, perhaps, part of leadership. But what exactly is charisma, and how is it perceived? We can start with a dictionary definition: "a personal quality attributed to those who arouse fervent popular devotion and enthusiasm." And another: "a personal magic of leadership arousing special popular loyalty; a special magnetic charm or appeal."[11] Synonyms are charm, magnetism, and presence. The term is derived from the Greek, meaning "divine gift" or "gift of grace." A student once said that whatever charisma is, watching or listening to the person who has it raises "goose bumps." We react emotionally to charismatic people. Their appeal attracts us and entrances us. One example of charismatic appeal is Ingrid Bergman's beauty in the film *Casablanca*. It is enhanced by slightly out-of-focus filming, which creates an aura, giving her an almost supernatural or "divine" appearance.

If charisma is "a personal quality attributed" by devoted followers, as the dictionary states, can we be more specific about what that personal quality is? Probably not. Sociologist Max Weber introduced the term to scholarly usage and noted that it denotes "exceptional powers or qualities," but it isn't clear just what those are.[12] We'll have to be satisfied by saying charismatic people are somehow compelling in their appearance, voice, and manner. People often perceived as charismatic include Martin Luther King Jr. and John F. Kennedy—King for his soaring rhetoric, Kennedy for his looks, dash, and eloquence. Many people feel that President Kennedy moved and spoke in a graceful way that seemed smooth, strong, and self-assured. Martin Luther King Jr.'s voice and delivery were charismatic. Both the words and music were moving. When we listen to the end of his famous "I have a dream" speech, the power of the final phrases "free at last, free at last, thank God Almighty, we are free at last" compels our attention and stirs our emotion.[13]

Leadership scholars define charismatic leadership as the strong articulation of a vision and a mission, clear willingness of the charismatic leader to take risks and make sacrifices to achieve the vision, and empowering words and behaviors that express both high expectations to followers about their own efforts to accomplish the mission, and confidence that they will succeed.[14] Leadership scholars also emphasize the fact that charisma is ultimately in the eye of the beholder. Psychologist Edwin Hollander wrote that charisma is "accorded or withdrawn" by followers, depending on whether the leader's behavior and message are arousing and motivating.[15] Another psychological perspective is that once certain individuals in a group are perceived as leaders, based on having attractive qualities that represent the best qualities of the group, followers will attribute charismatic qualities to those individuals and construct charismatic images of them. Perhaps the best way to think about charisma is that it's a two-way street. The charismatic leader or hero has to have certain qualities, but followers have to be willing to acknowledge and attribute those special qualities based on their own needs and commitments. Sigmund Freud put it well, writing that people's need for strong leadership takes the leader halfway in attracting the devotion of followers, but the leader must have the personal qualities, including "a strong and imposing will," and devotion to an ideal, that inspire confidence and admiration[16].

Abraham Lincoln offers an interesting example of charisma, in part because there are no films of him, or even audio recordings of his speeches. Charismatic reactions came from people seeing and hearing him in person, viewing his photographs, or reading his speeches. In person, Lincoln was a striking figure. Historian Shelby Foote described the effect: "Thousands touched him, heard him, saw him at close range, and scarcely one in all those thousands ever forgot the sight of that tall figure, made taller still by the stovepipe hat, and the homely drape of the shawl across the shoulders. Never forgotten, because it was unforgettable, the impression remained, incredible and enduring, imperishable in its singularity—and finally, dear."[16]

At the same time, photographs of Lincoln were very widely distributed, both in the United States and in Europe. One Frenchman commented that it wasn't obvious that pictures of Lincoln would help the cause of attracting people to his leadership. By ordinary standards, he was pretty ugly. Lincoln himself often made jokes about being far from handsome. When a political opponent called him two-faced, Lincoln asked whether anyone could believe that if he had another face he'd choose to wear the one they saw. But Shelby Foote again comments, this time on Lincoln's face: "You saw it not so much for what it was, as for what it held. Suffering was in it; so were understanding, kindliness, and determination." A soldier who saw Lincoln when he visited the army wrote, "None of us to our dying day can forget that countenance.... Concentrated in that one great, strong, yet tender face, the agony of the life and death struggle of the hour was revealed as we had never seen it before. With a new understanding, we knew why we were soldiers."[17]

These appraisals of Lincoln nicely fit the Great Eight formulation. He appeared Caring and Selfless, Strong, Resilient and Reliable, and Smart. This made him Inspiring and paved the way for the perception that he was Charismatic. We noted that charismatic leadership involves articulation of and sacrifice for a cause, and the capacity to empower followers. As the soldier wrote, Lincoln's countenance revealed his commitment and gave the writer himself new clarity about the purpose of the struggle and his own commitment to it.

Of course, it is Lincoln's words more than his image that move people today just as they moved those who heard him when he spoke. Long before Martin Luther King Jr., Lincoln was an orator who used rhythm, metaphor, and biblical phrasing to shape eloquent arguments. In his first inaugural address he assured his countrymen that "the mystic chords of memory" would again touch "the better angels of our nature." In his 1862 message to Congress he argued that "in giving freedom to the slave, we assure freedom to the free—honorable alike in what we give and what we preserve. We shall nobly save or meanly lose the last, best hope of earth.... The way is plain, peaceful, generous, just—a way which, if followed, the world will forever applaud, and God must forever bless." And in his second inaugural address he pointed the way forward, declaring, "With malice toward, with charity for all, with firmness in the right as God gives us to see the right, let us strive on to finish the work we are in ..."[18] Taken together, Lincoln's image, Lincoln's words, and the story of his struggle give him and his memory "magnetic charm" and "a personal magic of leadership arousing special popular loyalty." That is, they made him charismatic.

The Need for Heroes and the Perception of Charisma

We've mentioned that people's needs and motivations can nudge them toward perceiving certain individuals as charismatic. Yet very often we aren't aware of all of our needs, or if we are aware of them, how they are affecting our perception of other people. Psychologists talk of "unconscious impression goals," where we are looking to find certain qualities in other people without being aware of it, and even if we are aware, without realizing how those goals affect our perceptions. There is a powerful example of unconscious impression goals at work in a study of potential leaders. College students were asked to imagine that they were screening candidates for a position in a small high-tech company. One group of participants was informed that the company was doing well. Another was told that it was in trouble—it was falling behind the competition and there were debilitating conflicts between individual employees. The students then read 32 statements describing a candidate for a job with the company. Half of the statements suggested leadership qualities, and half were irrelevant to leadership. The students then wrote open-ended descriptions of the candidate's qualifications for group membership based on the statements. The results showed that when students read about a troubled group, they wrote about leadership qualities in the potential employee. They had formed an unconscious goal to find a leader when the group was in trouble, and they unconsciously believed that they had found him. This didn't happen when the group was doing well.[19]

The larger message of this study is that we have "implicit theories of leadership" that make us think that a successful group has good leadership, and that a failing group *needs* good leadership. In the latter case we look for it. And in the present study, the participants found it. Various statistical analyses showed that they did so by misremembering leadership qualities belonging to someone else as belonging to the candidate they assessed. In short, the students formed the goal of finding a leader and convinced themselves that the potential candidate fit the bill. All of this, the results showed, happened unconsciously.

People's needs for heroes and heroic leaders interact in subtle ways with the ways leaders present themselves. Military historian John Keegan skillfully explores this interplay in his book examining heroic leadership, *The Mask of Command*. Keegan says that leaders of all kinds, but especially commanders sending their soldiers into battle, must employ theatrics and artifice to present themselves in accord with their followers' needs and expectations. Similarly in combat, commanders must conceal aspects of themselves that do not fit with what their armies require.[20]

In discussing what he calls the heroic leadership of Alexander the Great, Keegan describes his theatrical abilities and his inspiring oratory. Alexander knew just how and when to make an appearance on the battlefield. He took great risks in order to inspire feats of bravery from his soldiers. He knew how to speak to large armies on a personal level, addressing small groups at a time, in ways that connected with their hopes and fears. Alexander was handsome, charismatic, and had a natural flair for the mysterious and dramatic. He was also extremely well educated. His teacher was Aristotle. Not a bad mentor. He tamed the horse Bucephalus before a large audience, a feat deemed impossible. Alexander noticed that the horse was terrified of his own shadow. Simply by facing Bucephalus into the sun, so that his shadow was behind him, Alexander calmed and rode him. No one who watched understood what seemed like magic. But Alexander understood that the Macedonian armies needed someone with the stature of a hero to lead them on one of world history's most ambitious and successful military campaigns. He carefully crafted his persona to fit his followers' image of the hero.

Scripts: A Special Kind of Schema

The way we think about heroes involves more than images of what heroes are like. As we explained in Chapter 1, we also have mental models or images of how people become heroes. Such images are called *scripts*, which psychologists define as mental representations or images of how events unfold.[21] Scripts are a particular kind of schema, specifically an event schema. An example of a script is one for having a meal at a restaurant. We expect to be greeted when we enter, shown to a table, handed a menu, and so forth. In recent years, a part of the script, somewhat irritatingly, is that the server will come around after, or maybe even before, we have taken the first bite of our entrée and ask, "Is everything all right?" And of course, the script specifies that we say, "Oh yes, thank you very much." Scripts, like schemas in general, are essentially general ideas, or preconceptions, that generate expectations. They tell us how events will unfold. An example from sports is the script for what happens in a baseball game with a runner on first base and one out. If the batter hits a ground ball to the shortstop, fans who know the game expect the fielding team to attempt a double play. The shortstop will catch the ball, throw to the second baseman, who in turn will step on second base and fire to first. This all happens very rapidly, in less than 3 seconds. Someone who doesn't know the script will be lost as to what is happening and why. But the typical fan at the ballpark knows the script and anticipates exactly what happens as soon as the ball leaves the bat.

So we have heroism scripts, or what we also call narratives, about the sequence of events that lead to heroic behavior. We know, implicitly, that there are many kinds of heroism, and therefore many heroism scripts. Rick Blaine's final actions in *Casablanca* follow one common heroism narrative. Rick is initially hardened and self-centered: "I'm the only cause I'm interested in." But then he decides that the world war is more important than he is, and that he must put aside his love for Ilsa and help her escape with Victor Laszlo. McMurphy's journey to heroism follows much the same script. The self-centered individual with a shady past sees wrong that needs to be righted, and after getting drawn in, knowingly sacrifices his life to achieve that end. There are other heroism narratives. For example, people of modest abilities overcome great odds to accomplish worthy missions. David slays Goliath and saves his army. An innocent man, Papillon, makes a daring escape from a cruel prison in South America. In one way or another, heroes do what is right and show both courage and competence.

We've noted that our schemas about what heroes are like and our scripts about what they do to achieve heroism are varied. Our research shows that these schemas and scripts combine to produce numerous hero subtypes. Joseph Campbell called his 1949 book *The Hero with a Thousand Faces*.[22] We found several hundred hero subtypes appearing in various literatures. These can be grouped into several overarching prototypes, although any such classification is messy. However, to give a sense of the range of subtypes we can mention several. One is the Saint prototype, people who are almost entirely virtuous and benevolent. Jesus and Mother Theresa illustrate this prototype. Another is the Underdog prototype, people who overcome great obstacles. Sylvester Stallone's Rocky Balboa in the *Rocky* series and Daniel Larusso from *The Karate Kid* illustrate this category. And we can see another in many of actor Clint Eastwood's characters, such as Dirty Harry. They exemplify The Bad Boy group. They are rough customers to begin with, but they use their toughness to advance virtue.

ARCHETYPES AND THE EVOLUTION OF HERO SCHEMAS

Many of our schemas, whether they be stereotypes of people in different ethnic groups, our image of R. P. McMurphy, or a baseball script about a double play, clearly come from experience. We acquire a few beliefs, which may or may not be true, about a person, group, or event, and form overall schemas or scripts based on those beliefs. And then, as we have discussed previously, we base expectations on those mental representations. These expectations then guide our perceptions and memories. For example, we remember new information that is consistent with our schemas better than information that is unrelated to them. But one of the most intriguing ideas about schemas, especially those related to heroes, is that they are not based entirely on our individual experience, but also on our collective experience as human beings and on unconscious images inherited from the evolution of the human mind. These unconscious or latent images are called *archetypes*, and they figure prominently in the psychological theories of Carl Jung.[23]

Carl Jung himself is a hero to many scholars for his highly creative but also highly controversial theories of the structure and development of the human psyche. For other scholars his ideas lack sufficient basis in evidence. To fully understand how we think about heroes, we believe that they are worth careful consideration. Jung argued that one part of the psyche was something he called "the collective uncon-scious." He defined it as a storehouse of latent or potential images that have developed through human evolution. Jung called these latent images *archetypes*. By referring to the images as latent, Jung meant that they were not conscious images, but unconscious ones that could be activated, or made conscious, when something in an individual's experience fits the latent image.

Archetypes have form but not content. That is, they are general outlines, or general ideas, much like schemas. But unlike schemas, they are based on our collective experience over the course of evolu-tion, rather than individual experience. Jung wrote, "There are as many archetypes as there are typical situations in life. Endless repeti-tion has engraved these experiences into our psychic constitution, not in the form of images filled with content, but ... only as forms without content, representing merely the possibility of a certain type of perception and action."[24]

One example that illustrates these characteristics of an archetype is the *mother*. Throughout evolution, most human beings have had experiences with their biological mothers or others who have nur-tured them in a maternal way. This common experience creates a mother archetype, or a latent, unconscious outline of a mother figure. When a mother, or someone assuming a maternal role, actually appears in an infant's life and generally fits the inherited mother archetype, that archetype will be activated or elicited. Then the infant's experience with the mother will reflect the archetype in two ways. First, the archetype will guide the perception of the mother. In this sense, archetypes work just like schemas. Second, it will also guide the infant's emotional reaction to her. Since the preponderance of human experience with mothers is positive, the typical infant will have a positive emotional reaction to the mother and will want her to approach and stay close. In short, when an infant encounters a person corresponding to the mother archetype, that person is recognized and elicits a strong positive emotional reaction. More generally, we pay attention to—and are drawn toward or repelled from—objects or persons that fit a latent archetypical image.

Jung wrote about a large number of archetypes, including *God*, *magic*, *power*, and the *wise old man*. Most relevant for us, one of

Jung's archetypes is the *hero*. The fact that there is a hero archetype means that we are prepared to see individual people as heroic and react emotionally to those who fit the image. The archetype includes a general image of what the hero is like, that is, a hero schema, and also a heroism narrative, or script, containing general information about what heroes do.

Jung also discussed the ways archetypes combine to create more specific latent ideas. For example, there is a *demon* archetype, which can combine with the *hero* archetype to form a potential image of a "ruthless leader," an image that someone like Adolph Hitler can activate.[25] In this respect, the enduring fascination with vampires is particularly interesting. One recent discussion focuses on "the two main branches of vampire fiction: the vampire as romantic hero, and the vampire as undead monster."[26] Versions of the vampire narrative are as old as human consciousness and have taken form in many cultures at many different times. Different renderings of vampire myths contain different mixtures of *hero* and *demon* archetypes. Bram Stoker's well-known *Dracula* reveals more demon than hero. Yet today's readers of Stephanie Meyer's *Twilight* novels encounter a more heroic version, with a teenage girl entwined in a forbidden romance with an attractive vampire.

How valid are Jung's ideas about the collective unconscious and archetypes? It's hard to say, but there are several strands of evidence that suggest that human infants do have an inherited readiness to recognize and respond emotionally to other people. For example, studies of auditory perception show that infants can easily distinguish human voices from other sounds. We seem to be wired to attend to other people and to assess their significance for us. And studies of visual perception show that infants as young as 2 days old show strong preferences for gazing at human faces. Infants also systematically appraise features of human faces and show a remarkable ability to discriminate emotional expressions in those faces.[27] It makes good evolutionary sense for newborns to have inherited the capacity to respond to other people's emotions, as well as, for example, the capacity to suck and grasp.

Clues of another sort come from literary accounts of the ways people are drawn to certain natural features. Jung discussed natural archetypes such as *sun, wind, rivers,* and *fire.* In the first paragraphs of his classic novel *Moby Dick,* Herman Melville talked about the magnetic, and essentially archetypical, pull of the sea. His narrator Ishmael takes to a ship whenever he feels depressed, and he tells us: "almost all men in their degree .... cherish very nearly the same feelings toward the ocean with me." He goes on to note: "Take almost any path you please, and ten to one it carries you down in a vale, and leaves you there by a pool in the stream. There is magic in it." And he asks, "If Niagara were but a cataract of sand, would you travel your thousand miles to see it?"[28] Melville was clearly suggesting a water archetype that pushes or pulls human beings toward rivers, streams, and seas. Was Melville right? Think of what we pay for water views today.

HERO ARCHETYPES AND PERCEPTIONS OF PRESIDENTIAL GREATNESS

The idea that we have hero archetypes and that they can combine with other archetypes or schemas has been used to help explain how both laypeople and historians assess the "greatness" of U.S. Presidents. Students of the presidency have been conducting greatness polls since 1948 when Arthur Schlesinger, Sr. first queried historians and classified presidents into categories of great, near great, average, and so forth. In recent years such polls have proliferated, and have surveyed ordinary citizens as well as scholars. In 2000 C-SPAN published polls of both historians and viewers. In 2009 C-SPAN again published the results of polls, this time just of historians.[29] Of great interest here is how laypeople assess presidents, and also how little their assessments differ from the experts. It may be that the overlap between scholarly ratings and the ratings of the U.S. population as a whole reflects the fact that both rating sets are rooted in the same information interpreted in terms of the same archetypes.

Let's first consider a study of laypeople. In the summer of 2007, Rasmussen Reports released a study of the American public's approval ratings of the 42 U.S. Presidents from George Washington to George W. Bush.[30] The results were based on a national telephone survey of 1,000 randomly selected adults. The six presidents receiving the highest favorable ratings constitute a familiar list. In order of percent favorable totals, they are Washington, Lincoln, Jefferson, Theodore Roosevelt, Franklin Roosevelt, and Kennedy. All of these are usually at or near the top of "greatness ratings" reported for scholars in numerous studies, although Kennedy's rating is less stable than the others'. One of the most interesting findings was the percent of respondents who said "not sure," that is, they had no opinion or knowledge about various presidents. The data showed that only 12 were known by at least 90% of the respondents. The well-known group included the five most recent presidents (George W. Bush, Bill Clinton, George H. W. Bush, Ronald Reagan, and Jimmy Carter) and seven others, including the six just mentioned with the highest favorable ratings, and the president with the highest unfavorable rating, Richard Nixon. These results raise questions about which presidents people know and what they know about them. And since these ratings are so similar to scholarly greatness ratings, they again raise questions about why this similarity exists, and whether scholars and ordinary citizens rely on the same information and schemas or archetypes.

One obvious explanation for the similarity of ratings is that the opinions of experts trickle down in some way to the nonexpert, as the concept of the "two-step flow" of communication suggests. The idea here is that the media influence local "opinion leaders" who influence the public more broadly. On the other hand, psychologist Dean Keith Simonton argues that experts use the same leadership schemas and the same conveniently available information as nonexperts in assessing presidents. He argues that both groups operate from a leader schema based on the three dimensions of meaning that we discussed earlier. The schematic leader, just like the schematic hero, is strong, active, and good. Furthermore, the argument goes, information people have about specific presidents activates the leader schema to varying degrees. In most cases, if available information suggests that a particular president was in some way strong, active, or good, the leader schema will be activated and the missing pieces of the overall image will be filled in schematically.[31] Those who are strong and active, for example, will also be perceived as good. Any new information about the president will then be assimilated into that positive schema, at least until the information cannot fit the schema, and alternative schemas replace it. For example, Richard Nixon is often seen as strong and active, but definitely not good. Thus, he is known, but gets high disapproval ratings. He fits a villain schema more than a hero schema.

Furthermore, Simonton speculates that the leader schema is in fact archetypical. He argues that the strong, active, and good presidential image is based on the schema of an "ideal or archetypical leader" and that the leader archetype has "transhistorical, even cross-cultural relevance" and "may even possess a sociobiological substratum."[32] In other words, Simonton endorses the idea of a leader archetype, very much the same as Jung's hero archetype, that shapes our perceptions and evaluations of U.S. Presidents.

We've done further research to learn more about how ordinary people appraise the men who have been Presidents of the United States and also to help us understand how their assessments might be related to hero archetypes. We start with Simonton's idea that what we "know" about presidents is quite limited, and go on to consider whether even a relatively small amount of readily available and highly salient information might activate hero archetypes which generate strong opinions about the presidents.

Relevant here is a theory similar to Simonton's idea that people's opinions of presidents are based on powerful leader schemas and relatively little information. That theory is a model of opinions put forth by psychologist Robert Abelson over 40 years ago. In making sense of his own research on voting, Abelson suggested that people are much more influenced by simple arguments and "compelling little summarizations" that "make the social rounds" than general principles or philosophy, and that people worry very little about opinion consistency. He argues that "there are limits on the typical man's intellectual reach" and that "his organizing capacities and efforts are usually applied over a small content area."[33]

From this general perspective Abelson suggests that people's political thinking might be dominated by independent "opinion molecules." An opinion molecule is made up of a *fact*, a *feeling*, and a *following*. That is, its elements are some item of information, which may or may not be true, some pro or con emotional orientation, and a perception that significant others feel that same way. For example,

"It's a fact that when my Uncle Charlie had back trouble, he was cured by a chiropractor. You know, I feel that chiropractors have been sneered at too much, and I'm not ashamed to say so, because I know a lot of people who feel the same way." This example not only includes the fact, feeling, and following pieces that make up the opinion molecule, it also illustrates Abelson's idea that the function of opinion molecules is to "bestow conversational and cognitive security—they give you something to say and think when the topic comes up."

Both Simonton's discussion of leader schemas and Abelson's opinion molecule approach suggest the following: Most people have a small amount of information about most presidents; that information may fit the leader schema; and if it does the schema then guides the opinions people form about presidents. With this overall formulation in mind, our own research sets out to explore the following questions: First, what presidents do people know at all? Second, is there evidence for what Abelson might have called "presidential opinion molecules" that consist of *facts*, that is, specific beliefs about presidents—what they did, what they looked like, what personality traits they had—and *feelings*, that is, positive or negative assessments of these presidents?

We began by asking undergraduates at the University of Richmond to list as many presidents as they could in 1 minute. We were very much aware that the participant population, college students, is not representative of the U.S. public. One psychologist put the matter quite bluntly: College sophomores may not be people.[34] But this seemed like a good place to start, and we could compare our results with the broader Rasmussen survey. In fact, we began with the hypothesis that the number—and the names—of the presidents that the students in our studies would know or know about was roughly the same as those known in the Rasmussen poll. More specifically we predicted the Richmond students would typically know about a dozen well-known presidents, and that those would be substantially the same as the 12 presidents who were well known according to the Rasmussen poll.

Here's what we found. On average our students list about 15 presidents in 1 minute. Most of them had clearly run out of names before their 1 minute was up. Thus, they seem to know a little more than Rasmussen's survey respondents. Second, there are 10 presidents listed by more than half our participants. They are the first three presidents, George Washington, John Adams, and Thomas Jefferson; the four most recent presidents at the time, Ronald Reagan, George H. W. Bush, Bill Clinton, and George W. Bush; and three others: Abraham Lincoln, John F. Kennedy, and Richard Nixon. It was a little surprising that Franklin Roosevelt was not mentioned by more than half the students. But under a little time pressure only the most memorable presidents were mentioned.

Our list of 10 corresponds very closely to the Rasmussen 12. Of the first three presidents, our list includes John Adams, while theirs only lists George Washington and Thomas Jefferson. Also, Rasmussen includes Jimmy Carter, the fifth most recent president. And Rasmussen includes both Roosevelts. That is, we list Adams while they do not, and they list Carter and the two Roosevelts while we do not. But the nine overlapping are most suggestive. People tend to remember items at the beginning and end of lists. These tendencies are called primacy and recency effects.[35] So the common listings of Washington and Jefferson at the front end and Reagan, Clinton, and both Bushes at the tail end are not that surprising. The three who are neither first nor last in time are the most suggestive. Why are Lincoln, Kennedy, and Nixon so frequently remembered? Short answer: Lincoln and Kennedy are regarded as heroes. Nixon is regarded as a villain.

Why make this case? Remember that one of the Great Eight traits of heroes is Selfless. Heroes are people who unselfishly give their all. And remember that charismatic leaders are those who put themselves at risk. Lincoln, Kennedy, Martin Luther King Jr., and Mohandas Gandhi paid the ultimate price: They were assassinated. Nelson Mandela spent years in jail. And of course Randle Patrick McMurphy knowingly put himself at risk for lobotomy and ultimately death. We may not think very rationally about assassination, but Simonton's research shows that assassinated presidents tend to have high greatness ratings. This may be because assassination is one of those vivid *facts* predicted by the opinion molecule idea, and perhaps we automatically think of assassins as bad, and therefore their targets as good.

Our research supports the idea that assassination is highly salient. We flashed names of well-known Americans on a computer screen and asked students to type in the first word or short phrase that came to mind when they read the name. Several presidents were included, and for some there were very strong associations. For example, when the name Bill Clinton was shown, most participants immediately typed in "Monica" or some other word or short phrase referring to the scandal that nearly forced Clinton out of office. For Lincoln and Kennedy people most often mentioned assassination or the good things they accomplished or handled well, such as "emancipation" in Lincoln's case or "missile crisis" in Kennedy's case. These results suggest that assassination is vivid and salient, and when an admired person is assassinated, a *hero* archetype is activated. Historians have discussed how both Lincoln and Kennedy were idealized and became heroic after they were cut down by bullets.

If our evaluations of Lincoln and Kennedy are related to the *hero* archetype, what about Nixon and a villain archetype? We have a couple of relevant clues. First, Simonton's research shows that scandal is one of the most powerful predictors of presidential greatness ratings, in the negative direction. Second, Richard Nixon is strongly associated with scandal. In general, if a president is linked to scandal, that fact is very salient, and it hurts his reputation. It generally wipes out anything else that doesn't fit that image. For example, Warren Harding is almost always at or near the bottom of presidential greatness ratings. He was president for a little over 2 years, before he died in office, of natural causes. If people remember anything about Harding, it is the scandals that marked his administration. The same is true for Ulysses S. Grant. Grant served 8 years as president and is belatedly being recognized for his achievements in economic and foreign affairs, as well as his efforts on behalf of African Americans and Native Americans. But for decades all that even knowledgeable observers bothered to mention about Grant were the scandals associated with his administration, though never with him personally.

As for Nixon, our study of people's immediate associations to famous names showed that Watergate was overwhelmingly linked to Nixon's name. Only the link between Bill Clinton and Monica Lewinsky was stronger. It seems clear that in Nixon's case, the Watergate scandal is so salient that it swamps anything else in people's view of him. He comes off worst in the Rasmussen survey, and he is rated quite poorly by historians, despite being given very high marks for leadership in foreign affairs. Time will tell about Bill Clinton. He left office with very high approval ratings, despite being impeached, and has made some significant diplomatic contributions in the past few years. Also, the Lewinsky affair is viewed as a private failing by many people, in contrast to the constitutional crisis caused by Watergate. Thus far, Nixon seems to activate a villain schema much more than Bill Clinton. We'll have to wait to see if that continues.

3

REDEMPTION

Back from the Brink

For years, Diana, Princess of Wales, had been forced to cope with relentless paparazzi. As the beautiful, beloved, but often troubled ex-wife of Charles, the future King of England, she drew as much attention from the media as anyone in the world. Late on the night of August 31, 1997, Diana and her close friend, Dodi Al-Fayed, left the Hotel Ritz Paris by a rear exit and got into the back seat of a hired Mercedes-Benz. The car was driven by the hotel's acting security manager. Tragically, as it turned out, he had been drinking heavily. Chased by several vehicles filled with press photographers, the driver sped through a tunnel, lost control of the Mercedes, and crashed into a concrete pillar. Efforts to save Diana's life failed, and she was pronounced dead at 4:00 a.m. Al-Fayed and the driver were also killed.

An enormous outpouring of grief focused the world's attention. Roughly 2.5 billion people from all corners of the earth watched the televised funeral from Westminster Abbey. But the week between Diana's death and her funeral did not pass uneventfully. Al-Fayed's father suspected that there was a conspiracy to kill Diana and his son. He believed that it might have grown from opposition from the royals or others to a romantic relationship between the mother of two heirs to the British throne and an Islamic man. And for several days Queen Elizabeth herself refused to express publicly her own or the royal family's sense of loss from the death of one of their own. Prime Minister

Tony Blair attempted to deflect increasing anger at the Queen and the monarchy itself. He praised Diana as "the People's Princess." Finally, on the day before the funeral, the Queen met with mourners outside Buckingham Palace and appeared on television to praise her former daughter-in-law.

The funeral itself was a spectacle that deeply moved most of those in attendance and the many millions watching on television. Diana's two sons, William and Harry, walked behind the coffin with their father, and the entire royal family attended the service. Singer Elton John performed a new version of the song he originally wrote to honor Marilyn Monroe, "Candle in the Wind," and eulogies were delivered by Diana's brother and others. Rosary beads given to Diana by Mother Teresa were placed in the coffin with the princess.

How did Diana achieve such stature? Her early life showed little promise. She was an indifferent student at best, although she was an excellent swimmer and diver. She did show unusual interest in social service and won a school award for community spirit. Even though Diana was descended from royalty, she began a career as a kindergarten assistant. She also did cleaning work for her older sister, Sarah. At about that time, Sarah was dating Charles, the Prince of Wales, and direct heir to the British throne. As Diana grew older, Prince Charles took an interest in her as a possible mate, even though she was still in her teens. Their romance grew, and they were officially engaged in early 1981, when Diana was 19 years old.[1]

While Charles had been a familiar international figure for many years, Diana was unknown to most people. But when she burst onto the scene for the first time, she struck the public as an extremely beautiful and poised, yet down-to-earth young woman. It was easy to see her as the future queen. When the two were married in the summer of 1981 millions of people around the world watched the fairy-tale wedding on television.[2] People without TVs drove miles to rent motel rooms so that they could wake up before dawn to watch the ceremony. The future King of England marrying the beautiful Diana matched the world's script for a royal wedding, and viewers hoped that their marriage would follow the familiar narrative of their childhoods. They wanted to believe that Charles and Diana would "live happily ever after."

But, of course, that didn't happen. They lived happily for only a few years. Diana gave birth to sons William, in 1982, and Henry, or "Harry," in 1984. But problems soon rocked their marriage. Charles rekindled his romance with a former girlfriend, Camilla Parker-Bowles. He had had a relationship with her before his marriage to Diana, and he is married to her at present. When Diana was alive, she was asked about Camilla in a televised interview. She remarked that "there were three of us in the marriage, so it was a bit crowded."[3] In turn, Diana engaged in a number of affairs of her own. While there was pressure on the pair to maintain at least the public semblance of a happy marriage, the stresses were uncontainable. Not surprisingly, the couple officially separated in 1992. A divorce was finalized in 1996.

Both before and after the separation the tabloid press was often critical of Diana. She was blamed for poor relationships with the royal family, her flamboyant dress, and even her choice of charities. While she was acknowledged as a devoted mother, her overall image was tilted toward that of the spoiled bimbo. But another part of Diana's life was also noticed, and increasingly appreciated. Like the typical English princess, Diana supported numerous charities. But despite some criticism, she expanded that traditional role. She gave conspicuous support to AIDS charities, going so far as allowing herself to be photographed touching a person infected with HIV. And she became involved in raising awareness of extremely serious illnesses such as leprosy. Diana persevered in these roles and played a large part in changing common views of AIDS sufferers.

Perhaps most enduring was Diana's prominent support for the International Campaign to Ban Landmines. She became increasingly involved with this endeavor toward the end of her life and brought it into much clearer public focus. When she died, both Diana's commitment to the cause and the cause itself were considered anew. The earlier image of Diana as a beautiful but self-centered lightweight gave way to one that emphasized her unselfish devotion to humanity and the common good. The Campaign to Ban Landmines won the Nobel Peace Prize shortly after her death. That award is widely recognized as a posthumous tribute to Diana, Princess of Wales.

HEROISM AND REDEMPTION

Diana's life and death illustrate the centrality of themes of redemption in our understanding of heroism. *Time* magazine wrote 10 years after Diana's death that she was "the flawed heroine" who played a charismatic role in the millennium-old narrative of British royalty.[4] That narrative was captured by William Shakespeare 400 years ago and it is still being played out today. Its power comes from the fact that heroes typically work on the edge of tragedy. They frequently pull themselves back from the brink of disaster or tumble over it. In Diana's case, not only did she change her life, but her wrenching death focused people on the deep commitments she had made toward helping some of the most unfortunate people on the planet. The popular perception that she had redeemed herself made her a lasting hero.

Our studies of heroes show that people redeem themselves in two basic ways. They make a moral turn, or they achieve new levels of competence. Or they may do both. No matter the method, the result is the same. The redeemed hero achieves her or his goals by making moral choices or through hard work. The hero does the right thing and summons the capacity to do it successfully. As with other facets of heroism, we see redemption in the behavior of both real and fictional individuals, as well as in our perceptions of them. Let's consider two examples.

Former First Lady of the United States Betty Ford famously redeemed herself by winning her personal struggle with alcohol dependency and drugs. Betty Ford served as First Lady during her husband Gerald Ford's term as U.S. President, from 1974 to 1977. She had always been an extremely independent and outspoken woman. Raised in Michigan, she struck out for New York City after high school and started a career as a dancer and model. But she was pressured by her family to move back to the Midwest. She then got married and divorced before age 30. The year after the divorce, she married Gerald Ford. At the time of the wedding, Ford was running for Congress for the first time. The ceremony was actually delayed until late in the campaign because Ford worried about how voters might react to him marrying a divorced ex-dancer. But he won, and Betty and Gerald began an unusually happy marriage that lasted until the former president died in 2006.[5]

But it wasn't all marital bliss. On the one hand Betty Ford was completely open in revealing the intimate side of their relationship. And they were quite intimate. When she was first lady she commented that one magazine interviewer asked her about almost everything, except how often she had sex with the president. And she added that "if they'd asked me that I would have told them. As often as possible."[6] On the other hand Betty had been a heavy drinker for most of her adult life. And when her children were young she was hospitalized for a painful pinched nerve. Doctors prescribed pain killers and over time she became addicted to pills as well as to alcohol. In her book *Betty: A Glad Awakening* she wrote that she had been taking "the sleeping pills, the pain pills, the relaxer pills, the pills to counteract the effects of other pills."[7]

When the spotlight was on her as first lady, she backed off her use of drugs and liquor. But feeling bitter and useless after Gerald Ford's narrow loss to Jimmy Carter in the 1976 presidential election, she became increasingly dependent on prescription drugs and alcohol. At the same time she dismissed the dangers of drinking and taking pills, sinking deeper and deeper into her destructive habits. Then all that changed abruptly. A year after the Fords left the White House, the president and the four Ford children orchestrated an "intervention." They all told Betty that she was in serious trouble and needed treatment for her addictions.

Betty's first reaction was disbelief. But she soon entered treatment and overcame her addictions. It was not easy, but she worked hard to get clean and sober. Then she took the monumental step that has made her a hero to so many people. In 1982 she established the Betty Ford Center in southern California for the treatment of drug addiction and alcoholism. The Center has been extremely successful. She served as Chairman of the Board from 1982 until 2005, when she was succeeded, at age 87, by her daughter Susan.

Betty Ford redeemed herself with great personal effort. She had the help of her close-knit family and many professionals. But she summoned her own personal resources and found the strength to make a major change in her own life. Then she found a creative way to help others do the same. Ford was presented with a Presidential Medal of Freedom by President George H. W. Bush in 1991 and with a Congressional Gold Medal in 1999, at the age of 81.

One of the reasons that Betty Ford's story has been so inspiring, and has so greatly supported the work of the Betty Ford Center, is that it is consistent with a common narrative of redemption through personal effort. A very different example of the same theme involves one of the heroes listed by anonymous research participants in the study we described in Chapter 1. Who, you may have asked, is Frank Champi, one of the heroes appearing in Table 1.1? Frank Champi not only illustrates redemption through dramatic personal achievement but also the fact that many heroes are unique to our own personal experience. Champi was the second-string quarterback on the Harvard football team in 1968. That year, both Harvard and Yale entered the final game of the season—The Game it is called by many—undefeated and untied. But Yale was heavily favored, and was ranked 16th in the country. True to form, Yale took a 22–0 lead in the first half. At that point, the Harvard coach inserted Champi into the game. In a recent documentary film, Champi revealed how angry and scared he was. He was totally unprepared and wondered why the coach was making him take the fall in a lost cause. At that point Champi had no thought of winning. His only goal was not to make a fool of himself.[8]

But things changed. Champi led Harvard to two touchdowns in the middle of the game, and they trailed 22-13. Then Yale seemed to regain total control. They scored again and led 29-13, and were driving toward another score with just over 3 minutes left. Then Yale's world turned upside down. They fumbled. Harvard moved down the field, and Champi threw a touchdown pass with 42 seconds left. Harvard scored the two extra points and recovered an onside kick. On the last play of the game, with time expired, Champi threw another touchdown pass and then threw again for a two-point conversion. The game ended tied, 29-29. And Champi was a hero (to Harvard, not to Yale). Even though the final score was even, the feelings of both teams were expressed perfectly by an unforgettable *Harvard Crimson* newspaper headline: HARVARD BEATS YALE: 29-29.

A different kind of redemption narrative emphasizes moral turning points, where an individual who has not thought or acted morally in the past decides that he or she must now follow a different path, even though the path is strewn with difficulty. As with cases involving redemption through personal effort and achievement, heroism through redeeming moral commitments is often illustrated more purely and poignantly in fiction. The 2008 film *Gran Torino*, directed

by and starring Clint Eastwood, provides a striking example.⁹ The
movie focuses on aging Korean War veteran Walt Kowalski, an angry
and alienated Ford factory worker residing in a rapidly changing area
of Detroit. Kowalski's wife has just died, and he has hostile relationships with his two sons and his grandchildren. His wife had won a
deathbed promise from a young priest that he would get Walt to
rejoin the church and go to confession. Walt is having none of it.

Most annoying to Walt are the changing demographics of his neigh-
borhood. Formerly all white, it is now also home to African Americans,
Hispanics, and Asians. Some of the young ones are loud and disrespectful. Right next door lives a large extended family of Hmongs
from Southeast Asia. While they are completely well behaved, even
by Walt's standards, his racism dominates his perceptions of the
entire household. He calls them gooks, zipperheads, eggrolls, and
swamp rats. However, things begin to change one night when a gang
of thugs, led by a cousin of his neighbors, tries to beat up the teenage
boy, Thao. Walt comes out his front door with a rifle and threatens
the attackers. When one tells Walt to go back in the house, he snarls,
"Yeah? I blow a hole in your face and then I go in the house … and
I sleep like a baby…. We used to stack f—s like you 5 feet high in
Korea .. use ya for sandbags." Not surprisingly, the hoodlums take
off. Walt deflects the family's thanks: "I'm no hero. I was just trying
to get that babbling gook off my lawn."

Over time Walt grows fond of Thao's older sister, Sue Lor, and
takes Thao under his wing. He is won over partly by huge quantities
of food, which his neighbors insist he accept as thanks, and by their
kindness and respect. He realizes that he has more in common with
his Hmong neighbors than with his own family, who seem overanx-
ious for their inheritance. And despite his crude manners, they feel
close to him. Sue Lor appreciates that Walt hangs out with Thao:
"You teach him to fix things, you saved him from that …. cousin of
ours…. And you're a better man to him than our own father was.
You're a good man."

At first, Walt doesn't experience himself as a hero or even as a
good man. But when the gang of cousins shoots up the neighbors's
house with automatic weapons and violently rapes Sue Lor, Walt
makes a fateful choice. He tells his priest: "Thao and Sue are never

going to find peace in this world as long as that gang's around." To Thao he says, "You got your whole life ahead of you, but for me, I finish things." The priest tries to pull Walt back from violence, pleading that he "go in peace." Walt replies, "Oh, I am at peace." He goes unarmed to the gang's home. He provokes them into shooting him, but he has orchestrated the killing so that there are witnesses. The entire gang is arrested and clearly headed for lengthy prison terms. Thus, in the end Walt does what he feels is the right thing. He has overcome his racism and becomes a martyr for the well-being of his friends.

Although the real example of Betty Ford's struggle with addiction and Walt Kowalski's fictional struggle with racism are very different, they both illustrate a central facet of the way we think about redemption. Both individuals are facing a traumatic life passage, where they must choose whether to reroute their lives or continue down a road of ruin, for themselves or for others. These moments are known in research on authentic leadership as "trigger events."[10] Trigger events are typically traumatic or disastrous happenings that cause us to clarify very quickly what is fundamentally important to us. They bring our values into sharp relief and lead us to change the way we live so that we can make our actions align with our attitudes. They also lead us to become increasingly honest with others in our lives about what really matters.

In cases like Betty Ford's, the trigger event is something that causes us to realize that we have reached a dangerous bottom in some central part of our lives. We can then commit to reclaiming ourselves and fighting to overcome our weakness, or risk becoming something we really do not want to become. In cases like Walt Kowalski's, the trigger event is something that makes us realize we have to make a moral commitment, a commitment that may be perilous but is surely right. In both such cases part of the insight is that there is something about our lives which we want desperately to fix. In Betty Ford's case it is her addictions. In Walt Kowalski's case it is the racism that grew out of atrocities that he committed during the Korean War. He won medals for killing young Koreans, but he has always known at some level that it was wrong. The rape of Sue Lor makes him realize that he can only atone for his earlier wrong and achieve personal peace if he does something equally significant that is right.

REDEMPTION AND THE MOTIVE TO ACHIEVE

The impressive thing about Princess Diana's commitment to help people less fortunate, and Betty Ford's commitment to overcome substance abuse, is that they both managed to find within themselves the motivation as well as the capacity to achieve their goals. It wasn't easy. How does it happen? Where does the commitment to accomplishing difficult goals come from?

Part of the answer can be found in some classic research by David McClelland and his colleagues on "achievement motivation."[11] McClelland was one of a number of psychologists who studied human needs and motives during the 1950s. They believed that understanding motivation was essential to understanding more fully the human condition. One influential theory emphasized a motivational hierarchy, such that lower needs needed to be satisfied before higher needs could be addressed.[12] This formulation included physiological needs, safety needs, the need to belong and be loved, the need to be competent and to achieve, and, finally, the need to fulfill one's potential. McClelland focused on three needs that fit the hierarchical theory quite well: the needs for affiliation, power, and achievement. He taught us a great deal about achievement motivation.

The need to achieve is closely related to needs that can be observed in very young children. Infants are curious; they want to understand their environment. Part of understanding their environment is examining and manipulating the objects they find there. They want to explore what things are, and what they can do with them. Watch a child play with a puzzle or with a set of tinker toys. The child will look, examine, manipulate, and see what can be made from the pieces. At a later age, we'll observe the child's desire to have an effect on the environment and to be competent in dealing with it. During the elementary school ages, heading into middle school, this desire is seen in children's efforts to develop what's been called a *sense of industry*, a "sense of being able to make things and make them well and even perfectly."[13] If they acquire this sense, achievement becomes intrinsically satisfying. And as they develop the skills to make and use more and more objects and implements, for example, as they learn to play musical instruments, their intellectual capacities grow along with those other skills.

But it's not a sure thing that children will develop a sense of industry and a drive to achieve. Some people have stronger achievement needs than others. Child rearing is one major factor influencing the outcome. Parents who emphasize independence and initiating new activities are more likely to have children with an intrinsic need to achieve. Being warm and rewarding efforts toward autonomy are also factors. Another is the overall culture's emphasis on achievement.[14]

We can't do much more than speculate about particular individuals such as Princess Diana and Betty Ford. In Diana's case we know that her parents went through a bitter divorce when she was 8 years old, that she initially lived with her mother after the divorce, but that her father soon won custody of Diana and her younger brother in a lawsuit. When Diana was 15 years old, her father remarried, and Diana did not get along with her stepmother. During these years Diana went to various schools, where she struggled academically. It would appear that her life circumstances were not the kind that would favor a high need for achievement. She did show an independent interest in becoming a ballerina, but she was too tall to make it as a professional.

Diana's interest in dance links her to Betty Ford. As a young teenager Betty taught children to dance, and after high school she wanted to begin a dancing career. But her father had died from carbon monoxide poisoning in the family garage, perhaps by suicide, when Betty was 16 years old, and at first her mother refused to let her go to New York City to strike out on her own. However, Betty did study dance under Martha Graham during two summers at Bennington College in Vermont, and she did perform once at New York's Carnegie Hall with one of Graham's troupes. But her mother continued to oppose Betty living in the city, and Betty returned to Michigan when she was 23 years old. Again, the stars didn't point toward a high need for achievement.

However, personalities are not shaped only by parents and childhood experiences. Adult life happens, and events elicit new motives, or perhaps rekindle old ones. Both Diana and Betty Ford clearly showed drives to achieve as their lives evolved. Diana worked hard for the causes that were important to her: AIDS awareness and banning land mines. Betty Ford worked hard to make the Betty Ford Center an outstanding success. How does this happen?

One key to understanding people's motives and where they put their energies is the kind of "self-guides" that they develop. Social psychologist E. Tory Higgins has been studying two different self-guides for over 20 years. Depending on the individual and the situation, people might be more concerned with *ought* self-guides, that is, what they should do, and what their obligations and responsibilities are. Or they might be more concerned with *ideal* self-guides, that is, what they would ideally like to be, and what their hopes, dreams, and aspirations are. When ought self-guides operate, people become more concerned with preventing disaster, with responsibility, protection, and safety. Their mode of self-governance is "assessment," studying situations carefully, and avoiding mistakes. They endorse sayings such as "The road to hell is paved with good intentions" and "Let the buyer beware." When ideal guides operate, people are more concerned with advancement, growth, and accomplishment. Their mode of self-governance is "locomotion," that is, moving, achieving, and getting into a flow. They are more likely to say, "If at first you don't succeed, try, try again" and "Never put off till tomorrow what you can do today."[15]

The assessment and locomotion modes are nicely illustrated by the literary characters Don Quixote and his companion, Sancho Panza. Quixote, the famous knight errant, was action oriented, sometimes without thinking too carefully or listening to good advice from others. He literally and unforgettably tilted at windmills. Sancho Panza is often pictured scratching his head or his beard, wondering what his idealistic but unrealistic boss will do next. He followed the assessment mode, trying to get Quixote to look before he leapt or galloped off to defend the honor of a lady he imagined was in distress.

People in the locomotion mode rather than the assessment mode are more oriented toward achievement. They are active, decisive, open to ideas, and highly involved in their work. They worry less about what others think of them and what the rules are. Although the locomotion mode, guided by ideal self-images, fosters effort and achievement more so than the assessment mode, each system of self-governance has its ups and downs. The high-achieving individual in the locomotion mode may be tempted to cut corners and disregard other people's norms and expectations, including their moral standards.

The locomotion orientation is illustrated by two significant figures in American history. One was John Stevens, who for about a year and a half was chief engineer during the construction of the Panama Canal. Stevens was an indefatigable railroad engineer who accomplished miracles in building tunnels and bridges to get trains over the continental divide in the northern United States. When he got to Panama he was extremely active and action oriented. He told one of his staff: "You won't get fired if you do something, you will get fired if you don't do anything." If you do something wrong, you can correct that," but there is no way to correct nothing."[16] Canal construction quickly became a beehive of activity. A more famous example is President Franklin Delano Roosevelt. FDR has been described as having an "active-positive" personality.[17] He reveled in activity, in trying things, in improvising. As he fought the Great Depression in the 1930s, the emphasis was action. If something didn't work, he'd try something else. The effect was electric. The country was impressed and reassured, knowing that the president would keep plugging and keep creating new ways to battle the faltering economy.[18]

Redemption through hard work, reflecting a locomotion orientation, is nicely illustrated in the case of the late Senator Ted Kennedy. Shortly before Kennedy died in 2009, the title of a new book concisely summarized the trajectory of his life. It was called *Last Lion: The Fall and Rise of Ted Kennedy*.[19] Ted was the youngest of Joseph and Rose Kennedy's nine children. Joe Kennedy put enormous pressure on his four sons, Joe Jr., Jack, Bobby, and Ted, to succeed. He emphasized ideal guides and locomotion over ought guides and assessment. Jack Kennedy once said he could always feel his father's eyes sticking him in the back. And Joe Kennedy didn't mind flaunting the rules, in his business or in his relations with women other than his wife. The boys all tried to achieve, but in different ways. Joe, Jr. was groomed to run for president, while Jack was headed into journalism. But when Joe was killed during a daring bombing mission over the English Channel during World War II, Jack headed into politics and was elected President of the United States in 1960. At the time, little brother Ted was still in his twenties.

Ted wanted to achieve in his own right, and decided to run for the U.S. Senate after he became old enough to be eligible. He was elected, served conscientiously, and lived first through the tragedy of President Kennedy's assassination, then 5 years later through the assassination of his older brother Bobby. While Ted was consistently a good senator, his personal life after Bobby's death became tumultuous. There was too much alcohol and too many women. And then in 1969, his life, and his career, hit bottom. Late one summer night, after a cookout on the tiny Massachusetts island of Chappaquiddick, Kennedy drove off a bridge, in the company of a young woman. Kennedy escaped, but the young woman, Mary Jo Kopechne, drowned. Kennedy didn't report the accident until many hours later. The ensuing scandal wrecked the promise of his political career.[20]

Despite Chappaquiddick, Kennedy's effective work in the Senate continued, and by 1980 it seemed once again that he might be elected president. He ran for the Democratic Party nomination against the incumbent president, Jimmy Carter, but was soundly defeated. His family was actually relieved. There would be no more worries about the assassination of a third Kennedy brother. And that brother completely committed himself to passing effective legislation in the U. S. Congress.

Over the next three decades Ted Kennedy's stature and effectiveness as a senator only grew. And after marrying Victoria Reggie in 1992, his personal life settled down. The name of the game became accomplishment and achievement. Through building close personal relationships with political opponents as well as allies, he managed to pass landmark legislation on issues such as health care, education, and the rights of the disabled. He compromised on specifics without ever compromising his principles. By the time of his death, Kennedy was widely known as the Lion of the Senate, and as one of the most effective senators in American history. In his early years, Kennedy's mode of self-governance had always tilted toward locomotion rather than assessment. But in his last 30 years he developed strength in both areas. While locomotion supplies the drive for achievement, research shows that achievement itself happens best for those who govern their behavior using both ought and ideal guides, combining assessment with locomotion. Kennedy's achievements testify to those findings. The title *The Fall and Rise of Ted Kennedy* reflects the reordering of his life, and his achievement of hero status through redemption.

MORAL COMMITMENT AND REDEMPTION

Many of the heroes we have discussed thus far chose moral behavior at crucial turning points in their lives. Rick Blaine turns away from indulging his passionate feelings for Ilsa and joins the international fight against Germany's Third Reich. Irena Sendler makes the costly decision to resist the Nazis by smuggling children out of the Warsaw ghetto. Randle P. McMurphy gives his life to help and empower mental patients who have been controlled and undermined by "the Combine." In each case, events create inescapable choice points that confront individuals with the decisions that define their lives and legacies. In *Gran Torino*, gang violence completely beyond Walt Kowalski's control places him in a situation where he must either condone rape and the brutal intimidation of his neighbors or, at great risk to his own life, act to protect them. The presidency of perhaps America's greatest leader, Abraham Lincoln, well illustrates exactly this kind of choice point.

As suggested earlier, moral decisions are not made in a vacuum. Lincoln understood this better than most. In an 1864 letter explaining his momentous decision to issue the Emancipation Proclamation the year before, Lincoln wrote, "I claim not to have controlled events, but confess plainly that events have controlled me."[21] This was not completely true, as Lincoln well understood, but he was acknowledging that his decision to free slaves had to recognize political and constitutional realities. For his entire life, Lincoln had believed that slavery was wrong. In the same letter he wrote, "If slavery is not wrong, nothing is wrong." And he was elected president as the candidate of a new political entity, the Republican Party, that had been founded primarily to oppose slavery. Yet on the first day of his presidency, in his inaugural address, his opposition to slavery seemed tepid. At the very beginning he stated, "I have no purpose, directly or indirectly, to interfere with the institution of slavery in the States where it exists. I believe I have no lawful right to do so, and I have no inclination to do so."[22] He even stated that he would not disturb Southern "property," seemingly adopting the Southern point of view that slaves were "a species of property." Was Lincoln being hypocritical?

The answer is more complicated. From all that we know about Lincoln, we can safely say he abhorred slavery. He wrote that he could "not remember when I did not" think and feel that slavery was wrong. But when he became president he did not heroically act on that unequivocal moral belief. He was hemmed in by both constitutional and political constraints. He had to act within those realities. And in combination they compelled him to put aside, at least for a time, his opposition to slavery.

On the constitutional side, in taking the oath of office, Lincoln swore to "preserve, protect, and defend the Constitution of the United States." He rightly pointed out that he had no constitutional power to emancipate slaves or abolish slavery. He could constitutionally oppose extending slavery, and he did so. But he could not constitutionally interfere with slavery in the states where it was legal and flourishing. On the political side, when Lincoln took office, war had not started, and eight slave states had not yet seceded from the Union. He hoped to keep all of them, most importantly Virginia, from breaking away. But as Lincoln said, "events controlled" him. Soon after his inauguration, Confederate forces fired on Fort Sumter in the harbor off Charleston, South Carolina, and the war was on. Virginia, Tennessee, North Carolina, and Arkansas quickly joined the rebellion. Now the question was whether he could hold the four so-called border states, Delaware, Maryland, Kentucky, and Missouri. It wasn't going to be easy.

Lincoln understood the importance of keeping those four states in the Union. If Maryland seceded the federal capital, Washington, DC, would be surrounded by Confederate territory, Maryland to the north and Virginia to the south. And Kentucky loomed even more important. Lincoln wrote a friend: "I think to lose Kentucky is nearly the same as to lose the whole game. Kentucky gone, we cannot hold Missouri, nor, as I think, Maryland. Those all against us, and the job on our hands is too large for us."[23] His political realism shone through when he responded to a supporter who claimed that God was on his side: "I hope to have God on my side, but I must have Kentucky."[24] And Lincoln knew that if he threatened slavery in any way at all in those crucial states, they too would secede and destroy the Union.

So Lincoln held his ground and made no move against slavery, the South's "peculiar institution."

But events unfolded, and the constitutional and political calculus changed with them. Early in the war, slaves began to escape from their masters when Union armies approached. Union commanders didn't want to deal with them or further inflame passions about slavery. They initially attempted to send the slaves back home. But one Union commander, Benjamin Butler, refused to return slaves to a Confederate officer who came under a flag of truce to ask Butler to do just that. First, Butler noted the absurdity of a rebel fighter asking that his ownership of slaves be protected in accord with the constitution of the nation that he was trying to destroy. Of more consequence, Butler said that slaves should be regarded as "contraband of war" and like other property captured in wartime, be destroyed or confiscated. Butler also decided that it would help the war effort if escaped slaves did work such as building fortifications for the Union rather than for the Confederacy. By keeping slaves, and employing them, the South's resources would be diminished and the North's enhanced.

Butler's policy confronted Lincoln with a dilemma. If he embraced it he might both violate the U.S. Constitution, which called for the return of escaped slaves, and also lose the crucial allegiance of the border states. On the other hand, the strongest support for the war came from abolitionists who wanted Lincoln to destroy slavery. The Congress made his dilemma even more pressing, passing Confiscation Acts in 1861 and 1862 that essentially made Butler's unofficial policy official. Lincoln had to decide.

Decide he did, using all his political skill to prepare the nation for what became the Emancipation Proclamation of January 1, 1863. In a famous open letter in the summer of 1862, Lincoln wrote that his clear goal was to save the Union. He explained further: "If I could save the Union without freeing *any* slave I would do it, and if I could save it by freeing *all* the slaves I would do it; and if I could save it by freeing some and leaving others alone I would do that." On the one hand these words seem to reflect the indifference to slaves and slavery that can be heard in the inaugural address. However Lincoln added that he was stating his "view of *official* duty; and I intend no modification of my oft-expressed *personal* wish that all men every where could be free."²⁵ More importantly, for the first time Lincoln here states, implicitly, that he believes that his official duty not only permits but actually requires him to free slaves if, but only if, freeing slaves is necessary to saving the Union.

In about a month Lincoln took the decisive step and declared that in 100 days he would declare slaves in states still fighting against the Union "thenceforth, and forever free." And of course none of those states stopped fighting. Therefore, on January 1, 1863, Lincoln issued the famous Emancipation Proclamation, declaring slaves free in the rebelling states. Furthermore, it also said that freed slaves would be "received into the armed service of the United States." The proclamation justified these steps "as a fit and necessary war measure for suppressing" the rebellion. In later letters to friends who questioned his policy, Lincoln elaborated that political and constitutional justification. He argued that that he had become convinced by the course of the war that freeing slaves *and* enlisting them to help in the war effort was an "indispensable necessity."

The argument went something like this. While Lincoln had no constitutional authority to free slaves, his most basic obligation was to uphold the U.S. Constitution. He could only do that, of course, if he preserved the Union. He explained, "I was, in my best judgment, driven to the alternative of either surrendering the Union, and with it, the Constitution, or of laying strong hand upon" slavery, while hoping "for greater gain than loss" in military terms. While he made this constitutional argument, Lincoln was well-aware of the political risks. He would gain support from abolitionists, but he might lose the support of moderates, including many military officers who wanted to preserve the Union but not free slaves. But Lincoln had made his commitment, and it completely fit his moral convictions. His "judgment and feeling" abhorred slavery, and now he found a way "to act officially upon this judgment and feeling."²⁶ At the defining moment of decision he stated, "My whole soul is in it," and he made sure that his hand was steady and his signature firm when he signed the Proclamation.²⁷

In the months following the Emancipation Proclamation, Lincoln came under intense pressure, especially when the war was going badly, to rescind it. And at times he believed he might make peace earlier if he did. He was sorely tempted. But he never really wavered, and in defending his decision to do what was right for African Americans, his passion can be heard in his eloquence. He wrote a group of political allies who questioned whether it was wise to free and arm blacks. He argued not only had the policy been effective from a military point of view, but that it was morally right: "You say you will not fight to free negroes. Some of them seem willing to fight for you; but, no matter...." He then went on to explain, "... negroes, like other people, act upon motives. Why should they do any thing for us, if we will do nothing them? If they stake their lives for us, they must be prompted by the strongest motive—even the promise of freedom. And the promise being made, must be kept." He argued that blacks were fighting for a peace that would "come soon, and come to stay; and so come as to be worth the keeping in all future time.... And then, there will be some black men who can remember that, with silent tongue, and clenched teeth, and steady eye, and well-poised bayonet, they have helped mankind on to this great consummation."[28]

It's inspiring to hear the passion and conviction in Lincoln's voice after his public policy more perfectly coincided with his private priorities. His ultimate decision to make the moral choice raises a number of important psychological questions. Where does our morality come from? How are our moral "judgment and feeling" shaped? And what determines whether we act in accord with our morals? The heroes we've studied thus far help us answer these questions. Let's try to understand how.

MORAL CONVICTION AND MORAL COMMITMENT

How does a person like Irena Sendler decide to risk her life to help smuggle innocent children out of the Warsaw ghetto? What made Princess Diana commit herself to the fight against AIDS and land mines while risking disapproval and ostracism from the royal family? How did Abraham Lincoln maintain his belief that slavery was wrong when he could do nothing to end it, but then move with decisiveness and passion when events gave him an opening? The riddle of moral conviction and moral action is complex. We'll begin to untangle it by looking first at what children learn in the home, and how they learn it.

Learning, Imitation, and Identification

Psychologists have looked to child rearing and family dynamics for decades in an effort to understand moral thought and moral behavior. Much of the early research on these questions was influenced by studies of animal learning which emphasized various kinds of conditioning. Researchers would jokingly ask, "Does the name Pavlov ring a bell?" and trade stories about training rats to press bars using food pellets for reinforcement. And it's clear—as a very broad statement—that human beings perform more of the behaviors for which they are rewarded or reinforced, and fewer of the behaviors for which they are punished. So in that quite general sense, one of psychology's oldest principles, "the law of effect" formulated before 1900 by Edward Thorndike, holds up. Thorndike studied how cats learned to escape from what he called a puzzle box. He claimed that behaviors that led to reward were "stamped in" and that behaviors that led to punishment were "stamped out."[29]

With many qualifications, that statement is true. And it has obvious application to children learning to perform, or not perform, a range of behaviors, good and bad. Children praised for sharing are likely to share more. Others deprived of dessert or television time for hitting their siblings are likely to hit less. Noted psychologist B. F. Skinner used such observations to make the general argument that behavior is under the control of its consequences. People do what they are reinforced for doing, even though in many cases it isn't easy to predict what they will find rewarding or reinforcing, or how rewarding and reinforcing it will be.[30] Betty Ford, for example, discovered early in her life that alcohol was a very powerful reinforcer. It controlled her behavior more than she thought it would. She drank heavily, without worrying too much about where that might lead her.

Starting in the 1960s researchers went beyond the idea that behavior is controlled by direct reward and punishment. Studies of how children learned aggressive behaviors began to focus on imitation. In classic experiments by Albert Bandura and his colleagues, young children behind a one-way mirror watched adults kick, hit, and scream at a plastic "Bobo" doll, the kind that bounces back when it is knocked down. When the children had a chance to play with the Bobo doll themselves, they would imitate the adult, who served as a model, in very precise ways. If the model hit the doll with a wooden mallet, the children would do that as well. Later experiments showed that children would imitate filmed models as well as live ones, suggesting that children learn aggressive behaviors from seeing aggressive models on television.[31]

The idea of reinforcement didn't disappear once psychologists started studying imitation, or what came to be called social learning. For example, it turned out that the consequences of a model's behavior make a big difference. If a model's aggressive behavior is praised by another adult, children imitate the model more. If the model is scolded for being a bully, children imitate the aggression less. These findings led to the concept of *vicarious reinforcement*, that is, the idea that one person's behavior is strengthened or weakened depending on whether another person is observed being rewarded or punished for performing the same behavior.[32]

Another important finding about social learning is that children pay careful attention to who the model is. For example, a model who controls a collection of enticing toys is much more likely to be imitated. In general, people who have more status or power are more imitated than people who have less status or power.[33]

Taken as a whole, the research on vicarious reinforcement and social learning suggests a crucial distinction. There is a difference between learning a behavior and performing it. In the studies on modeling, it is quite clear that children learn the behaviors that they observe, independently of who the model is, or the consequences for the model. But just because a child, or an adult, learns a behavior, doesn't mean that he or she will actually imitate or perform it. Among other things, children learn whether good things or bad things happen to people who behave in certain ways, and they govern their actions accordingly.

The distinction between learning and performance is especially important in the case of moral behavior. Very often people know what's right. Whether they act on that knowledge is something quite different. Abraham Lincoln strongly believed that abolishing slavery was right. Taking steps toward that goal was a much more complicated matter. As he said, events controlled him. In saying so he seemed to anticipate B. F. Skinner, who argued that behavior is under the control of its consequences. Lincoln knew the consequences of doing the right thing, or the wrong thing, and his behavior was largely under the control of what he understood those consequences to be.

Beyond Imitation: Identification

A different perspective on the acquisition of morality emphasizes a concept broader than imitation, the idea of identification. Whereas imitation refers to learning and copying specific behaviors, identification refers to a more general wish to be like and therefore act like another person. Our overall sense of identity, of who we are, is based in large part on the sum of the identifications we have made with various people throughout our lives. In this way our identity changes as we adopt new identifications with people we choose to be like, or drop old identifications with people we no longer admire or wish to be like.

One of the first psychologists to develop a theory of identification was Sigmund Freud. His formulation grew out of his analysis of the way young children resolved conflicting feelings about their parents during the resolution of the Oedipus complex. Many readers already know something about this controversial theory. Freud proposed that young boys form erotic attachments toward their mothers and view their fathers as rivals for their mothers' love. Similarly, young girls form erotic attachments toward their fathers and view their mothers as rivals. However, both boys and girls grew to fear that their attachments and jealous feelings would lead to conflict and punishment. As a result, they repressed these emotions and identified with the same-sex parent. Boys strived to be like their fathers, since their fathers seemed so successful in commanding their mothers' affections, and girls similarly strived to be like their mothers. Boys hoped that their mothers would admire them for their similarity to their fathers, and girls hoped that their fathers would admire them for their similarity to their mothers.[34]

While there is very little direct evidence to support Freud's theory of the Oedipus complex, his idea of identification as a powerful force in shaping behavior and morality has stood the test of time. Children identify with numerous people, real and fictional, but parents are most often very significant early identification figures. They are the original role models. Through identification, then, what a parent teaches with words, or demonstrates with actions, is a powerful determinant of morality. Interestingly the research on observational learning is consistent with parts of Freud's theory. As Freud suggested, children are most likely to identify with and imitate models who have high status and who control resources that children would like for themselves. As noted previously, that's exactly what researchers studying social learning found.

Of the cases considered in this chapter, Ted Kennedy provides the best example of a boy identifying strongly with his father, Joseph P. Kennedy. Like his older brothers—Joe Jr., Jack, and Bobby—Ted admired his powerful and successful father. In many ways all four brothers modeled themselves after their father. However, for the three brothers who lived well into adulthood—Jack, Bobby, and Ted—their identification with their father provided an incomplete model for how to live a significant and moral life. All of them developed an independent and more altruistic moral philosophy. We have to go beyond principles of imitation and identification to explain that kind of growth and change.

Cognitive Development and Morality

To get us started thinking about the development of a mature moral philosophy, consider the following dilemma:

> In Europe, a woman was near death from cancer. There was one drug that doctors thought might save her. It was a form of radium a druggist in the same town had discovered. The drug was expensive to make, but the druggist was charging 10 times what it cost him. He paid $200 for the radium and charged $2,000 for a small dose of the drug. The sick woman's husband, Heinz, went to everyone he knew to borrow the money, but he could only get together about half of what it cost. He told the druggist that his wife was dying, and asked him to sell it cheaper or let him pay later. But the druggist said, "No, I discovered the drug and I'm going to make

money from it." So Heinz got desperate and broke into the man's store to steal the drug.[35]

Should Heinz have stolen the drug? What would you say if you were asked that question? What reason would you give for your answer? Psychologist Lawrence Kohlberg studied the responses of young boys over a 20-year period and developed a theory of moral development to account for changes in their moral reasoning over time. Children began at what Kohlberg called Preconventional Morality or Level I. At this level they are concerned with rewards and punishments. In the Heinz example they talk about having to go to jail, or about Heinz losing his wife. But by the teenage years, the boys articulate what's called Level II or Conventional Morality answers. They talk about what other people will think of them and what society and the law require. For example, they might mention a sense of honor as com-pelling them to steal the drug to save their wife, or not wanting to be dishonest or a criminal as reasons not to steal the drug. Finally, start-ing in late adolescence or early adulthood, some people begin reason-ing at Level III, using Postconventional Morality. Here they become more concerned about following mutually agreed-upon moral prin-ciples and their own ethical values. Their thinking revolves around abstract principles such as justice and equality. They might decide that stealing drugs is the right thing to do, even though it violates the law. What matters in this case is not what choice people make, but how they think about it.

There are two crucial points about Level III Postconventional Morality. First, it very much involves taking other people's perspec-tives into account and thinking about the common good as well as one's own interests. Second, not many people, even as mature adults, get to this level of thinking. A few do, but most don't. And it's not clear just what propels people to Level III. To begin with, they must be intelligent enough and thoughtful enough to reason at a high level. And then some event or experience must confront them with moral questions or moral decisions, leading them to use their ability to make ethical choices. Earlier in this chapter we discussed "trigger events" that cause people to examine and question their values, and decide the kind of person they want to be going forward, and the kinds of lives they want to lead. These are the kinds of experiences that can stimulate higher levels of moral reasoning and more intellectually developed moral commitments.

We've discussed several people who illustrate this kind of growth. Princess Diana was jarred out of a conventional life dominated by conventional morality when she discovered Prince Charles' infidelities and encountered disdain from the tabloid press, and even some of the royal family. She decided to concentrate on being a good mother to her two sons and working on causes that she independently believed to be important, whether they were conventional choices or not. Although we can't know whether her moral reasoning was on Level II or Level III, she made commitments that reflect an emphasis on important moral principles, such as equality and the value of human life.

We get a much clearer sense of Level III Postconventional moral reasoning by studying the 1963 speech in which President John F. Kennedy asked the nation's support for civil rights legislation. First, Kennedy appealed directly to the country's conscience and morality. He explicitly asked "every American" to "stop and examine his conscience" and stated, "We face, therefore, a moral crisis as a country and a people." "It is as old," he argued, "as the Scriptures." Second, he invoked principles of equality and justice, and values as fundamental as the Golden Rule. He reminded the nation that "it was founded on the principle that all men are created equal" and declared that "every American ought to have the right to be treated as he would wish to be treated." He appealed to "a sense of human decency" and asked "who among us would be content with the counsels of patience and delay" in the face of injustice. Not every listener was prepared to think at this level, but as a leader Kennedy tried to raise the nation's level of moral reasoning.[36]

The Possibility of Moral Behavior: Evolutionary Perspectives

President Kennedy's morally based appeal for civil rights legislation met with ultimate success, but only after his assassination galvanized the country's commitment to honoring his legacy. The difficulty of passing civil rights legislation raises questions about the human capacity for moral reasoning and moral action. Are human beings inclined to be moral, so that the ethical teachings of parents and others resonate with basic human tendencies? Or do those appeals fall on essentially deaf ears? The work of evolutionary psychologists suggests that we may, happily, be much more disposed toward moral behavior than we ordinarily think.

Let's start with the recognition that many prominent researchers today believe strongly that human evolution has prepared us for complex thinking. This view holds that complex conceptual systems unique to humans are easily built on primitive "cognitive modules" that humans share with other primates. Furthermore, we are not only built to think in complex ways, but our capacity to think in complex ways lays the groundwork for thinking and acting in moral ways. An evolved conscience is one of the complex ways of thinking that spurs moral behavior.

In short, "cooperative, and altruistic behaviors and moral virtues have evolved in humans." They have done so because it is adaptive to take other people's perspectives and to treat them kindly and fairly. It is in the interest of both the more powerful and less powerful to help one another survive and adapt. Such cooperation and altruism enables groups as a whole to flourish, and it helps individuals. For example, people who have altruistic mates benefit from their mates' altruism. Not surprisingly then, "moral virtues are attractive to potential mates." As a result, it is in our evolutionary interest to appear altruistic. Being altruistic increases the individual's chances of reproducing and our species' chances of survival. Furthermore, emotions supporting moral behavior have evolved alongside tendencies toward helpful and altruistic inclinations. We have sympathetic concern for victims, and feelings of closeness, love, and empathy. And we have evolved a sense of fairness that puts limits on cheating in our interactions with others.[37]

Some of you may be asking, with so many evolved tendencies toward moral thought, altruistic emotions, and cooperative behavior, Why is there so much evil in the world? Why do people cheat so much? Why is there so much killing? Part of the problem is that doing the right thing is harder than knowing what that right thing is. We'll conclude this chapter talking about the difficulties we face in self-regulation, in doing what we know is the right thing.

Self-Control as a Muscle

You can see how self-control challenged several of the individuals we've introduced in this chapter. The most dramatic example is Betty Ford. She knew she had problems with alcohol and drugs, but she was addicted. Her self-control wasn't up to beating that. Princess Diana was afflicted with eating disorders, and thus she couldn't exert the control over her life that she wanted. Ted Kennedy had problems with drink and with an appetite for women. What determines whether people are able to control their impulses, their fears, and their weaknesses? It does happen, of course. In the clutch, quarterback Frank Champi controlled his fear and anger in the Harvard-Yale football game and won. But it was difficult. In all these cases, people want to do the right thing, but sometimes they just can't. Is there some way to understand why not? Does our understanding offer any help?

Most of us encounter self-control challenges. We have to resist the temptation to have another drink, the desire to ignore our diet, or perhaps the temptation to start an extramarital affair. Others struggle to force themselves out of bed to keep to their exercise schedule or make themselves go the library to study for an exam. In all of these cases the person must restrain or override one response to make another possible. Recent research shows that this kind of self-control is psychologically exhausting. It requires willpower, or ego-strength, and this, it turns out, is a psychological resource that is easily depleted. Studies show that if a person has recently had to exert self-control, at least for a time, he or she will have trouble summoning the strength to do it again.[38]

One way to think about this is that the person's self-control muscle is fatigued. This is true even if the two kinds of self-control are quite different. For example, one study showed that people who had just had to resist the temptation to eat sweets gave up more quickly on a frustrating task. In another experiment, white students discussed racial politics either with other white students or with a mixed-race group. In the mixed-race group, many white students found that they had to be more careful what they said. They had to be careful not to offend the nonwhites. This requires self-regulation, and their capacity to self-regulate in the immediate future was apparently tired. When they had to attempt a color-naming task that was fairly easy but did require suppressing an initial response, they performed poorly. Imagine them being shown the word BLUE written in red letters and being asked to name the color of the letters. It's harder to say "red" when the red letters spell the word "blue." People must suppress the tendency to say "blue" when they see that word in print. In line with the idea of self-regulatory muscle fatigue, the participants from the mixed-race groups did worse on this kind of color-naming task.

In short, exerting self-control is psychologically tiring. Like a muscle, it gets worn out and doesn't function as well when it's fatigued. There are a number of interesting ways that the depletion of self-control resources can be counteracted. First, all psychological processes use physiological resources, and it turns out that self-control uses glucose. Some fascinating research shows that drinking a glass of lemonade with sugar restores glucose levels and reduces the fatigue or depletion of self-control. More useful perhaps is the finding that people can keep their self-control muscle in shape by exercising it carefully, just like any other muscle. For example, a person having trouble carrying out her intention to exercise regularly at 2:00 in the afternoon can make a decision first thing in the morning to exercise at 2:00 without fail. That's an easy decision to make early in the morning. But consciously making that commitment makes it more likely that she will honor it. When 2:00 comes around, she isn't faced with what may be a decision requiring great strength. She has already made her decision and proceeds to carry it out without any second thoughts. The decision is made when it's simple, not when it's hard.

In short, redeeming ourselves through effort and achievement or through moral commitment requires self-control. It's not enough to *know* what is right. We must *do* what's right. We must rise to the occasion. Practicing self-control in small ways will make us better able to exercise it in big ways. Keeping our self-control muscle in shape enhances our ability to make good on our life-defining commitments.

4

OBSTACLES

Triumph over Adversity

She was a muscular athlete whom the media derisively called "man-ish" and "muscle moll." Because she even dared to participate in sports, she developed a reputation as a freak. College physical education instructors told their female students that she was an example of what *not* to become. A reporter for the *New York World-Telegram* wrote, "It would be much better if she and her ilk stayed at home, got themselves prettied up and waited for the phone to ring." She would have won an Olympic gold medal in the high jump, but the judges disqualified her because she used a jumping technique that only men were permitted to use.

Her name was Babe Didrikson Zaharias, and she was quite possibly the greatest athlete—male or female—in human history.[1] Zaharias was born with the name Mildred, but as a child playing sandlot baseball she hit so many towering home runs that her friends named her after Babe Ruth, the great Yankees slugger. She became accomplished in every sport she tried: basketball, track, golf, baseball, tennis, swimming, diving, boxing, volleyball, handball, bowling, billiards, skating, and cycling. When asked if there was anything she didn't play, she said, "Yeah, dolls." As a child growing up, she knew her life's ambition. "My goal was to be the greatest athlete who ever lived," she said (p. 34).

In 1930, at the age of 19, Babe Zaharias' basketball skills drew the attention of Employers Casualty Company, who wanted her to rejuvenate the company's semiprofessional women's basketball team. She was hired to do office work and play on their team. Between 1930 and 1932 she led Employers Casualty to two finals and a national championship. Zaharias was voted All-American each season. Employers Casualty became aware of her exceptional athletic versatility and thus expanded its women's sports program beyond basketball. At the 1932 Amateur Athletic Union Championships, Zaharias represented the company as a one-woman team in eight of ten track and field events. She took first place in six events: shot put, javelin, baseball throws, 80-meter hurdles, long jump, and high jump. She finished fourth in the discus throw. In 3 hours, Zaharias singlehandedly accumulated 30 points, eight more than the entire second-place team, which had 22 athletes. She also broke world records in javelin, 80-meter hurdles, high jump, and baseball throw.

At the 1932 Summer Olympics in Los Angeles, Zaharias qualified for five Olympic events, but women at that time were only allowed to compete in three events. She won the first women's Olympic javelin event with a throw of 143 feet, 4 inches, and she set a world record in winning the first Olympic 80-meter hurdles with a time of 11.7 seconds. In the high jump, she and Jean Smiley both broke the world record at 5 feet, 5 inches, but Smiley received the gold and Zaharias the silver when the judges ruled that her head-first jumps were illegal. Today, this jumping style is common among all world-class athletes, male and female.

After the Olympics, in search of another challenge, Babe Zaharias took up golf.[1] Rarely do people excel at golf when they first pick up a golf club in their twenties, but like all sports, the game came easily to Zaharias. She began winning golf tournaments immediately, including the first tournament she entered, the 1935 Texas Women's Invitational. She demonstrated a brashness that was unusual for her generation. She was known for saying, "The Babe is here. Who's coming in second?" (p. 55). The upper-class golfing establishment was unhappy with her unfeminine looks, attire, and mannerisms. At that time, most of the prestigious golf tournaments were amateur events, and to keep Zaharias from participating in them, the U.S. Golf Association stripped her of her amateur status. Years later she regained her amateur standing, and in 1943 she proceeded to win 17 consecutive tournaments. By the end of her career, Zaharias had won 55 professional and amateur golf championships. She was the fastest player ever to win 10 tournaments (1 year, 20 days), the fastest to win 20 (2 years, 4 months), and the fastest ever to win 30 (5 years, 22 days).

Zaharias' golf game was unlike any woman's game, before or since. Her drives off the tee were routinely 50 to 100 yards longer than those of her opponents. Legendary golfer Byron Nelson once said that he knew of only a few men who could outdrive her. Legendary sportswriter Grantland Rice once said of her, "The Babe is without any question the athletic phenomenon of all time, man or woman." He added, "She is beyond all belief until you see her perform. Then you finally understand that you are looking at the most flawless section of muscle harmony, of complete mental and physical coordination, the world of sport has ever seen."[2] Her unparalleled athleticism drew big crowds wherever she competed. Gene Sarazen observed that "people wanted to come and see this freak from Texas who could play golf, tennis, and beat everyone swimming up and down the pool."[3]

To achieve her amazing feats, Babe Didrickson Zaharias was able to overcome significant obstacles. Chief among them was society's prejudice against women, especially women who dared to defy the stereotype of females as soft, passive, and submissive. She also had to overcome the golf establishment's vendetta against her. But these obstacles were nothing compared to the daunting challenge that awaited her. In 1953, Zaharias was diagnosed with colon cancer. She underwent a colostomy to remove cancerous tissue. Her doctors told her that she would never be able to play championship golf again.

The cancer diagnosis did not deter Babe Didrickson Zaharias. Wearing a colostomy bag, she began competing in tournaments again 14 weeks after surgery. The difficulty of playing world-class golf while wearing a colostomy bag should not be underestimated. Film footage of Zaharias swinging a golf club during this time shows that the bag restricted her swing and was an obvious distraction to her. Remarkably, within a year of her cancer surgery, she won five tournaments, including the 1954 U.S. Women's Open, which she won by a staggering 12 strokes. With this win, she became the second-oldest woman ever to win a major Ladies Professional Golf Association championship tournament. The Golf Writers of America awarded her the Ben Hogan Trophy as comeback player of the year.

The Associated Press voted Babe Didrickson Zaharias the Greatest Female Athlete of the first half of the twentieth century. The wire service also voted her Female Athlete of the Year six times—once for her track dominance and five times for her golfing accomplishments. The Guinness Book of World Records lists her as the most versatile female athlete in history.[4] She was a true pioneer in the world of women's sports. Toward the end of her life, she assumed significant leadership roles that helped shape the future of women's golf. In 1949, she helped establish the Ladies Professional Golfers Association, and she served as this organization's president for several years.

Sadly, Zaharias' cancer returned in 1955, and she died the next year at the age of 45. Her tombstone in Galveston, Texas, reads "Babe Didrikson Zaharias—1911–1956—World's Greatest Woman Athlete." To millions, she was undoubtedly a hero who achieved her dream of becoming the world's best athlete in an era that neither encouraged nor rewarded women for pursuing such dreams. Even when cancer ridden, she won golf tournaments. Zaharias was truly a sports legend who triumphed over several different kinds of adversity.

OVERCOMING OBSTACLES

Struggle is a central, inescapable part of the human experience. Heroes separate themselves from the rest because they don't allow struggle to stop them from achieving great things. Zaharias is not the only great athlete who struggled and yet succeeded in conquering the sports world. Ben Hogan won golf championships soon after nearly dying in a car accident. Lance Armstrong won multiple Tour de France titles after overcoming testicular cancer. Hall of Fame footballer Jack Youngblood played in the NFC Championship Game and Super Bowl XIV with a broken leg. Pete Gray, known as the "one-armed wonder," played major league baseball despite having lost his right arm in a childhood accident. A quote from Booker T. Washington nicely sums up our beliefs about struggling through life's challenges. He wrote, "Success is measured not so much by the position that one has reached in life as by the obstacles which he has overcome."[5]

Witnessing athletes prevail over obstacles to achieve greatness can no doubt be inspiring to us. But while athletic achievement is entertaining, it is hardly the most noble of activities. Our most iconic heroes overcome daunting challenges to achieve *morally* worthy goals. Consider the classic children's tale of *The Little Engine That Could*. A train filled with toys and gifts for children breaks down and asks several passing trains to pull it over a big hill. All the big trains refuse to help, but one little blue train agrees to try. Although the little train is small and struggles mightily to climb the hill, it *thinks* it can make it, and sure enough, with great effort the train succeeds in bringing the toys to the children. The story is timeless because it teaches us that a combination of optimism and hard work is essential for overcoming seemingly insurmountable obstacles. Also important is the fact that the train doesn't achieve its goal for personal glory. Rather, there is a moral payoff at the end: toys for children.

The themes portrayed in the *Little Engine* story are so powerful to us that we can be deeply moved when we hear true stories of people who embody the qualities of the little train. Consider the remarkable story of the Antarctic explorer Ernest Shackleton, whose goal was to be the first to lead a team from one side of the icy continent to the other.[6] By itself, this goal involved perilous challenges, but these challenges were dwarfed by a series of unexpected and nightmarish obstacles. As he neared Antarctica, Shackleton's ship *Endurance* encountered unusually thick ice floes, and in mid-January they trapped the vessel, forcing the crew to make winter quarters in the ship, and on the ice.

Crossing the Antarctic was now out of the question; survival was now paramount. Shackleton was optimistic that during the following spring, the floe would break up enough to set *Endurance* free. However, when the ice eventually began to move, it simply crushed *Endurance*. All 28 men barely managed to get into three small life boats, escaping the floe before they were also trapped and crushed. They faced almost certain death by rowing and sailing through cold wind and waves for days to Elephant Island, a small speck of land at the end of a peninsula stretching into the South Atlantic. Somehow, Shackleton buoyed his team's spirits, guided them through these ferocious storms, and managed to reach the island.

Shackleton decided that the only hope of rescue was to sail before winter set in again with five other men in the largest of the life boats, 800 miles across the South Atlantic to the whaling station they had left more than a year before. Then he would hire a ship to return to rescue the other 22 men. Struggling through icy hurricanes, the six managed to find South Georgia. Shackleton and two others immediately set out on a dangerous march across the island to the whaling station. Once there, Shackleton sailed a ship back to rescue the three others at the landing site. Finally, after several failed attempts, Shackleton sailed another ship from Chile that rescued all 22 men on Elephant Island just before that vessel too was trapped in the ice. Shackleton's relentless drive to rescue his stranded men under the most dire circumstances has been called one of the most vivid displays of heroism and extraordinary leadership in human history.

What is the psychology behind our great appreciation for those who successfully overcome obstacles? In 1972, psychologist Harold Kelley proposed the principles of *augmenting* and *discounting* to explain how we come to understand others who either struggle, or fail to struggle, to achieve big goals.[7] As an example, we'll use baseball pitcher Jim Abbott, who reached the major leagues in 1989 despite having been born with only his left hand. During the act of pitching the ball, Abbott would rest a right-handed thrower's glove on the stump of his right forearm. After releasing the ball, he was quickly able to slip his left hand into the glove in time to field any balls hit at him. Opposing teams tried to exploit this fielding disadvantage, but they never could. In 1993, while playing for the New York Yankees, Abbott threw a no-hitter against the Cleveland Indians. He was a true star, especially in the eyes of disabled Americans for whom Abbott provided tremendous inspiration.

As observers of Abbott's baseball performances, we recognize that his disability inhibited his ability to become a star baseball player. Harold Kelley theorized that when we observe someone successfully overcome an inhibitory force, then we are left to conclude that the person has an especially strong dispositional quality that can account for the success. In short, our beliefs about Abbott's ability level are *augmented* because he had such a large obstacle to overcome. While the principle of augmentation can explain why Abbott is perceived as a hero, the principle of discounting can explain why some people can achieve success but will find it difficult to be viewed as heroes. Imagine people who are born into wealth and have every advantage growing up.

If these people succeed wildly in life, their ability levels will be *discounted* because they had so few obstacles to overcome.

Kelley's theory can explain why the friend we play tennis with always seems to complain about her sore back or twisted ankle before playing a friendly match with us. If she beats us despite the injuries, then she will be viewed as heroic in conquering her obstacles. Psychologists call this tendency of people to advertise their obstacles *self-handicapping*.[8] Our tennis friend may announce her injuries to protect her self-esteem in the event of losing to us, or to enhance her self-esteem in the event of beating us. It is human for us to want to self-handicap. In Jim Abbott's case, the obstacle was plainly visible, but sometimes the obstacles are unseen variables that observers have trouble taking into account when evaluating others' behavior. This leads us to the distinction between internal and external obstacles, which we discuss next.

Internal versus External Obstacles

Ernest Shackleton's heroics stemmed from his ability to overcome the vicissitudes of the external world. But people also triumph over their inner obstacles, such as Rick Blaine's broken, bitter heart in Casablanca. Rick also contended with the Nazis, showing that he had both internal and external forces to contend with. Jim Abbott's amazing baseball career shows us that significant personal challenges can assume a physical form. Actor Robert Downey Jr.'s successful battle with drug addiction illustrates how the line between internal and external obstacles can sometimes be blurred. Clearly Downey had personal issues that led to his drug use, but the drugs themselves were external obstacles.

To illustrate personal challenges, and how people overcome them, we will tell you the story of a remarkable man named Nick Vujicic.[9] Born in Australia, Vujicic entered the world with no arms or legs, and only a small foot with two toes protruding from his left thigh. As a child, Vujicic was obviously very different from other children and thus was bullied mercilessly. As a result, he became depressed and suicidal. Eventually, he learned to become grateful for just being alive and grew in his motivation to overcome his physical shortcomings. Vujicic started by learning to use his two toes to grip objects; eventually, he learned to use a computer, throw tennis balls, and operate a telephone. He eventually graduated from college with a double major, established the nonprofit organization *Life Without Limbs*, and has become a highly popular motivational speaker. He has also become a youtube sensation, giving speeches on overcoming fear and rejection, depression, suffering, and unanswered prayers.

Responses to Vujicic's speeches from youtube viewers attest to his heroic qualities:

- "You are the angel amongst us. God bless you—what an inspiration to speak with kids."
- "I know that God has put him on earth for a reason. To let us know that anything is possible. Thank you, Nick."
- "You are amazing, Nick. You give me the strength to overcome anything."
- "Nick, you are an awesome inspiration!!"
- "Nick, you are a very great legend, and your angelic face and smile is enough to change millions of people's lives."[10]

Another example of person challenge involves the story of Karl Merk, a German dairy farmer who lost both arms in a work accident, and in 2008 became the world's first recipient of a double arm transplant.[11] Responses to online news coverage of Merk's ordeal show that people strongly resonated to his courageous struggle with disability, with the many painful medical procedures associated with the transplant, and with regaining use of his new arms. Hope and inspiration were the main theme of readers' responses, as these excerpts attest:

- "Merk brings hope for those living with similar disabilities."
- "Merk certainly brings hope to my life. My daughter is having her foot amputated very soon. The fact that they have done this now with arms gives me hope that some day my daughter will be able to have her own foot."
- "Here is a story that brings hope for those living with similar disabilities."
- "It's great to hear some uplifting inspiration news and my congratulations to this man for his courage and bravery."[12]

In addition to admiring Merk's heroic personal struggle with the double arm transplant, there was also an equally strong appreciation for the heroic actions of his 40-person medical team. The challenges this surgical team faced were considerable indeed. Never before had such a large amount of foreign tissue been transplanted to a person. Five subgroups of surgeons working in two operating theatres gathered at 10 p.m. the night of the operation, one on each side of the patient and the donor, who had died only hours before. The fifth group removed a leg vein from the donor. First, the surgeons exposed Merk's muscles, nerves, and blood vessels and prepared them for connection to the donor's tissue. Before the bones of the donor could be cut, the blood vessels in his arms were filled with a cooled preservation solution. Both the donor's arms were then removed exactly at the point matching Merk's arm stumps. The bones were the first body parts to be joined, after which arteries and veins were grafted together to enable blood circulation as quickly as possible. The surgeons then, in order, attached onto Merk the muscles, tendons, nerves, and finally the skin.

The procedure was arduous, lasting more than 15 hours. It was also successful. As this book heads into print, Merk is slowly regaining the feeling in his arms, holding hands with his wife and children once again. His medical team is confident that he should regain full use of his new limbs within 2 years.

It's important to note that when Merk's story received widespread media attention in the fall of 2008, people were just as responsive to the heroism of the medical team as they were to Merk's heroic journey. Some excerpts of people's reactions to the medical team:

- "The brilliant talent of the surgeons is hard to believe. The hope that they gave that man can't be surpassed."
- "The miracle of these dedicated surgeons puts me in awe."
- "What a wondrous achievement, giving this man his life back. They could never have given him a greater gift."
- "The hard work and heroic actions of these talented doctors is remarkable."[13]

Adversity + Selflessness = Superhero

While Merk earned people's admiration by overcoming the challenges of his disability and rehabilitation, the surgeons were venerated for selflessly applying their medical talents toward the goal of restoring Merk's arms. Thus, we can learn a couple of important lessons about what makes someone a hero. The first lesson is that we are clearly moved by witnessing someone triumph over great adversity. If a person successfully conquers a great challenge, he or she *has a very good chance* of being viewed as a hero. Why only a very good chance? Why doesn't overcoming a stiff challenge guarantee heroic status? The reason is that heroism requires that the person's actions be directed toward achieving a socially admirable goal. Some great efforts are unworthy of our applause, as when a criminal works tirelessly to foil rigorous law enforcement. Merk achieved heroic status by bravely trying to piece his life back together—a noble goal. Moreover, his medical team attained heroic stature for accomplishing the worthy objective of conquering a daunting medical challenge.

The second lesson about heroism is reflected in people's comments about the surgical team, who were lauded for working toward the goal of helping Merk. People who show great selflessness in the service of helping others are often judged as heroes. And, in the case of the medical team, selflessness combined with beating adversity made for an especially powerful perception of heroism. Merk's team, along with Shackleton's rescue team, were very much like the *Little Engine That Could*. They attained heroic status by surmounting formidable obstacles to achieve the mission of helping others.

From what we have been able to glean from the results of our studies, the surest path to heroism involves this combination of beating adversity and serving others. A vivid example of this two-component blueprint for heroism is found in the moments after two jet planes struck the twin towers of the World Trade Center in New York on September 11, 2001.[14] While thousands of trapped citizens raced down stairwells to escape the burning structures, hundreds of firefighters, police, and paramedics chose to climb *up* the stairs to offer assistance. These rescuers faced the perilous task of clearing an escape path, dowsing flames, and treating victims. Hundreds of lives were saved by the selfless actions of these emergency workers, who performed their jobs in the face of horrific adversity. When the buildings collapsed, there was an immense outpouring of grief for all the lost lives in the building, and especially for the rescuers who were killed.

In the wake of the September 11th attacks, the emergency personnel who perished that day were honored in speeches and in more
permanent physical tributes. Numerous monuments and memorials
were erected nationwide, and a postage stamp was issued depicting
firefighters raising the American flag. President Bush commented
that the attacks brought out "the best of America," including "the
daring of our rescue workers."[15] Dozens of Web sites continue to
honor the heroes from September 11th, and many of these sites
include poems and essays commemorating the day's heroism. Several
poems contain a biblical quote from John 15:13, "Greater love has no
one than this: that one lay down his life for his friends."[16] A stanza
from another poem reads:

> They didn't do it for the glory
> They didn't do it for the fame
> They only did what they knew was right
> They are heroes that have no name.[17]

The reverence felt for the 9/11 firefighters serves as a strong
reminder to us that a central recipe for heroism involves a combination of sacrifice and altruism. Among Christians, of course, Jesus
Christ is believed to have suffered horribly to save human beings
from sinfulness. Great epic tales from both Western and non-West-
ern traditions all tell stories of a strong courageous hero who estab-
lishes either a great religion or a great nation. The *Aeneid* tells the
story of Aeneas's brave journey from Troy to Italy and the founding
of the Roman Empire. The African epic of *Sundiata* tells a similar
story of Sundiata's great triumph over adversity in establishing the
Mali Empire. In Mesopotamian mythology, *Gilgamesh* chronicles the
story of a king who overcomes many supernatural challenges to build
the great city of Uruk. These and many similar tales demonstrate that
humans across time and geography have always been enamored
with the hero who suffers deeply to accomplish something noble
and great.

The popularity of fictional superheroes in our popular culture can
be attributed, at least in part, to the appeal of the person who triumphs over adversity and makes extraordinary sacrifices to achieve
an altruistic goal. Superheroes encounter great challenge in at least

three different ways. First, superheroes usually have an origin story featuring great pain and hardship. Batman must overcome the trauma of witnessing his parents' murder; Superman must overcome being orphaned as a small child from his home planet; Spiderman must overcome feelings of rejection, inadequacy, and loneliness; and Xena must overcome past hardships and her own past sins as a ruthless warlord. Many of us can relate to painful early childhood memories, and we bestow superhero status to those who not only overcome severe childhood setbacks but use them to serve the greater good.

The second way that superheroes encounter great challenge is seen in their unique weakness or Achilles heel that renders them vulnerable. For Superman, the weakness was exposure to the substance kryptonite; for the Green Lantern, it was wood; for the Incredible Hulk, it was anger. Superheroes, it seems, not only must conquer early life traumas but also a chronic, unavoidable shortcoming throughout their life span that impedes their ability to perform noble acts. For all of his superhuman strength, kryptonite reduces Superman to a helpless weakling, and he must rely on help from his ordinary human allies—Lois Lane or Jimmy Olsen—to restore his strength.

What is most interesting is that Superman's weakness is essential to his popularity. If he were 100% invincible and had no obstacles to surmount, we would be unable to relate to him. All human beings experience struggle of some sort, allowing us to identify with others who also struggle. More importantly, we witness Superman achieving great things *despite* his vulnerability to kryptonite. So not only does he have a debilitating limitation, he demonstrates an unstoppable desire to overcome it so that he can serve others. Human beings inherently know that there is nothing to admire about a person who effortlessly succeeds. The struggle makes the hero.

The third way that superheroes face great challenge is represented in the human (or sometimes superhuman) opposition they face. All superheroes encounter exceptionally evil, cunning villains whom they must defeat. Superman's nemesis is Lex Luther; Batman squares off against the Joker, the Riddler, and the Penguin; The Green Lantern battles the Vandal Savage. Not surprisingly, these villains frequently use the superheroes' origin story or unique weakness against them, heightening the superheroes' struggle to conquer evil. What is especially interesting about these villains is that their story of origin is often not unlike that of their superhero counterpart. The villain is often damaged by family tragedy or by some debilitating accident, but unlike the hero, this setback breeds anger, hatred, and evil. Thus, we become particularly impressed with the superhero, whose courage and ability to turn setback into redemption represents a sharp contrast to the villain's meek surrender to setback.

It is important to remember that superheroes must be supremely challenged to do their good work. If doing the right thing comes too easily to heroes, they won't be judged as heroes. If a person could simply snap her fingers to save someone from a burning building, her action would certainly be celebrated, but because anyone could have (and would have) done the same thing, it is unlikely she would be deemed a hero. Heroism requires an uncommon ability to do something exceptional, something rarely seen and involving great sacrifice. Heroes do not do their work by performing simple pain-free acts. There must be either extraordinary effort or extraordinary sacrifice directed toward accomplishing a socially redeeming goal. Such is the stuff of heroes.

Different Types of Adversity: Physical, Emotional, and Social

Obstacles come in many different forms. Shackleton battled the elements, while Karl Merk and Nick Vujicic were faced with the challenge of overcoming considerable physical disability. Still others are confronted with the challenge of overcoming great emotional turmoil. Our lead character from *Casablanca*, Rick Blaine, was madly in love with Ilsa, and he could easily have made the choice to spend the rest of his life with her. But doing so would require breaking up Ilsa's marriage with Victor Lazlo, stranding Victor in Casablanca where he would undoubtedly be imprisoned, and severely harming the Allied resistance movement of which Victor was the leader. Not only does Rick make the selfless choice to insist that Ilsa leave Casablanca with Victor, he must kill a Nazi officer to get them on the plane. In doing the right thing, Rick has sacrificed everything: the love of his life, his business, his position in Casablanca, his freedom, and possibly his life. His heroism is forever etched in pop-cultural history because he overcame two difficult emotional hurdles (Ilsa jilting him earlier, and his current love for her) along with a major physical hurdle (the Nazis). On top of this, his overall objective was supremely laudable (helping the Allied cause).

Sometimes doing the right thing is challenging because the people around us are pressuring us to do the wrong thing. Overcoming these social pressures can seemingly be just as formidable a task as overcoming physical or emotional obstacles. Consider the results of a classic social psychological study conducted in 1951 by Solomon Asch.[18] The participants in this study arrived at an experiment with seven others whom they thought were also participants but were actually Asch's accomplices. Asch told everyone that the study was a test of people's visual judgments. He showed everyone two cards, a left card portraying one vertical line and a right card displaying three lines of varying length.

Asch asked all eight people—only one of which was the actual participant—to choose which of the three lines on the right card matched the length of the line on the left card. The task was repeated several times with different cards. On some occasions Asch's accomplices unanimously chose the wrong line. In these instances, Asch found that about one-third of the participants went along with the clearly erroneous majority. The task was simple and the correct answer was obvious. So then why did the participants conform to the wrong answer so willingly? Interviewed after the experiment, most of them said that they did not really believe their conforming answers, but had gone along with the group for fear of being ridiculed or judged to be "peculiar." A few of them said that they really did believe the group's answers were correct.

The results of Asch's study are especially unsettling given that the accomplices never actually "pressured" the respondents to give the incorrect response. If there had been actual arm-twisting to give the majority response, we imagine the rate of conformity might have been much higher, but the conforming rate was still high despite the absence of overt pressure. Asch was clearly disturbed by the results of his study; he wrote: "The tendency to conformity in our society is so strong that reasonably intelligent and well-meaning young people are willing to call white black. This is a matter of concern. It raises questions about our ways of education and about the values that guide our conduct."

We suspect that Asch's call for better education and values may overlook the fact that most ordinary, nonheroic people are smart, good-hearted folks who simply find it difficult to overcome the obstacle of social pressures. Consider the case of Angel Arce Torres, who in 2008 was crossing a street in Hartford, Connecticut, when a car plowed into him, sending him flying and leaving him lying crumpled and bleeding in the middle of the street.[19] The driver of the car did not stop, but even more disturbingly, passing cars and people on the sidewalk nearby did nothing to help Torres. As he lay in the street, nine cars passed him without stopping. More than 40 seconds went by before anyone even stepped off the sidewalk to get a closer look. But no one went over to Torres' body to try to help or even divert traffic.

Finally, after about a minute and a half, a police car responding to a different call happened upon the scene and an ambulance was called. Sounding much like Asch, Chief of Police Daryl Roberts expressed outrage in a news conference, saying, "We no longer have a moral compass. *It's a clear indication of what we have become* when you see a man lying in the street, hit by a car, and people just drive around him" (emphasis added).[20]

But is the story of Angel Torres a clear indication of what we have become? If Shackleton had been unable to surmount the icy storms, would anyone dare call him a coward? Probably not, because physical hurdles such as snow and wind are much more tangible and visible than psychological ones like social pressures. Park Street, where Torres was hit, is part of a notorious high-crime area, with many residents unwilling to help police lest they be labeled a "snitch" by others. Torres needed a hero who was willing and able to overcome this powerful yet unseen pressure to avoid involvement.

Even those who wanted to help Torres may have been reluctant to do so because of a phenomenon social psychologists have identified as *diffusion of responsibility*.[21] Put simply, this refers to the idea that the more people who are available to help, the less responsibility for helping any one person feels. The bottom line is that doing the right thing requires much more than good values and a willingness to help others. It also requires an ability to overcome easily overlooked social and psychological obstacles that can lure people into doing the wrong thing. Note also how doing the wrong thing is often doing the easy thing. It is easy to do nothing, to avoid possible ridicule, rejection, or harm. Becoming a hero is hard because it often violates the most cherished instinct we have: self-preservation. When we dare to leave our comfort zone, to confront adversity rather than cower from it, then we are demonstrating heroic tendencies.

Heroes somehow overcome hidden forces that discourage heroic acts. Social pressures do not deter them. This is no easy feat given that people routinely underestimate the power of these unseen obstacles to heroism. Psychologist Stanley Milgram conducted a classic study of obedience to illustrate just how much we fail to appreciate the power of social influence to lead us toward cowardly, unheroic acts. In Milgram's study, the experimenter led participants to believe they were delivering painful shocks to another participant, who was actually the experimenter's accomplice and never actually received the shocks.[22] The majority of participants delivered the maximum voltage shocks to the accomplice, who could be heard screaming in pain, and they obeyed the experimenter simply because he told them that doing so was required for the experiment. About a third of the participants were "heroes" of sorts, refusing to harm the accomplice and exiting the study, but most could not overcome the powerful situational forces at work pulling them toward obedience. These results were unanticipated and stunned Milgram. Prior to the study, Milgram described the procedure of his study to both laypeople and psychiatrists, the vast majority of whom predicted that he would find little or no obedience. Thus, we see that not only do strong social forces often impede heroism, we also are often blind to the magnitude of these forces and are prone to miscalculating their impact.

Physical versus Moral Courage

Heroes must display courage to overcome forces that inhibit good behavior. Usually this courage is *moral* courage rather than *physical* courage. People display physical courage when they risk life and limb to overcome a great obstacle, as when a mountain climber scales a dangerous mountain. There is little or no moral component to physical courage; there is only a willingness and an ability to triumph over physically challenging circumstances. Many people are deemed heroes solely because of their physical courageousness: Amelia Earhart for setting many speed and distance aviation records, Sir Edmund Hillary for conquering Mount Everest, Chuck Yeager for breaking the sound barrier, and Neil Armstrong for walking on the moon. None of these actions fed a hungry baby or saved a life. But they were all impressive demonstrations of overcoming great physical challenges.

Now consider the concept of moral courage. People who display moral courage are not necessarily risking personal safety, but they are challenged to perform the morally correct action in the face of popular opposition and possible risk to personal reputation or financial standing. Morally courageous individuals might include the participants in Milgram's study who disobeyed the experimenter's orders to continue delivering painful shocks. They may also include whistleblowers who expose corporate or government cover-ups. A notable example of a morally courageous whistleblower is Jeffrey Wigand, a former vice president of a major tobacco company.[23] He became known as a whistleblower when on the CBS news program 60 *Minutes* he exposed his company's practice of "impact boosting," which refers to intentionally enhancing the effect of nicotine in cigarettes. Wigand claims that after he exposed his company's morally questionable behavior, he was harassed and received anonymous death threats. While he was vilified as a disloyal snitch to those within the company, he was hailed as a hero to nearly all outsiders who appreciated his morally courageous stance against deadly nicotine addiction.

Heroes are especially admired when they combine both physical and moral courage. U.S. Senator John McCain's experience as a prisoner of war during the Vietnam War exemplifies the physically and morally courageous hero.[24] McCain was flying his 23rd bombing mission over North Vietnam in 1967 when his fighter jet was shot down by a missile over Hanoi. McCain fractured both arms and a leg while ejecting from the aircraft, and he nearly drowned when he parachuted into a lake. After the North Vietnamese pulled him ashore, they crushed his shoulder with a rifle butt and bayoneted him. McCain was then transported to Hanoi's main Hoa Lo Prison, nicknamed the "Hanoi Hilton."

McCain was badly wounded, but his captors refused to treat his injuries, beating and interrogating him to get information. Weeks later, he was finally given marginal medical care but only after the North Vietnamese discovered that his father was a top admiral. McCain was in a chest cast for 2 months and, with his hair turned prematurely white, he was sent to a different prison camp on the outskirts of Hanoi, where he shared a cell with two other Americans. He was not expected to survive his injuries, but he somehow made enough of a recovery to be placed in solitary confinement for 2 years.

At this point in McCain's story, he had shown mostly physical courage in withstanding torture and confinement, but in 1968 an opportunity for moral courage was presented to McCain when the North Vietnamese offered him early release. They did so to appear merciful for propaganda purposes, and also to demoralize other longtime prisoners of war. McCain, to his credit, turned down the offer; he would only accept early release if every prisoner taken in before him was released as well. His refusal to be released infuriated his captors, and so in August of 1968, a program of severe torture began on McCain. He was subjected to rope bindings and repeated beatings every 2 hours, and at the same time he suffered from dysentery. Further injuries led to the beginning of a suicide attempt, which was stopped by guards. After 4 days, McCain made an anti-American propaganda "confession." He has always felt that his statement was dishonorable, but as he later wrote, "I had learned what we all learned over there: Every man has his breaking point. I had reached mine." Many American prisoners of war were tortured and mistreated in order to extract "confessions" and propaganda statements, and most all of them eventually yielded something to their captors. McCain subsequently received two to three beatings weekly because of his continued refusal to sign additional statements.

A lesser-known story of moral courage appeared in the life history of Ulysses S. Grant.[25] Required by his father to attend West Point, Grant was an average student, fought well in the Mexican War, got married, and was assigned to an army post in California. Grant was lonely and miserable, as his wife was in St. Louis, and this separation from her may have led to his growing alcohol problem and his early resignation from the army in 1854. After losing money in bad business ventures in California, he moved to New York City, where he continued to struggle financially. Grant borrowed money to return to his family in St. Louis, started more business ventures in farming and in real estate, and, when those undertakings failed, moved his family to Illinois in 1860 to work for his father's business.

At this point in his life, Grant was hardly a success or a hero, but he quickly hit his stride. When the Civil War broke out, he volunteered for the Union army and quickly moved into a command rank. The soldiers under him had a reputation for being hard-heads, but under Grant's leadership they very aggressively won a number of battles, earning Grant a series of promotions. In February of 1862, Grant secured the first major Union victory, capturing Fort Donelson. Promoted to General, he continued to preside over many impressive victories and is credited for turning the war in the union's favor. Vastly popular, he served two terms as U.S. President, after which he traveled the world to great fanfare. But once again his bad business instincts doomed him; he was swindled of his life savings by a man named Ferdinand Ward, and to make matters worse, at the same time he discovered that he had throat cancer. Days before Grant died, he published his memoirs, earning him and his family almost a half million dollars.

Grant's moral courage is manifested in several ways. First, he showed considerable bravery fighting for a morally just cause while serving with distinction in the army. Moreover, during his presidency, he fought hard for the rights of African Americans, lobbying fiercely for the passage of the 15th amendment, which gave blacks the right to vote. Grant is also credited for crushing the Ku Klux Klan in South Carolina in 1872. Grant showed moral courage by working for racial equality at a time when doing so was both uncommon and unpopular. He was able to overcome extreme opposition from racist friends and lobbyists. Grant was the last president until Lyndon Johnson to propose and pass civil rights legislation, and he was the last until Eisenhower to send troops to a Southern state to suppress terrorism and guarantee minority rights.

The Appeal of the Underdog

Grant deserves credit for helping blacks achieve equal rights, just as Karl Merk's medical team deserves credit for helping Merk reacquire a set of limbs. We tend to have a soft spot in our hearts for people who are down on their luck, disadvantaged, harmed, or struggling. Such people are underdogs, and it is rare to find anyone who doesn't root for a deserving underdog. Underdogs often need our help, and people are often credited with heroism for going beyond the call of duty to help underdogs overcome their struggles. Underdogs, by definition, struggle to achieve some worthy goal. And we love underdogs who successfully overcome their challenges. For this reason, tales of underdog triumphs permeate our culture.

One of the earliest underdog stories is recounted in the Bible, which tells the memorable account of how the young David defeated the giant Goliath:

> And there went out a champion out of the camp of the Philistines named Goliath whose height was six cubits and a span. And when the Philistine looked about, and saw David, he disdained him: for he was but a youth. And the Philistine said unto David, Come to me, and I will give thy flesh to the air, and to the beasts of the field. And David put his hand in his bag, and took thence a stone, and slang it, and smote the Philistine in his forehead, that the stone sunk into his forehead; and he fell upon his face to the earth.[26]

What has made the story of David and Goliath so important in Judeo-Christian cultures? Most likely its importance lies in the lessons for living that it teaches us. In the story, everyone was afraid of the seemingly invincible Goliath. Not even King Saul, the tallest man in Israel, had stepped out to fight the giant. When Goliath hurled threats and insults at the people, David didn't hesitate or waver. While everyone else cowered in fear, David ran to the battle because he knew that action needed to be taken. We can see that the story of David and Goliath urges readers to show courage in the face of daunting challenge. David displayed both physical and moral courage because he risked personal injury to do the right thing.

Another moral of the story is the lesson of trusting oneself and trusting God. Because David was skillful and comfortable with the simple slingshot he wielded, the story encourages readers to trust one's own skills and resources, and to have trust in the familiar gifts and talents that God has provided. A recurring theme throughout the Bible is the idea of being open to divine help and being receptive to God's miracles. Goliath embodied the opposite principle; he was a mere mortal defying an all-powerful God. From the Judeo-Christian God's perspective, God will fight for us and with us when we encounter profound challenges. When we believe we are not alone when tackling our problems, we are open to receiving courage and can fight more effectively.

Modern movies abound with David and Goliath-like stories of underdog triumph in the sporting world: *Rocky*, *The Bad News Bears*, *Seabiscuit*, *Miracle*, *Hoosiers*, *Something for Joey*, *Breaking Away*, *Cinderella Man*, and many more. Consider the many fairy tales and other children's fables that focus on the underdog's ability to overcome evil or other adversity: *Little Red Riding Hood*, *Jack and the Beanstalk*, *Hansel and Gretel*, *Bambi*, *Beauty and the Beast*, *The Little Engine That Could*, *The Three Little Pigs*, *Snow White and the Seven Dwarfs*, and many more. Stories about underdogs seem to touch something deep in the human psyche. People, animals, or even inanimate objects perceived to face difficult challenges against a strong opponent seem to inspire our support.

Why might people root for underdogs? In many cultures there are numerous popular underdog stories and tales of success spawned from humble origins that fascinate people of all ages. Many cultural narratives relate stories of people facing difficult challenges, such as King Sisyphus condemned in Hades to roll a stone toward the top of a hill for eternity. We believe that such narratives reflect a script or archetype of struggle which engages support and sympathy. In the United States, the idea of the "American Dream" and the Horatio Alger stories of rags to riches, embodied by individuals such as Andrew Carnegie, nourish our aspirations to overcome the imposed limitations of underdog status. These heroic accomplishments of underdogs may serve as an inspiration as well as a guide for socially sanctioned behaviors. They may also provide hope to the masses who aspire to successfully overcome the obstacles present in their own lives and may suggest that the world can be a fair place in which all individuals have the potential to succeed.

These underdog stories are powerful because without exception, all of us have experienced struggle and have been small and powerless early in life and when first enrolled in schools, jobs, and social organizations. Therefore, it may be relatively easy for us to take the perspective of those who are also struggling or competing against formidable odds. We may find stories such as those of David and Goliath and *The Little Engine That Could* compelling because we have also been in psychologically similar situations. Because of our own experience of being an underdog and frequent exposures to many cultural narratives of underdogs, we easily recognize, identify, and sympathize with the struggles of an underdog. There may be other plausible explanations for the underdog effect. First, if people perceive rooting for the underdog as unusual, doing so may satisfy their need for uniqueness. Second, if people perceive rooting for the underdog as just or fair, doing so may satisfy their need for fairness or equity. Third, when we see underdogs succeed, it provides us with hope that we too can prevail in difficult circumstances. Fourth, watching an underdog succeed is much more dramatic, satisfying our need for exciting entertainment. Fifth, since we expect the underdog to lose, rooting for him or her costs very little, but the vicarious rewards of an expected success of a disadvantaged protagonist are great.

One thing is undeniably true: The tendency to root for underdogs is deeply engrained in us. To illustrate just how powerful the underdog phenomenon is in our psyche, we conducted a study in which participants sat at a computer screen and observed a circle moving along a horizontal line. Soon the line begins to slope into the shape of a "hill" and the circle begins to move up the incline. The participants in the study were assigned to one of four different conditions. In one condition, the circle maintained its speed as it traversed the hill. In a second condition, the circle's speed noticeably declined as it moved up the hill. In a third condition, the circle slowed as it traversed the hill and was passed by a second circle that is not slowed at all by the hill. In the fourth condition, the speedy second circle not only passed the first circle, it "bumped" the first circle backward down the hill, as if trying to prevent it from successfully ascending it.

Figure 4.1 A circle appearing to struggle up a hill in our studies. Our participants liked, rooted for, and sympathized with this circle. See Kim et al. (2008), published in the *Journal of Applied Social Psychology*.[27]

We asked participants in all four conditions to indicate how much they liked the circles, rooted for the circles, and sympathized with the circles. We were not at all sure what kind of results we would get. After all, these were simple geometric shapes displayed on the computer screen. Why should participants like a circle or root for a circle at all? These circles were clearly not living things, and we included no instruction suggesting that participants view them as alive. Nevertheless, our findings were clear: People liked the circle more when it struggled up the hill than when it didn't struggle. In addition, they showed stronger liking for the struggling circle when it was passed by a faster circle than when it struggled alone. Finally, our participants' liking and sympathy for the struggling circle was the strongest, by far, when it appeared to be harmed by the faster circle. This aggressive faster circle was, by far, the most significantly disliked circle.

Our participants were also visibly agitated when they witnessed the struggling underdog circle being harmed. After the study was completed, they reported to us that such an aggressive act directed toward an "underdog" was completely out of line and unacceptable. These findings stunned us. People appear to become emotionally attached to any entity, even an inanimate one, simply because that entity resembles the characteristics of a living underdog. The underdog phenomenon is such a powerful part of our thinking that we anthropomorphically ascribe human traits of courage and strength to inanimate objects that resemble heroic underdogs.

Underdogs Are Not Always Loved

Do people always give underdogs their unconditional support? The results from our program of research on underdogs suggests that the answer to this question is no. There is no doubt that underdogs attract our sympathy, but the results of our studies indicate that our love for underdogs is limited and qualified by a number of factors. Here's what we've discovered about the limitations of the underdog phenomenon:

1. While underdogs attract our sympathy, we really only pull for underdogs when their fate has minimal impact on us or others. This is why we are more likely to support underdogs in sporting events than in other contexts that matter more, such as in the business world. The consequences are low if the underdog team loses a basketball game, but the consequences are high if the small underdog appliance store charges more for a DVD player than does Walmart.

2. We root for underdogs only when we believe they are expending maximum effort to perform at their highest level. When the underdogs are perceived to be coasting, we actually like and respect the top dog more than the underdog.

3. We love underdogs the most when they have an unlikely— but not impossible—chance to prevail. A small but reasonable possibility of success is apparently necessary to assure us of a sufficiently high emotional payoff if the underdog triumphs. If an underdog has absolutely no chance of success, the results of our studies show that we will not root for the underdog.

4. People's emotional support for an underdog does not translate into respect. In our studies, we've found that people root for underdogs but also believe that underdogs produce work that is inferior to that of top dogs. Only after underdogs prevail are we convinced that they have meritorious qualities.

What do these findings suggest about underdogs and underdog heroes? They tell us that underdog heroes in sporting contexts are especially powerful because our goal in witnessing sporting events is to be entertained, and nothing entertains us more than watching an underdog prevail. This explains the proliferation of underdog sports heroes in books and movies. Our findings also tell us that our love for underdogs is reserved only for those who work the hardest, and that witnessing the rewards of hard work affirms a cherished value about good work ethics. Finally, our research tells us that people who do the seemingly impossible, who defy the odds, who have no right to succeed but somehow do, are judged to be the most heroic. Those who sacrifice the most and surprise us the most with their success are heroes in our eyes.

OBSTACLES IN PERSPECTIVE

As we have seen in this chapter, the ability to overcome obstacles is one of the principal ingredients in the recipe for heroism. These obstacles and challenges come in many different forms: physical, personal, social, and emotional. We've also seen that people often underestimate the impact of social and psychological obstacles to heroism because these obstacles tend to be invisible to the naked eye. We've also learned that heroes who overcome obstacles in the service of performing moral actions are especially revered. That is, a hero like Shackleton who overcomes winter hurricanes to rescue his men in Antarctica is more highly revered than a hero who overcomes winter hurricanes simply to be the first to cross Antarctica. In other words, moral courage trumps physical courage.

Underdogs who defy great odds to overcome obstacles are especially admired. In fact, the underdog who prevails is powerful to us because it taps into the deeply engrained archetype of the hero that all of us have. In all children's stories, and in many adult ones, the ideal heroic scenario features the nobility of the great struggle against adversity to achieve a worthy goal. While being an underdog is no guarantee that one will be loved, it is clear that underdogs who exert superhuman effort and unexpectedly prevail become some of our most cherished cultural heroes.

One of the most important requirements that we have for our heroes is that they experience struggle, and succeed despite it. If success comes too easily to them, they aren't heroes. In 2009 golfer Phil Mickelson's wife and mother were both diagnosed with breast cancer at roughly the same time. Somehow, despite these distractions, Mickelson was able to win the PGA tour championship. In 1993 Michael Jordan was devastated by his father's murder, retired from the NBA, but then came back later to regain his status as the NBA's greatest player. We are moved by stars who continue to shine, or who somehow shine brighter, despite experiencing great personal tragedy.

But what about the accomplishments of people who face less visible inner struggles? Their heroism often goes unnoticed and unappreciated. It is not unusual for talented stars to wage largely unknown battles with depression, stage fright, personal loss, or worse. Celebrities such as Elton John, Paula Abdul, Mary-Kate Olsen, Wynnona Judd, and Kate Moss have all struggled with eating disorders. Harrison Ford, Jim Carrey, Brooke Shields, and J. K. Rowling have each overcome depression. Actress Mackenzie Phillips has admitted to a heroin habit and stated that her father sexually abused her for years. In 2007, actor Owen Wilson attempted suicide by slitting his wrists. Obviously battling personal problems, Wilson continues to display his talent in successful movies, and we greatly admire his perseverance and courage.

Without struggle, there can be no hero. It is unlikely that Bill Clinton, who served as president during a time of peace, will ever be viewed as a hero. Without crises, leaders are doomed to be viewed as nonheroic. Just as there are heroic people, there are also heroic situations, or moments in time, that give rise to heroism. These heroic moments are fraught with the kind of adversity that is necessary for heroism to emerge. Because Bill Clinton never had the opportunity to shepherd America through economic depression or war, his heroic potential was never truly tested. Heroic moments never came his way. The heroes we have described in this chapter—Ernest Shackleton, John McCain, Karl Merk, and Nick Vujicic—all faced heart-wrenching and sometimes horrific hardship. No sane person would want to experience their suffering. Yet these heroes prevailed while others caught in similar heroic moments could not or would not. This fact tells us that while heroic moments may provide heroic opportunities, only a select few of us are able to rise to the occasion. Heroic moments are thus a necessary but not sufficient condition to produce heroism. The heroes among us muster up the courage to conquer these heroic moments.

On the surface it may seem that many of our heroes were unsuccessful in their struggles. John Belushi and Chris Farley are two comedians who died from doing speedballs, a combined injection of heroin and cocaine. Many rock music stars, such as Jimi Hendrix, Janis Joplin, and Kurt Cobain, also succumbed to drug addiction. Yet, to most people, these late great heroes have retained their heroic status. Why? One reason may be that these stars shone brightly despite the dark clouds in their lives. In short, they were able to prove before their deaths that they were able to conquer their inner demons long enough to attain greatness. Another reason why we cherish dead heroes is that death itself may have a profound effect on how we evaluate people, especially our heroes. In Chapter 6 of this book we explore in great detail the role of death in shaping our judgments of people. Suffice to say, our emotional connection to heroes becomes greatly magnified when they encounter the one obstacle that no one, not even the greatest of heroes, can overcome: human mortality.

5

EVIL

Challenges to Heroism

The curly-haired man stood at the podium before a sea of hostile onlookers. There was great tension in the air as they waited for him to speak. His close friend had been murdered in cold blood just minutes earlier by a band of people, not unlike those in the crowd, who believed his friend to be a power-hungry traitor. The previous speaker, one of the killers, had won over the crowd by justifying the murder as essential for the public good. The curly-haired man was seemingly backed into a corner. Although he was angry at his friend's death and wanted to avenge it, he also knew that his own life was in jeopardy if he dared to contradict the killer's speech and the prevailing sentiments of the emotionally charged mob before him.

"Friends, Romans, countrymen, lend me your ears," he began.[1] "I come to bury Caesar, not to praise him." (Act 3, Scene 2, line 58). This opening line delivered by Mark Antony instantly disarms the crowd. They now believe that he is one of them: a true patriot, on board with the bloody coup. Having established his credibility, Antony continues to mask his true feelings, at least temporarily, by affirming the crowd's beliefs about Caesar's wrongdoings. "The evil that men do lives after them," he tells them. "The good is oft interred with their bones; so let it be with Caesar." (Act 3, Scene 2, line 60).

At this point, Antony decides to take a chance. In a very slow and measured way, he begins to undermine the previous speaker's argument about the danger that Caesar posed to fellow Romans. He begins by confirming the crowd's beliefs about Caesar's alleged danger: "The noble Brutus hath told you Caesar was ambitious: If it were so, it was a grievous fault, and grievously hath Caesar answer'd it." (Act 3, Scene 2, line 62). To maintain a connection with the crowd, Antony next compliments Brutus by calling him "an honorable man" (Act 3, Scene 2, line 63). He then begins to use the term "honorable" repeatedly, and sarcastically, to characterize Brutus as he picks apart the killer's justification for his violent act. Antony begins listing Caesar's many accomplishments, but he does so by coupling them with the charge of ambition and Brutus's "honorable" nature. In this way, he allows the crowd to see the merits of Caesar's life while questioning the merits of the people who ended it. "He hath brought many captives home to Rome whose ransoms did the general coffers fill," exclaims Antony (Act 3, Scene 2, line 65). He then asks, "Did this in Caesar seem ambitious?" (Act 3, Scene 2, line 66). The crowd's silence speaks volumes. "When that the poor have cried, Caesar hath wept: ambition should be made of sterner stuff: yet Brutus says he was ambitious; and Brutus is an honorable man." (Act 3, Scene 2, Line 69).

The momentum has now swung in Antony's favor, and he deftly milks the moment. He reminds the crowd that on three occasions Caesar turned down the opportunity to be crowned king. "Was this ambition?" asks Antony. "Yet Brutus says he was ambitious; and, sure, he is an honorable man." (Act 3, Scene 2, Line 71). To drive home the injustice of Caesar's murder, Antony wraps up his speech with emotional, dramatic flair: "You all did love him once, not without cause: what cause withholds you then, to mourn for him? O judgment! Thou art fled to brutish beasts, and men have lost their reason. Bear with me; my heart is in the coffin there with Caesar, and I must pause till it come back to me." (Act 3, Scene 2, Line 75).

With these simple yet effective words, Antony turns a hero into a villain, and a villain into a hero. Brutus, once viewed as the savior of Rome from the tyrant Caesar, is now seen as the wretched assassin of a great Roman legend. Caesar, once viewed as a power-hungry despot, is now a heroic martyr. In Shakespeare's play *Julius Caesar*, all that separates the hero from the villain is a finely crafted speech by Mark Antony, a speech that beautifully illustrates how heroism and villainy are often in the eye of the beholder. More than we realize, only a fine line divides good from evil, and the position of the line can be affected by a few skillfully crafted words and fleeting emotions.

In *Julius Caesar*, confusion sometimes reigns among the characters themselves about whether a particular individual is heroic or villainous. Antony clearly maligns Brutus for slaying his friend Caesar. Yet, at the end of the play, when the armies of Brutus and Cassius lay defeated and Antony reflects back on what Brutus did, he acknowledges that Brutus was the "noblest Roman of them all" (Act 5, Scene 5, line 45). Standing over Brutus's dead body, Antony observes that most of Caesar's assassins were motivated by greed and envy, while only Brutus genuinely believed that his actions served Rome's best interests. Antony then gives Brutus the most honorable burial possible. We are left to puzzle whether Brutus is a hero, villain, or neither. Even Antony acknowledges the confusion by noting that "the elements [were] so mix'd in him" (Act 5, Scene 5, line 52).

No one understood the razor-thin edge between heroism and villainy better than William Shakespeare. Many tragic figures in Shakespearean plays were conflicted individuals like Brutus who believed they were doing the right thing but were misled by prideful motives, villainous sidekicks, or both. *King Lear* is a striking example. Lear's ego is stroked by the false flattery of his two evil daughters, to whom he bequeaths his kingdom. Only later, when it is too late, does he realize their true nature and that he is responsible for the death of the daughter whom he disinherited. In *Macbeth*, the lead character more closely resembles the path of Brutus. Three witches appear before Macbeth, offering the prophecy that he will become king. He shares this prophecy with his wife, Lady Macbeth, whose own ambition becomes ignited. She challenges Macbeth's manhood, encouraging him to murder King Duncan. The murder is carried out, precipitating the unraveling of the couple's sanity and life. Although they exercise poor judgment and harm others, Brutus, Lear, Macbeth, and Lady Macbeth are not the embodiment of evil. Shakespeare portrays them as ordinary people, manipulated by circumstance and prone to ambition, who succumb to greed or vanity.

We thus see that many Shakespearean tragic figures can perform heinous acts and yet attract sympathy. Shakespeare had an intuitive understanding that unequivocal evil is rare. Yet, it is clear that he could create characters who were unambiguously malicious. In *Julius Caesar*, the character of Cassius, for example, is one of Shakespeare's most blatantly evil characters. Just as heroes have sidekicks who bring out the best in the heroes, villains also can have sidekicks who bring out their worst. Cassius serves as such a sidekick to Brutus. He knows that Brutus and Caesar are good friends, but he begins a campaign of undermining that friendship by appealing to Brutus' vanity and his love for the Roman Empire. Cassius recalls a time when he saved Caesar from rushing waters and questions whether such a man deserves the reputation of a god. To Brutus he asks: "Brutus, and Caesar; what should be in that Caesar? Why should that name be sounded more than yours?" (Act 1, Scene 2, line 50). Cassius exploits Brutus' vanity and pride by noting that "everyone doth wish you had but that opinion of yourself which every noble Roman bears of you" (Act 2, Scene 1, line 44).

Cassius continues to stroke Brutus' ego while also painting a fearful image of Caesar as a man whose rapid ascent to power will inevitably corrupt him. In a famous soliloquy, Brutus ruminates: "'tis a common proof, that lowliness is young ambition's ladder, whereto the climber-upward turns his face; but, when he once attains the upmost round, he then unto the ladder turns his back, looks in the clouds, scorning the base degrees by which he did ascend: so Caesar may…." (Act 2, Scene 1, line 59). The murderous seeds planted in his head by Cassius, Brutus reflects about what he must do to stop what appears to be Caesar's runaway ambition. "And therefore think him as a serpent's egg which hatch'd, would, as his kind grow mischievous; and kill him in the shell." (Act 2, Scene 1, line 65).

Perhaps the most treacherously evil villain in Shakespeare's entire body of work is the character of Iago in *Othello*. Unlike Brutus or Lear or any other Shakespearean tragic figure, there is nothing noble at all about Iago or his motives. He plots against people who have been promoted ahead of him. He plants incriminating evidence against people who stand in his way of his ambitions. He engineers fights that will slay innocent others. And he deceives and manipulates others, especially Othello, to serve his petty interests. Shakespearean critic A. C. Bradley said that "evil has nowhere else been portrayed with such mastery as in the evil character of Iago."[2] Samuel Taylor Coleridge described Iago as having "motiveless malignity."[3] The strongest indictment against Iago's character is that he is not just a villain in his own right. Like Cassius, he is also an influential sidekick, bringing out villainous tendencies in others. Othello is the main recipient of Iago's evil influence. Believing Iago to be an honest and true friend, Othello received false information from Iago that his wife Desdemona has been unfaithful to him. Acting on Iago's lies, Othello kills her.

What is Shakespeare's message about evil? For one thing, the pure unadulterated evil that we see in Iago is rare. The Bard teaches us that evil actions usually stem from one of two sources: human weakness and social influence. Human weakness in Shakespeare's world is best exemplified by the seven deadly sins as described by Christian theology: pride, envy, wrath, sloth, greed, gluttony, and lust. The downfall of many Shakespearean tragic figures can be traced to the human tendency to succumb to one or more of these sins. Villainous sidekicks tend to nurture these basic human vices in others, most often bringing pride, envy, and greed to full fruition. Shakespeare is telling us that we are most prone to perform evil acts when we allow others to fan the flames of our destructive tendencies.

Also, as seen in Mark Antony's speech, we learn from Shakespeare that humans are capable of seeing either great good or great evil in others, depending on how these tendencies are described or framed by skillful persuaders. Shakespeare understood that the fine line between good and evil exists in the hearts and minds of fallible humans whose minds can change quickly depending on which schema—hero or villain—is activated. Brutus activated the villain schema when describing Caesar to the crowd, after which Antony more effectively triggered the hero schema. Shakespeare recognized how much his audience—including, of course, Mark Antony's audience—could resonate emotionally to characters whose traits embody the classic hero or villain schema. Shakespeare also realized that the line between good and evil within a single person is often blurred, and his most intriguing characters—Brutus, Lear, MacBeth—embodied traits that tapped into both the hero and villain schemas.

WHAT IS EVIL? A TALE OF TWO CITIES

Two cities, separated by nearly 5,000 miles, illustrate the difficulty of pinpointing the exact nature of evil. First there is the city of Richmond, Virginia, nestled along the mid-Atlantic seaboard of the United States. The former capitol of the Confederacy, Richmond boasts a beautiful tree-lined road leading into the center of downtown called Monument Avenue. Along the median strip of the road are four elaborate statues, some as high as 60 feet tall, of Confederate heroes Robert E. Lee, J. E. B. Stuart, Jefferson Davis, and Stonewall Jackson. In no other city in the world are defeated war heroes so visibly celebrated. To this day, members of the Sons of Confederate Veterans gather periodically on Monument Avenue to remember their heroes. Of course, many people sympathetic to the Union cause view these same immortalized men as villains, and on occasion these two groups will clash. The slippery dichotomy between hero and villain remains vividly on display in Richmond, Virginia.

Sometimes there is no such moral slipperiness. There are some behaviors that are so obviously good, or so obviously bad, that the vast majority of us can reach agreement about which ones are moral and which ones are not. A compelling example of this distinct moral dichotomy can be found on a single street in another fascinating city: Budapest, Hungary. One of the main roads leading into downtown Budapest is Andrassy Avenue, lined with beautiful homes, boutiques, and neo-renaissance palaces. At the end of Andrassy Avenue sits a very picturesque and regal monument called Heroes' Square, which displays 14 magnificent statues of legendary Hungarian heroes. These heroes were former kings, princes, and statesmen who advocated human rights and played pivotal leadership roles in shaping Hungarian society. Occupying thousands of square feet, Heroes' Square is a visually impressive sight, commands attention, and memorializes the best of human nature.

But if you walk just one-half mile down Andrassy Avenue from Heroes' Square in Budapest, you encounter another remarkable structure that memorializes the worst of humanity. The building is called the House of Terror, located at 60 Andrassy Avenue. Here stood the headquarters of the Nazi party during its occupation of Hungary in 1944 and 1945. When the Soviet army drove the Nazis out and began their own 45-year subjugation of Hungary, this same building then served as their communist headquarters. The House of Terror is now a museum that showcases the atrocities committed against Hungarian citizens during the Nazi and Soviet eras. A tour of the building reveals many artifacts and rooms used to detain, interrogate, torture, and kill innocent civilians. It is a chilling sight.

Monument Avenue in Richmond and Andrassy Avenue in Budapest both exemplify the two faces of evil. In Richmond we learn that evil resides in the eye of the beholder, with the nobility or wretchedness of an act being open to interpretation. In 1861, didn't the American South have the right to leave the union if the majority of its citizens favored such a split? Reasonable people could (and did) disagree on this issue. But in Budapest we learn that there are some actions so heinous that any reasonable person would judge them to be evil. In 1945, wasn't it clearly wrong for the Nazis in Budapest to murder 400 Jews on the banks of the Danube River? The answer is yes, and there is no reasonable interpretation of the event that would condone such a slaughter.

Webster's dictionary defines evil in two ways: as *morally objectionable behavior* and as *that which causes harm or destruction or misfortune.* Let's take a look at these definitions more closely, starting with morally objectionable behavior. How does one define what is objectionable? The answer is that it depends on who is doing the objecting. If you believe in *moral nihilism*—the idea that there is no such thing as good or bad—then you believe that anything goes and nothing is objectionable. Few people hold this position. Many more believe in the idea of *moral relativism*, which is the notion that determinations of good and bad depend on the situation or on one's cultural values. You may believe that killing another human being is wrong, but you may believe it's entirely appropriate to kill someone in self-defense. Or you may believe that circumcision is wrong but you accept that other people or cultures practice it. Finally, there is the idea of *moral universalism.* Proponents of this idea argue that some moral codes are better than others, and that a universal ethic can be inferred by drawing from the best existing moral codes that are common across all cultures.

From these three moral philosophies, we can imagine three different approaches to villainy. Moral nihilists would argue that there can be no villains since there is no such thing as wrongdoing. Moral relativism is a far more interesting and controversial form of morality, and we've encountered examples of it numerous times in this book. In *Casablanca*, the Germans viewed Victor Lazlo as the villain but an American or French audience would certainly regard Major Strasser as the bad guy. In *One Flew over the Cuckoo's Nest*, Nurse Ratched and her staff probably viewed McMurphy as the villain, whereas the Chief and the other patients no doubt judged Nurse Ratched as villainous. In *Julius Caesar*, one moment Brutus and Caesar were hero and villain, respectively, and the next moment their roles were reversed completely. And in Richmond, Virginia, moral relativism ran rampant during the Civil War. If you lived in the north, Abraham Lincoln and Ulysses S. Grant were your heroes. If you lived in the south, Jefferson Davis and Robert E. Lee were your heroes.

From a moral relativistic viewpoint, evil is so subjective and slippery that some relativists might even agree with the moral nihilists that evil doesn't truly exist. In 1983, when Ronald Reagan called the Soviet Union an "evil empire," moral relativists were outraged. "How can peace between the two nations be achieved if each believes the other to be evil?" asked moral relativists. If only each country would realize that evil is in the eye of the beholder, then any differences that exist between two nations can be seen merely as cultural variations—neither right nor wrong—that can be valued and respected.

But this kind of reasoning on the part of moral relativists may be problematic. Why? Because moral relativism may fail to recognize that some actions are more morally defensible than others. For example, slavery has been justified with the argument that certain human races are inferior to others—an obviously false premise. The practice of slavery in pre–Civil War America or the practice of apartheid in South Africa was wrong despite the beliefs of those societies. The treatment of the Jews in Nazi society was morally repugnant regardless of the moral beliefs of the Nazis. According to the prime minister of Iran, gays in Iran must have their homosexuality beaten out of them, as it is viewed as wrong. The current view is that sexual orientation is hard-wired into people, much like skin color, and thus is a valid alternative to heterosexuality.

The key word in that last sentence is the word "current." Morality evolves over time. Our notions of good and evil have changed and grown as the human race has changed and grown. Frederick Nietzsche touched on this idea in his 1887 book *On the Geneology of Morals*.[4] According to Nietzsche, our concepts of right and wrong are born out of social conditions. For example, ancient Romans considered traits such as *strength* and *power* to be good, virtuous qualities. The Roman slaves, from whom Christianity evolved, quite understandably considered these Roman virtues of strength and power to be evil because they were cruelly directed at the slaves. To survive such treatment, slaves were compelled to show the opposite qualities of meekness and gentleness. From this master–slave social arrangement, a new form of slave morality evolved in which gentleness, charity, and pity were seen as virtues.

If morality evolves, then moral universalists must concede that one's notions of right and wrong must therefore reflect the era in which one lives. Most reasonable Americans today believe that slavery is wrong, but this belief wasn't held a few hundred years ago. And not only does morality evolve, it evolves at a different pace in different parts of the world. Long after slavery was abolished in one part of the world, it still thrived in another. It took centuries for the "inferiority of races" argument to become debunked and for this debunking to take hold in nearly all corners of the world. Moral universalists may argue that some moral actions are more defensible than others, but like evil itself, defensibility is in the eye of the beholder, too.

When it comes to defining evil, clear-cut answers can be elusive. Legitimately different conceptions of right and wrong exist between cultures and across time, supporting the moral relativists' position. Some issues like slavery would seem to defy legitimacy no matter what culture or time period it occurs in, supporting the position of moral universalists. But slavery was once universally accepted as appropriate, suggesting that everyone can be wrong. And this leaves us exactly where we began this chapter with Mark Antony's speech, in which a few simple yet powerful words proved that our conceptions of evil are slippery and dynamic.

EVIL BY CHOICE OR EVIL BY NATURE?

According to Christian theology, the human tendency to make bad choices stems from the concept of original sin as described in the Bible's Book of Genesis. The story of Genesis is simple, yet it effectively illustrates human fallibility. The first humans, Adam and Eve, live in paradise in the Garden of Eden, and they are told by God that they will die if they eat fruit from the Tree of Knowledge of Good and Evil. While wandering the garden one day, Eve encounters a snake who asks why she avoids eating from the tree. Eve explains God's admonition, but the serpent tells Eve that she will not die if she eats the fruit; instead, she and Adam will "be as gods, knowing good and evil." Eve is thus persuaded to eat the fruit. Later Adam realizes what she has done, and he also eats the fruit so that he can stay with her. At this point God finds them, confronts them about their transgression, and expels them from paradise.

Temptations to make bad choices can be found everywhere, not just in the Garden of Eden. When we go to the bank, we see plenty of cash in the bank teller's drawer, and yet most of us, most of the time, resist the desire to take it. We see our cranky neighbor's beautiful automobile, and somehow we avoid the temptation to key it. We become furiously angry at someone, yet we manage to resist the urge to physically harm the person. Why? The simple answer is that we live in a society that has enacted laws that prohibit bad behavior. And why do we have such laws? Because there existed a time in human history, before such laws existed, when murder and theft were rampant. Thomas Hobbes, the famous English philosopher, speculated about what life was like without government, a condition that he called the *state of nature*. In that state, each person had a right, or license, to everything in the world. In the state of nature, humans found themselves in endless and inevitable conflict, a "war of all against all," producing lives that were "solitary, poor, nasty, brutish, and short."[5]

With the threat of criminal punishment hanging over our heads, most of us, most of the time, manage to avoid robbing banks, stealing cars, and killing our enemies. But as the story of Genesis teaches us, even when an authority figure threatens us with punishment, we still manage to misbehave on occasion. If you have ever watched the 11 o'clock news, attended middle school, seen the Jerry Springer Show, or witnessed a university faculty meeting, you will have seen some outrageously bad human behavior. So we are left with the question: Why do humans sometimes choose evil over good, even when the evil choice usually has obvious and severe negative consequences?

There is no simple answer to this question, but one can glean valuable insights from examining early humans' struggle for survival. Throughout most of human evolutionary history, it behooved people to choose short-term gain over long-term gain. Before the advent of modern agriculture, food was often scarce, and when food did become available one had to eat it immediately before it spoiled or before someone else ate it. Life expectancy was short and competition for mates fierce. Thus, one seized a potential mating opportunity immediately rather than risk losing out to a competitor. For tens of thousands of years, life for hominids was indeed nasty, brutish, and short, and any humans who were slow to gratify themselves were in jeopardy of not passing their genes on to the next generation.

In the previous chapter on overcoming obstacles, we noted several different types of situations that serve as impediments to people choosing the heroic act. Other people can influence us to choose an act of evil, as evidenced in Milgram's study of obedience.[6] Participants in that study administered potentially dangerous shocks to another person simply because they were told to do so by a man in a white lab coat. In another classic social psychology study, Phil Zimbardo at Stanford University randomly assigned participants either to the role of prisoner or to the role of guard in a simulated prison environment.[7] It was assumed that the intent of the study was to examine the effects of confinement among the prisoners. In reality, Zimbardo wanted to know how people given a small amount of power (the guards) would behave toward those who are powerless (the prisoners).

Zimbardo's findings were striking. After the simulated prison had been in operation for just two days, the guards began treating the prisoners in a dehumanizing way. The cruel behavior started gradually, beginning with extended prison counts, verbal insults, and mandatory pushups and jumping jacks. To punish the prisoners, some guards refused to allow prisoners to urinate or defecate, and some guards would not let the prisoners empty their sanitation buckets. Guards would sometimes punish prisoners by removing their mattresses, leaving them to sleep on concrete. Reminiscent of the Abu Ghraib prison scandal in Iraq, some prisoners were forced to go nude as a method of degradation, and some were subjected to sexual humiliation, including simulated sodomy. Zimbardo had to terminate the experiment early before anyone became seriously hurt.

There are several important things to keep in mind about Zimbardo's study. First, the guards were most hostile toward the prisoners when the guards believed they were not being observed by Zimbardo. This suggests that their bad behavior was genuine and not an act designed to please the experimenter. Second, the guards knew that the study was a prison simulation and that the prisoners had not really committed any crimes. Despite this knowledge of the prisoners' innocence, the guards still badly mistreated the prisoners. Third, after the study concluded, many of the guards expressed remorse for their bad behavior. Some said they couldn't believe they were capable of such cruelty.

These testimonials from Zimbardo's guards suggest a very important fact: Evil acts are not necessarily committed by evil people. None of Zimbardo's participants had any prior history of antisocial behavior. Like Milgram's participants, they were ordinary law-abiding citizens whose harmful actions resulted from their sensitivity to social forces. The ease with which humans can be cruel to each other, as shown in Milgram's and Zimbardo's work, is consistent with research on the psychological makeup of terrorists. Our intuitive belief about terrorists is that they must be deranged or insane in order to kill innocent people. But research on terrorism suggests otherwise. Terrorists are a product of a social system that exerts pressures on its members to perform any behavior that serves the group's cause, even if that behavior involves harming others. Terrorism results not from madness, but from strong social influence tactics that heighten one's allegiance to a group or religion. The frightening conclusion reached by almost all psychologists is that any one of us, under the right social circumstances, can be molded into a terrorist.

It seems clear that most people have the ability to discern good from evil. Sometimes people make the bad choice, as Eve did in the Garden of Eden, and as the majority of participants did in Milgram's and Zimbardo's studies. Like many of us who do the wrong thing, Eve was driven by pride and greed. Milgram's and Zimbardo's participants made the wrong choice because they were affected by social pressures. There are, of course, many people—including some psychologists—who believe that the wrong choice should be excused if the person making the choice was pressured by outside forces. We don't agree. We take the position that most of us, most of the time, are responsible for our wrong choices. Pressures to do the wrong thing can be, and often are, overcome. *Doing the right thing, even when difficult, is what heroes do.* Like Brutus in *Julius Caesar*, we all have the potential for villainy if we allow our choices to be ruled by primitive human drives or by the influence of others. And we all have the potential for heroism when we make the choice to rise above our petty natures and above corrupting social pressures.

While social pressure can lead to evil, it is also ironically true that people freed from social pressure can also be prone to evil. Lord Acton was famous for saying "power corrupts; absolute power corrupts absolutely."[8] There is actually a surprising amount of research that confirms this statement. Power frees people from restraint and accountability, and has the overall effect of disinhibiting goal-directed and instinctive behavior. And it sometimes leads us to disregard other people's perspectives as we focus on our own agenda. The research showing these effects doesn't compare more and less powerful individuals, but rather focuses on college students in a lab setting who are made to feel momentarily more or less powerful. In one study, participants who were made to feel powerful were more likely to get up and turn off an annoying fan than others who did not feel powerful. The latter just let the fan blow on them.

Other research has shown that people who felt powerful were more likely to eat the last cookie on a plate of shared snacks. And they were less careful about getting crumbs on the table. They went about satisfying their feeding instincts in an unrestrained way. And even sexual instincts were uninhibited. Both men and women who feel powerful are more likely to flirt. This finding underscores former Secretary of State Henry Kissinger's comment in 1973 that "power is the ultimate aphrodisiac."[9] And support for this idea comes from the real world as well as from the psychology laboratory. Presidential scholar Theodore H. White, in writing about President John F. Kennedy and First Lady Jacqueline Kennedy, noted that he "knew that Kennedy loved his wife—but that Kennedy, the politician, exuded that musk odor of power which acts as an aphrodisiac to many women."[10] According to White, only three Presidential candidates he had ever met had denied themselves the pleasures invited by that aphrodisiac—Harry Truman, George Romney, and Jimmy Carter. He was reasonably sure that all the others he had met had, at one time or another, on the campaign trail, accepted casual partners. "The noise, the shrieking, the excitement of crowds, and then the power, the silent pickup and delivery in limousines, set the glands alive in women as in men."

Being in a situation of power can corrupt us all, if we allow it. But these types of situations are not the only source of evil. We are all aware of individuals who are naturally evil, people for whom evil isn't a choice, nor the product of a situation, but is instead a vocation. In fiction, these people include Hannibal Lecter, the Joker, and Lord Voldemort. For his embodiment of pure evil, Hannibal Lecter was named the number-one movie villain of all time by the American Film Institute.[11] Hannibal Lecter is the classic psychopath, defined as a person who has no conscience, no empathy, and no remorse. What makes Hannibal such a fascinating figure is not just that he murders in cold blood. It is the way he does it. His charming and charismatic demeanor belies his ruthless cunning. Most horrifyingly, he eats his victims, sometimes one body part at a time, sometimes while they are still alive.

What draws us to Hannibal Lecter is our awareness that while he may be a fictional character, he is not unlike some notorious real-life serial killers. The story of Jeffrey Dahmer comes to mind. Between 1978 and 1991, Dahmer killed 17 people. The details of his murders, and his arrest, are quite gruesome. Dahmer often kept the body parts of his victims either in his refrigerator or in his bedroom.

Family members and neighbors frequently reported bad smells and the sounds of a power saw coming from his apartment. Upon his arrest, police found several corpses stored in acid-filled vats. Human skulls were found in his closet, and a human heart was found in his freezer. Dahmer later admitted to practicing cannibalism, commenting that human flesh "tasted like beef." Dahmer was a true psychopath. His father recalled that "there was something missing in Jeff. We call it a 'conscience,' that had either died or had never been alive in the first place."

INDIVIDUAL DIFFERENCES IN PERCEPTIONS OF EVIL

As noted earlier, cultures differ in their morality, and individuals within the same culture differ, too. In America, liberals and conservatives see the world through a very different moral lens, and thus they can have very different heroes and villains. A striking example is the sad case of George Tiller, the medical director of a clinic in Kansas that performed late-term abortions. Most conservatives oppose such abortions, while most liberals support the practice as long as there is some medical justification for it.

According to Kansas law, late-term abortions can only be performed if two physicians certify it to be medically necessary. Those physicians must be financially unaffiliated with the aborting doctor. In March of 2009, Tiller went on trial after being charged with consulting with a physician who was not unaffiliated. The trial received national attention, and both conservatives and liberals were vocal in reaching very different moral conclusions about the matter. Conservative columnist Jack Cashill compared the trial to the Nuremberg Trials of Nazi war criminals.[12] In stark contrast, liberal NYU Professor Jacob Appel described Tiller as "a genuine hero who ranks alongside Susan B. Anthony and Martin Luther King Jr. in the pantheon of defenders of human liberty."[13] Sadly, Tiller was shot and killed in May of 2009 by an anti-abortion activist. His story sparked a fierce debate between liberals and conservatives about the moral appropriateness of abortion, especially late-term abortion.

Jonathan Haidt, a professor of psychology at the University of Virginia, has studied how liberals and conservatives in the United States differ in their moral values. According to Haidt and his colleagues, liberals (the "left) and conservatives (the "right") share two core moral codes: *Do No Harm to Others*, and *Be Fair*. Both liberals and conservatives want to avoid harming others, and both strive for a society in which there is fairness and justice. But digging a little deeper, Haidt saw some significant differences in morality between those on the left and right. To understand these differences, Haidt argues that we must understand how liberals and conservatives differ in their worldviews.

According to Haidt, liberals live in "atom world." The idea here is that, first and foremost, liberals believe that individual human beings enjoy an existence that is independent of other individuals, much like atoms exist in isolation to one another. There are many different kinds of atoms in atom world, but none of them are connected, and each exists and thrives separately from other atoms. In contrast, conservatives live in "lattice world." From this perspective, individual human beings are far from independent entities. They are connected to other human beings, and these connections are seen in many types of important group memberships. In lattice world, a central part of one's self-identity resides in one's connection to family, religion, country, and other institutions.

It is easy to see how citizens of atom world could develop moral codes that differ very much from those of lattice world citizens. In liberals' atom world, as long as one does no harm and is fair to others, one leads a moral life. But for conservatives, the lattice-like structure of their world requires additional moral principles that go beyond avoiding harm and achieving fairness. In lattice world, the importance of group functioning mandates a moral emphasis on respecting authority and tradition. Citizens of lattice world also place a premium on cherishing their group identity and making this identity central to their self-concept. Moreover, to preserve the group's values, conservatives in lattice world strive to maintain the purity of the group. Table 5.1 displays the different moral codes valued by liberals and conservatives.

Given these differences in morality between liberals and conservatives, it certainly comes as no surprise that these two groups celebrate the accomplishments of very different heroes. Conservatives cherish

Table 5.1 Moral Codes Valued by Conservatives and Liberals[14]

Liberals	Conservatives
Do No Harm	Do No Harm
Be Fair	Be Fair
	Respect Authority and Tradition
	Value Group Identity
	Strive for Purity

traditional values and hence their heroes are traditionalists such as Sarah Palin and Bill O'Reilly. Liberals value progressives who challenge the status quo, and thus their heroes are Barack Obama and Jon Stewart. With their emphasis on preserving our national identity, U.S. conservatives' heroes are people such as Rudy Giuliani and Lou Dobbs, who are tough on illegal immigration. Less concerned with group boundaries, liberals' heroes tend to be more accepting of open borders; these individuals include Diane Savino and Ted Kennedy.

Because of their sensitivity to moral impurity, conservatives' heroes tend to reject gay marriage and rallied around Miss California Carrie Prejean's controversial endorsement of traditional marriage in 2009. Moreover, conservatives value the life of a fetus, particularly viable fetuses that George Tiller was terminating. Liberals' heroes, such as Nancy Pelosi, show greater support for the legal status of nontraditional relationships. Liberals also champion the right of women to choose whether to have abortions.

Overall, Jonathan Haidt and his research team deserve great credit for illuminating the differences in morality that exist between liberals and conservatives. Haidt argues that both groups can learn from each other. Liberals can learn what conservatives value and why some of these values, such as an emphasis on healthy group traditions, can have positive effects on society. Likewise, conservatives can learn how liberals' tolerance for individual differences can have an enriching effect on society. Haidt also points out, quite correctly, that most humans live in a lattice world, particularly nations in Asia, Africa, and the Middle East. The message here is that we have to understand the morality of lattice world dwellers if we truly want to understand and improve our relations with other countries.

DOUBLE STANDARDS AND SHIFTING
PERCEPTIONS OF MORALITY

When we judge the morality of others' actions, we'd like to think that our standards of evaluation are fairly consistent over time and from case to case. Research has shown, however, that people are not very consistent, and that their inconsistencies follow a predictable pattern. To illustrate this idea, we conducted the following study.[15] Participants were asked to imagine a scenario in which a football team accidentally gains access to the opposing team's playbook just prior to a big game. Participants were asked to judge the morality of using the playbook to gain an advantage in the game. Not surprisingly, most participants (70%) indicated that using the playbook would be unethical. However, their judgments changed significantly when we described one team as a heavy underdog in the upcoming game. When the team finding the playbook was described as the underdog, only 25% of our participants judged the team as being unethical. But when the team finding the playbook was the favored team—the top dog—almost all of our participants (93%) judged them as unethical.

The findings of this study suggest that our perceptions of good and evil are highly sensitive to the status of the people whom we are judging. Someone who is disadvantaged can get away with performing a morally dubious act, whereas someone who is advantaged cannot. We appear to hold advantaged people to a higher moral standard. This, of course, may partly explain the phenomenon of *schadenfraude*, the tendency to tear down heroes who fall from grace. We may love our heroes, but they had better show impeccable behavior.

But we suspect that our tolerance for misbehavior in our heroes is sensitive to the *type* of misbehavior they display. This idea is supported by the findings of a very clever study conducted almost a half century ago by social psychologist Elliot Aronson and his colleagues.[16] In this study, Aronson arranged for participants to witness a student being interviewed for a quiz show. Some participants learned that the student had a stellar record of achievement in academics and had impressive extracurricular activities. Other participants were told that the student had mediocre academic and extracurricular qualifications. Participants then witnessed the student accidentally spill coffee on the table at the end of the interview. Aronson asked participants to report how much they liked the student. The results showed that participants who witnessed the coffee mishap actually reported liking the star student *more* than did participants who did not witness the accident. In contrast, the mediocre student was liked less when he spilled coffee. Aronson explained the finding by suggesting minor errors can make extremely successful people appear more human and more likeable. Heroes, it seems, can endear themselves to others by appearing fallible in minor ways.

Most importantly, Aronson's study suggests the intriguing possibility that any double standards we may have in our evaluations of others may not only depend on whether they are heroic or nonheroic people. They may also be sensitive to whether the behavior being evaluated is indicative of ability or morality. In our football playbook study, the heavily favored team was disliked intensely when it committed the moral transgression of using the opposing team's playbook. Compare this result to the results of the Aronson study, which found that the stellar student was liked more when he committed the mistake of spilling coffee. Perhaps successful people can get away with minor lapses in ability but not with lapses in morality.

To test this idea, we conducted another study in which participants were instructed to imagine that a man was applying for a job and had to give a Powerpoint presentation as part of the job interview. Some participants were asked to imagine that the applicant was a hero—Microsoft software giant Bill Gates. Other participants were asked to imagine that the applicant was a young unknown man who was struggling to make ends meet. Participants were told that the Powerpoint presentation had slides containing several typographical errors. We again asked participants to indicate their liking for Gates and the unknown man. Figure 5.1 shows our results. Consistent with Aronson's results, the data showed that when Bill Gates' presentation had minor errors, he was liked more. But when the unknown struggling man's presentation had errors, he was liked less. When it comes to minor mistakes in competency, heroes are given the benefit of the doubt. In fact, we find those mistakes to be endearing. Sadly, we give

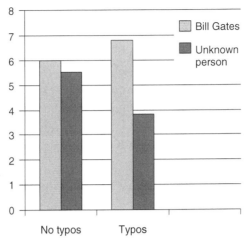

Figure 5.1 Liking for a hero and non-hero after a minor ability transgression.

nonheroic people no such margin for error, and we hammer them for making mistakes.

Interestingly, this double standard appears to reverse itself in the domain of morality. We asked participants to imagine that either Bill Gates, or an unknown struggling person, took a newspaper out of a newspaper vending machine without paying for it. In this instance, we found that participants were outraged at Bill Gates' thievery and showed a strong disliking for him. In contrast, participants were much more forgiving and understanding of the newspaper theft when it was performed by a struggling underdog person. In fact, participants' liking for the immoral underdog rose slightly, whereas their liking for the immoral Bill Gates plummeted. Figure 5.2 shows our results. It appears that a hero can get away with, and even benefit from, a small error in ability, but a hero cannot get away at all with a small moral indiscretion.

Although we may not condone a hero performing a moral indiscretion, we may take into account the *type* of moral indiscretion. For example, what do Bill Clinton and Tiger Woods have in common? They both cheated on their wives numerous times. Yet they have both retained their popularity in the eyes of most of the public. Why? We can think of several possibilities. One possibility is that their immoral actions were unrelated to the actions that propelled them to fame. If Jefferson had plagiarized the Declaration of Independence,

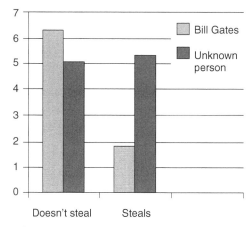

Figure 5.2 Liking for a hero and non-hero after a minor morality transgression.

or if Tiger Woods had cheated at golf, their reputations would no doubt be irreparably tarnished. Perhaps because their marital infidelity was unconnected to their heroic achievements, Jefferson and Woods have been able to retain their heroic status.

A second possibility is that cheating on one's spouse is viewed as a minor offense, and that people are generally forgiving of minor moral offenses. However, consider our participants' response to Bill Gates' hypothetical theft of the newspaper. His one-dollar crime is hardly a major offense, and yet it led to a substantial decline in people's liking for him. Thus, we suspect that the severity of their moral breakdowns—or lack of severity—may be insufficient to explain why Jefferson and Tiger have remained popular.

Perhaps the most compelling reason why people tend to forgive heroes who cheat on their spouses is that we tend to be very understanding of those who commit sins of the flesh, or sins involving bodily cravings. We may easily see the redemptive possibilities in sinners of this type. The story of actor Robert Downey, Jr. is worth telling.[17] Downey currently enjoys fabulous popularity as a television and feature film actor, most recently playing the role of Sherlock Holmes and the role of Tony Stark in the *Iron Man* movie franchise. But Downey has spent much of his adult years battling a severe drug addiction that has threatened both his career and his life.

Downey has had more than his share of drug arrests, time in rehab programs, and time in jail, but perhaps his low point may have been in 1996. That year he was arrested for possession of heroin, possession of cocaine, possession of a firearm, speeding down Sunset Boulevard, trespassing into a neighbor's home while under the influence, and falling asleep in the neighbor's bed. In 1999 Downey explained his self-destructive addiction to drugs this way: "It's like I have a loaded gun in my mouth and my finger's on the trigger, and I like the taste of the gunmetal." Stunningly, Downey has stated that his drug addiction began at the age of 8. His father, also an addict, gave him drugs as a child.

The good news is that movie fans now embrace Downey, and there is no shortage of reasons why. Some may have forgiven him for his wrongdoings, while others may not view drug-related misbehaviors as wrongdoings at all. Almost everyone can agree that Downey is to be applauded for his ability to conquer his inner demons and overcome his addictions. One day in 2003 Downey made a decision to stop taking drugs. He was driving north on the Pacific Coast Highway in California. "There I was," he recalled, "with tons of freaking dope in my car. I'd already been up for a couple of days, and I could have gone on a binge for the next couple of days. And it probably wouldn't have ended there." (http://tinyurl.com/26slnd3). But rather than going on one of the epic binges that had been his habit since his teens, Downey instead stopped the car, threw all his drugs into the ocean, and went to Burger King. Downey has been clean and sober ever since.

There are lots of stories similar to Downey's about people who engage in less than stellar behavior but are able to rehabilitate themselves, their image, or both. Some people, like Downey and like Betty Ford, hit their rock bottom and make the courageous decision to clean themselves up. Some, like St. Augustine who lived in the fourth century, discover God and attribute their turnaround to God's grace. Augustine is known for his contributions to philosophy and theology, but as a young man he was admittedly prone to stealing and womanizing. In his book *Confessions*—the first known Western autobiography—he tells the story of the day he and his friends stole pears from a neighbor's pear orchard.[18] Augustine speculates that he most likely would not have stolen anything had he not been in the company of others who were a bad influence on him. Thus, we see yet again another example of bad behavior resulting from negative social forces fanning the flames of one's greed and pride. To end the cycle of self-destruction, St. Augustine turned to religion and established himself as a brilliant thinker whose ideas have profoundly shaped modern psychology, philosophy, and theology. Today, St. Augustine is known as the great sinner who became a great saint.

As we saw in *Julius Caesar*, the perception of who is good and who is evil can change quickly. Sometimes a person is seen as having changed from evil to good when, in fact, the person hasn't changed at all. The 2007 movie *3:10 to Yuma* illustrates two such flip-flops in perception. In the film Ben Wade is an outlaw who, as a favor to the film's protagonist, allows himself to be taken to prison and even kills the film's psychopathic villain in the process. Just when we are led to believe that Wade has transformed himself from villain to hero, we see at the end of the film that he has escaped capture and will return to his criminal lifestyle. We are left to wonder whether Wade's redemption was real, and whether he is a good guy or a bad guy. Compared to the psychopath whom he killed, Wade was a saint, but if he was kind-hearted he was nevertheless a kind-hearted criminal. Evil, it seems, comes packaged not only in different shades of gray, but the lines between all the different shadings shift constantly and are open to different interpretations by different people.

Another example of perceptions shifting when the person being perceived has not really changed can be found in the story of golf legend Jack Nicklaus.[19] When Nicklaus arrived on the professional golf scene in the early 1960s, the undisputed king of golf was Arnold Palmer. No golfer in the history of the sport has been as loved and venerated by fans as Arnold Palmer. To watch Palmer play golf was to watch "every man" play golf. Unlike most golf pros, Palmer had a swashbuckling style of golf that involved taking chances with his shots, a strategy that brought him glorious successes as well as agonizing defeats. Also unlike most golf pros, Palmer connected with the crowds. He was handsome, dashing, wore a contagious smile, and bantered good-naturedly with golf galleries. And he never refused an autograph request. His charisma was off the charts. Legions of fans, called "Arnie's Army," followed him around the golf course and cheered his every move. Men wanted to be like him, and women wanted to be with him.

When Jack Nicklaus entered the golf arena, he was 10 years younger than Palmer and immensely talented. Most conspicuously, the two players differed in their style of golf, in their physical appearance, and in the way they carried themselves. While Palmer was charismatic, Nicklaus was robotic. Whereas Palmer took risks in his golf game, Nicklaus played conservatively. While Palmer was handsome and trim, Nicklaus was overweight and wore a crew cut. Whereas Palmer reached out to fans and connected with them, Nicklaus was all business on the golf course and concentrated solely on his game.

Playing in his first U.S. Open as a professional in 1962, Nicklaus defeated Palmer. Most golf fans were openly rooting for the popular Palmer and began to resent Nicklaus's threat to the Palmer dynasty. For a number of years, while Nicklaus made a habit of defeating Palmer in major golf championships, fans rudely rooted against him at tournaments. In golf, fans behave themselves better than in most other sports, but Nicklaus's success bred a resentment toward him that prompted some fans to shout "fat boy" at him. There was no doubt in the golf world that Palmer was the hero and Nicklaus was the villain.

Over time, however, perceptions of Nicklaus changed for the better. Two things happened to bring about this change. First, as the years passed by, Nicklaus kept winning golf tournaments. In fact, Nicklaus began accumulating a record of achievement in golf that has not been matched by anyone, not even Tiger Woods. Second, Nicklaus made a few minor changes to his appearance. He lost some weight, grew out his hair, and began to wear more fashionable clothing on the golf course. Suddenly, the dumpy and frumpy man who threatened a legend was now an attractive legendary figure himself. Without changing the way he conducted himself at all, Jack Nicklaus went from being golf's villain to golf's hero.

MORALITY: UNCONSCIOUS AND INACCESSIBLE

We've discussed how our notions of good and evil can be shaped by cultural forces. But are moral codes determined solely by culture? Marc Hauser, an evolutionary biologist at Harvard, would say no.

According to Hauser, evolution hardwired us to know right from wrong in a very basic way, with cultural influences also playing a large role in shaping these moral notions.[20] In the 1950s, linguist Noam Chomsky suggested that all human beings possess a universal linguistic grammar, a set of instinctive rules that underlie all languages.[21] In a similar way, Hauser argues that millions of years of evolution have produced a universal *moral* grammar in our brains that enables us to make ethical decisions and judgments. Hauser himself explains it best[20]:

> … there might be something like a universal moral grammar, a set of principles that every human is born with. It's a tool kit in some sense for building possible moral systems. In linguistics, there is a lot of variation that we see in the expressed languages throughout the world. The real deep insight of Chomskian linguistics was to ask the question, "Might this variation at some level be explained by certain common principles of universal grammar?" That allows, of course, for every language to have its own lexicon. The analogy with morality would simply be: There is going to be a suite of universal principles that dictate how we think about the nature of harming and helping others, but each culture has some freedom—not unlimited—to dictate who is harmed and who is helped. (p. 37)

From Hauser's perspective, human beings possess an innate "readiness" to develop a moral code. In a recent interview in *Discover Magazine*, Hauser acknowledged that "there's a huge amount of other work to be done. In the end, I will bet that the analogy [to language] will only go so deep. Morality could not be just like language. It's a different system. But my guess is that *there will be unconscious, inaccessible principles* that will be in some sense like morality. They will not be part of a child's education, and there will be a richness to the child's representations of the world in the moral area that will be as rich as they are in language" (p. 38; italics added).

Does Hauser's description of unconscious, inaccessible moral principles sound familiar to you? Earlier in this book, in Chapter 2, we described Carl Jung's theory of archetypes. Jung argued that humans are not born a blank slate, but are innately equipped with patterns of thoughts and images that have been molded by eons of hominid experience. The system of morality proposed by Hauser seems to bear some resemblance to the Jungian archetypes of good (the hero archetype) and evil (the demon archetype). Although they did their theorizing a century apart, both Jung and Hauser imply somewhat similar principles about our notions of right and wrong. Human beings may be biologically supplied with a readiness to develop a system of morality, largely outside of conscious awareness, that prepares them for encounters with good and evil. This system allows humans to develop explicit codes of appropriate conduct for humans to follow, and it is flexible enough to allow for cultural variations.

FINAL THOUGHTS ON EVIL

And so what do we conclude about evil? We've emphasized through-out much of this book that people mentally construct their heroes, and in this chapter we've discussed the mental construction of villains. You may recall the Great Eight from Chapter 2—the eight attributes possessed by heroes as reported by our participants. For villains, our participants generated the "Evil Eight"—the eight characteristics of villains. The results of our study showed that villains are seen as smart, greedy, mentally ill, vengeful, resilient, violent, immoral, and egotistical. As Table 5.2 shows, there are two traits that heroes and villains share, and they are the tendencies to be smart and resilient. To achieve any goal with effectiveness, whether the goal is noble or ghastly, one needs the basic tools of intelligence and the ability to work hard. The remaining traits of villains are primarily vices, with the exception of mental illness, which may reflect peoples' beliefs that evil perpetrators may not always be responsible for their actions.

In this chapter we've explored how people perceive evil. We know that bad behavior exists, and when it is extremely bad we are out-raged when we see it. Interestingly, we are also outraged when we realize that not everyone shares our outrage. In 2006, when Barry Bonds shattered the professional baseball record for career home

Table 5.2 Eight Traits Characterizing Heroes and Eight Traits Characterizing Villains, as Reported by the Participants in Our Study

Heroes: The Great Eight	Villains: The Evil Eight
Smart	Smart
Resilient	Resilient
Strong	Violent
Selfless	Greedy
Charismatic	Mentally ill
Caring	Immoral
Reliable	Egotistical
Inspiring	Vengeful

runs, there was strong evidence suggesting he had cheated by taking steroids to bulk up his body. While many fans were angered and viewed him as a villain, many other fans heartily embraced Bonds and viewed him as a hero. Some bad behaviors, like those displayed by Jeffrey Dahmer, are universally deplored, but other questionable behaviors, like those of Barry Bonds, are open to interpretation. Sometimes reasonable people can disagree about what's bad and what isn't, as when liberals and conservatives clash on issues of abortion, gay marriage, and capital punishment. But some bad behaviors, such as enslaving or murdering people, are so atrocious that they invoke universal censure from almost everyone. Not all moral codes are equally valid, but deciding which is the best morality for the greatest number of people is a daunting task for society.

Complicating matters even more, we have also learned in this chapter that the same person can view the same act differently depending on who is performing it. Recall the hypothetical scenario involving Bill Gates. When a rich person like Gates steals a dollar, we are outraged, but when a poor person steals a dollar, we are sympathetic. Double standards exist in our evaluation of bad behavior, with underdogs getting the benefit of the doubt more than top dogs. People are inconsistent in their recognition of evil, showing sensitivity to a moral transgressor's success and status in life.

Interestingly, people appear to be aware of these double standards and will often position themselves as the underdog to gain sympathy and understanding for their wrongdoings. In the Middle East, Israel and the Arab world have each claimed the status of underdog in their conflict to attract world sympathy and to deflect blame for their violent actions. Israel points to its small geographic size and to the fact that it is physically surrounded by larger Arab countries to justify its underdog label. In turn, Arab countries have claimed underdog status by virtue of their relatively weak economies and military capabilities. In American football, it is not unusual for each Super Bowl team to declare itself the underdog prior to the game. Doing so attracts sympathy, helps the team motivate its players, and excuses the team for poor performance in case it loses the game.

Most intriguing, we have seen how nature may biologically prepare us for developing a system of morality, in much the same way nature equips us for language. To survive over the ages, humans have needed a basis for deciding which people are good—the ones we would want to mate with and hunt food with—and which people are bad— the ones who might kill us or steal from us. Over the past few decades, psychologists have found that people form these evaluative good and bad judgments quickly, automatically, and without conscious awareness. The work of nineteenth-century psychoanalysts such as Freud and Jung have recently enjoyed a resurgence in popularity as their theories of unconscious judgments have been supported by experimental data. The work of modern evolutionary biologists points to a similar conclusion about good and evil. It is likely that our brains were designed to prepare us for good and evil, to identify each, and to emotionally respond to each. Moreover, as humans continue to evolve biologically and culturally, our notions of good and evil will also continue to evolve.

6

SHAPING

How Heroes Shape Us and
How We Shape Them

We're going to begin this chapter with a little quiz for you. Here's how it'll work. We'll describe a person to you, and your job is to guess who it is. Ready? Here goes.

This person was named "arguably the world's most powerful man" by CNN and Time.com. He was also called "arguably the most influential man in the world" by *The American Spectator*, "one of the 100 people who most influenced the twentieth century," and "one of the most influential people" of 2004, 2005, 2006, 2007, 2008, and 2009 by *Time*. This man is the only person in the world to have made all six of *Time*'s lists.

Can you name this person yet? No, it's not Barack Obama. Here are some more clues.

At the end of the twentieth century *Life* magazine listed this person as the most influential man of his generation, and in a cover story profile the magazine called him "America's most powerful man." Another top-selling magazine also ranked him number one in their list of the most powerful men in America. Barack Obama has said he "may be the most influential man in the country." In 1998 he made the top of *Entertainment Weekly*'s list of the 101 most powerful people in the entertainment industry. In 2003 he edged out both Superman and Elvis Presley to be named the greatest pop culture icon of all time by VH1. *Forbes* named him the world's most powerful celebrity in 2005, 2007, and 2008.

Have you identified this person yet? Here's another clue: There is one piece of information we're giving you about this person that is incorrect. Only one. The rest is true. Here's some more information.

Columnist Maureen Dowd wrote that this man "is the top alpha male in the country. He has more credibility than the president." *Vanity Fair* wrote that he "has more influence on the culture than any university president, politician, or religious leader, except perhaps the Pope." Bill O'Reilly said that he is "the most powerful man in the world, not just in America." This person's biographer wrote that he "has wielded an unprecedented amount of influence over the American culture and psyche ... There has been no other person in the twentieth century whose convictions and values have impacted the American public in such a significant way ... I see him as probably the most powerful man in our society."[1]

The results of a 2005 public poll revealed this man to be the ninth-greatest American in all of U.S. history. According to Gallup's annual most admired poll, Americans consistently rank him as one of the most admired men in the world. In 1996, he received the prestigious George Foster Peabody's Individual Achievement Award. In 1998 he received a Lifetime Achievement Award at the Emmy Awards ceremony. In 2002, he received the Bob Hope Humanitarian Award at the 2002 Emmy Awards for his services to television and film.

So have you guessed this person's identity yet? Who could possibly be greater than Elvis, Superman, the President, and the Pope? No, it's not George Clooney, Stephen Spielberg, Michael J. Fox, Roger Federer, Lance Armstrong, Tom Hanks, Tiger Woods, Jon Stewart, Robert Redford, Michael Jordan, Mel Gibson, or Paul McCartney. You may want to review all of our clues above before we reveal the answer below. Remember one of our hints: There is one fact we've given you about this person that is incorrect.

Give up? It turns out that clearing up the one false piece of information we provided is essential for correct identification. We told you that the person is a male. In truth, the person we described is a woman. Go back and replace all male pronouns with female pronouns, and see if you can now guess the person's identity. While you do that, we'll briefly explain why we began this chapter with this person and with this gender deception. First, this individual is a natural choice for a chapter on how heroes shape us. As her accolades indicate, no person male or female over the past two decades has had a more powerful and enduring impact on American society and pop culture. Her contributions have been remarkable, and we'll describe them shortly.

Our reason for deceiving you about her gender is to illustrate how deeply gender plays a role in shaping our thinking about heroes. If we had said from the outset that the person was a woman, you would likely have gotten the correct answer immediately. Why? Because until recently, women have been denied opportunities for heroism, and so there are far fewer female than male heroes on lists such as "greatest Americans" and "most powerful people." While this woman was named the ninth greatest American of all time in 2005, all eight individuals ahead of her on the list were males: Elvis Presley, Abraham Lincoln, Martin Luther King Jr., George Washington, Ronald Reagan, George W. Bush, Bill Clinton, and Benjamin Franklin. In fact, when we asked 50 participants (25 males and 25 females) to draw a picture of a hero, 39 of them drew a male (20 of the 25 male participants and 19 of the 25 female participants). This finding is consistent with research indicating that people's default belief about leaders is that they are males with stereotypically masculine traits. The fact that female heroes are relatively scarce means that the ones who do emerge are very well remembered.

In case you haven't figured it out, we will now tell you that the person we described is none other than Oprah Winfrey.[2] We suspect you were able to determine it was Winfrey as soon as we told you her correct gender. If you didn't correctly identify Winfrey, either you don't watch television or you underestimate her. We believe that Winfrey is highly deserving of the recognitions given her and that her influence matches or exceeds that of any male today. A brief look at her career reveals a truly remarkable person.

Winfrey was born in a small town in Mississippi and lived in extreme poverty for much of her childhood. She was teased at school for wearing clothes made of potato sacks. For years as a child she was sexually molested by a number of people, including an uncle, a cousin, and a family friend. Winfrey ran away from home at age 13 and became pregnant at age 14. Tragically, her baby son was born premature and died from medical complications soon after he was delivered.

Despite all of these obstacles standing in her way, Winfrey was intent on becoming a success. She threw herself into her schoolwork and became a model student. She joined her high school speech team, won an oratory contest, and earned a scholarship to attend Tennessee State University. A local radio station hired her part time as a news anchor, and shortly thereafter she was the anchor at Nashville's WLAC-TV. In 1983, Winfrey was asked to host WLS-TV's low-rated half-hour morning talk show, *AM Chicago*. Winfrey only needed a few months to catapult the show from the ratings basement to the penthouse. With Winfrey at the helm, *AM Chicago* became the highest rated talk show in Chicago, surpassing the *Donahue* show in popularity. The show was renamed *The Oprah Winfrey Show*, expanded to a full 60 minutes, and broadcast nationally beginning in 1986.

Winfrey is largely credited for revolutionizing the television talk show format. For more than two decades, *The Oprah Winfrey Show* has promoted books and literature, various forms of self-improvement, family values, and a stronger spiritual lifestyle. Appearing on her show, Roseanne Barr told Winfrey, "you're the African Mother Goddess of us all." Winfrey's show has helped propel nontraditional lifestyles (gay, lesbian, transgender) into the cultural mainstream. She singlehandedly jumpstarted Dr. Phil's television career. Oprah's Book Club has encouraged legions of Americans to read more, and a book plugged by Winfrey will sell a million more copies than it ordinarily would.

What have been the key reasons for Winfrey's unprecedented achievements? If you recall the Great Eight from Chapter 2, where we described the eight attributes of heroes, it can be said that Winfrey is one of the very few people who possess all eight traits. Let's briefly see how Winfrey embodies all these heroic attributes. First, Winfrey is obviously *smart*. And she's not just school smart; she has terrific interpersonal skills that have been honed from decades of interviewing guests of all types. Winfrey is also *strong*, although less in the physical sense and more in the area of emotional strength. Such strength would be necessary to see her through so much adversity early in life. Winfrey is also *caring*. She has received great praise for her ability to empathize with her guests, bringing them to tears, and coaxing astonishing self-disclosures from them on the air in front of millions of viewers. The *Wall Street Journal* coined the term "Oprahfication" to describe public confession as a form of therapy.

Winfrey is also *selfless*, having raised tens of millions of dollars for various charities and taking a leading role in animal rights activities. In addition, Winfrey is *charismatic*. She connects with her audience like no other talk show host. Television columnist Howard Rosenberg once wrote that Winfrey "is a roundhouse, a full course meal, big, brassy, loud, aggressive, hyper, laughable, lovable, soulful, tender, low-down, earthy and hungry."[3] Winfrey is also *reliable*. She is consistently true to her causes, her values, and her friends. Finally, Winfrey is *inspiring*. She has cultivated a fiercely devoted fan base that hangs on her every word. Some inspirational quotes attributed to her are as follows:

- "Where there is no struggle, there is no strength."
- "Do the one thing you think you cannot do. Fail at it. Try again. Do better the second time. The only people who never tumble are those who never mount the high wire. This is your moment. Own it."
- "Don't back down just to keep the peace. Standing up for your beliefs builds self-confidence and self-esteem."
- "Every time you state what you want or believe, you're the first to hear it. It's a message to both you and others about what you think is possible. Don't put a ceiling on yourself."
- "My philosophy is that not only are you responsible for your life, but doing the best at this moment puts you in the best place for the next moment."
- "Real integrity is doing the right thing, knowing that nobody's going to know whether you did it or not."
- "The big secret in life is that there is no big secret. Whatever your goal, you can get there if you're willing to work."

One extraordinary way in which Winfrey has shaped American society can be seen in the role she played to bring Barack Obama to the nation's attention as a viable presidential candidate in 2006. That year Winfrey began endorsing Obama for president before he had even declared himself a candidate. Once Obama became an official candidate, Winfrey publicly gave him her full support, and beginning in December 2007 she made occasional campaign appearances for him. Two University of Maryland economists, Craig Garthwaite and Tim Moore, conducted a study to determine Winfrey's impact on Obama's successful run for president. They concluded that Winfrey's endorsement of Barack Obama was worth 1 million votes to him in the Democratic primary elections. According to their analysis, if Winfrey hadn't endorsed him, Hillary Clinton would have gotten more votes than Obama.[4]

While interviewed on *Larry King Live* on CNN, King asked Winfrey why she was supporting Obama's candidacy for president. "Because I know him personally," she replied. "I think that what he stands for, what he has proven that he can stand for, what he has shown, was worth me going out on a limb for. And I haven't done it in the past because I haven't felt that about anybody. I didn't know anybody well enough to be able to say, 'I believe in this person.'" Winfrey proved that she could shape far more important things than America's tastes in reading, eating, and shopping. She played an instrumental role in electing a president and thus has forever altered the course of world events.

HOW HEROES SHAPE US

As psychologists, we devote our careers to studying people's emotions, thoughts, and behavior. And so when discussing how heroes have shaped us, we'll focus on those three areas. What are some notable examples of how heroes have influenced the way we feel, think, and act?

The Shaping of Feelings and Behavior

Let's start with feelings. The most dominant feelings that heroes invoke are feelings of inspiration. Heroes move us. Sometimes they bring us to tears. In June of 2009, *Sports Illustrated* reported a story that "gave gooseflesh to a phys-ed teacher in Pennsylvania, made a market researcher in Texas weak in the knees, put a lump in the throat of a crusty old man in Minnesota, and convinced a cynic in Connecticut that all was not lost." Jaded executives, self-described rednecks, and burly firefighters all cried when they read the story. The tale "reminds us that goodness and decency and honor still exist."[5]

The story is about a simple heroic act that took place during a college softball game in Ellensburg, Washington, on April of 2008. In the second inning, Western Oregon University's Sara Tucholsky hit an apparent home run over the left field fence. While running between first and second base, however, Tucholsky tore the anterior cruciate ligament of her right knee and could not complete her home run trot. Tucholsky lay in pain on the ground while umpires explained to coaches and players that the home run would be negated and Tucholsky would be called out unless she touched all four bases without any help from her teammates.

Playing first base for the opposing team was Central Washington University's Mallory Holtman. After hearing the umpire's interpretation of the situation and seeing the injured Tucholsky writhing in the dirt near first base, Holtman made the kind of selfless choice that only a hero would make. Holtman asked the umpire if she, herself, could carry Tucholsky around the bases to complete the home run. The umpire agreed that the rules did not prohibit the opposing team from helping Tucholsky. Holtman and teammate Liz Wallace gingerly lifted Tucholsky into their arms and gently carried the injured hitter to each base, including home plate. As they rounded the bases, Tucholsky thanked Holtman and Wallace, to which Holtman responded, "You hit it over the fence. You deserve it." The stunned crowd stood in applause at this unprecedented act of sportsmanship.

Were any lives at stake in this story? No. But that didn't prevent it from having a profound impact on people all over the world, not just in the United States. Reporters from dozens of media outlets, Japanese filmmakers, and television script writers descended on Holtman and her story. People from far and wide wrote to Holtman with offers of gratitude, money, and admiration. Clearly, Holtman's act of kindness struck an emotional cord. People recognized that Holtman did the right thing in a situation in which most people would have either done nothing or done the wrong thing. She performed the type of selfless act that defines heroism.

Another inspirational baseball story with more life-and-death consequences is that of Pittsburgh Pirates' right-fielder Roberto Clemente. Born in Puerto Rico in 1934, Clemente lived and played baseball in an era that was rather intolerant of non-white, non-English-speaking people. Yet on and off the field, he behaved with great dignity and class. During his career, Clemente accrued 3,000 hits, made 12 all-star game appearances, earned 2 most valuable player awards, 12 gold glove awards, and 2 World Series championships. He was clearly one of the greatest right fielders in baseball history.

But that's not how the world best remembers Clemente. Each winter, during baseball's off-season, Clemente spent much of his time involved in charity work. In late December of 1972, he heard that Managua, Nicaragua, had been devastated by a massive earthquake. Clemente immediately began arranging emergency relief flights from Puerto Rico. He soon learned, however, that the aid packages on the first three flights never reached victims of the quake. Apparently, corrupt officials had diverted those flights. Clemente decided to accompany the fourth relief flight to ensure that the relief supplies would be delivered to the survivors. The airplane he chartered for a New Year's Eve flight, a Douglas DC-7, had a history of mechanical problems and was overloaded by 5,000 pounds. Shortly after takeoff, the plane crashed into the ocean off the coast of Puerto Rico, killing Clemente.

Clemente's story is especially inspiring because he was much more than a legendary ballplayer. He had a great heart, and he died performing a selfless act. Clemente once said, "Any time you have an opportunity to make things better and you don't, then you are wasting your time on this Earth ."[6] He lived and died by those words.

Athletic heroes inspire us with their performances because they demonstrate difficult physical movements in an entertaining fashion. Mia Hamm inspired a generation of young female soccer players. Michael Jordan and Nancy Lieberman inspired millions of young basketball players. Roger Federer inspires millions of tennis players, and Annika Sorenstam millions of golfers. But deep down we know that these demonstrations of athleticism don't solve world hunger or bring world peace. And so athletes' *nonathletic behavior* can be their most inspiring acts. Witness the courage of Babe Zaharias and her fight with cancer, and the selfless sacrifice of Roberto Clemente. Mallory Holtman made headlines with her heroic kindness, not with her bat and glove. Holtman's example shows us that we don't have to be athletic geniuses like Michael Jordan or Mia Hamm to inspire millions.

Simple everyday people like Malloy Holtman can become the most inspirational heroes, especially if they remain hidden and humble. We call these heroes the *unsung heroes*. A book called *The Quiet Hero* describes the remarkable yet largely unknown heroism of George Wahlen during World War II.[7] In 1945, Wahlen was awarded the Medal of Honor by President Truman. He came home from the award ceremony, stuffed the medal in a dresser drawer, and told no one about it. His wife didn't know he was a national war hero until they had been married for many years. Content to take his story to his grave, Wahlen was finally convinced by family and friends to tell his story. Wahlen's Medal of Honor citation sums up his extraordinary heroism:

> For conspicuous gallantry and intrepidity at the risk of his life above and beyond the call of duty ... during action against enemy Japanese forces on Iwo Jima ... on 3 March 1945. Painfully wounded in the bitter action on 26 February, Wahlen remained on the battlefield, advancing well forward of the frontlines to aid a wounded marine and carrying him back to safety despite a terrific concentration of fire. Tireless in his ministrations, he consistently disregarded all danger to attend his fighting comrades as they fell under the devastating rain of shrapnel and bullets, and rendered prompt assistance to various elements of his combat group as required. When an adjacent platoon suffered heavy casualties, he defied the continuous pounding of heavy mortars and deadly fire of enemy rifles to care for the wounded, working rapidly in an area swept by constant fire and treating 14 casualties before returning to his own platoon. Wounded again on 2 March, he gallantly refused evacuation, moving out with his company the following

day in a furious assault across 600 yards of open terrain and repeatedly rendering medical aid while exposed to the blasting fury of powerful Japanese guns. Stouthearted and indomitable, he persevered in his determined efforts as his unit waged fierce battle and, unable to walk after sustaining a third agonizing wound, resolutely crawled 50 yards to administer first aid to still another fallen fighter. By his dauntless fortitude and valor, Wahlen served as a constant inspiration and contributed vitally to the high morale of his company during critical phases of this strategically important engagement. His heroic spirit of self-sacrifice in the face of overwhelming enemy fire upheld the highest traditions of the U.S. Naval Service.

There is a long list of unsung heroes, many of them only recently known, all of them with inspirational stories of courage and selflessness. These heroes include the following:

- Hope Makoni, a Zimbabwe woman who at age 14 was raped by her uncle. The incident left her pregnant and infected with HIV. Makoni now works tirelessly to protect Zimbabwe's youth from sexual abuse.
- S. Ramakrishnan, who was paralyzed from the neck down in an accident when he was 32 years old. Ramakrishnan decided to build a haven for severely disabled children and adults in India.
- Women Airforce Service Pilots, who during World War II broke the gender barrier by becoming the first women to fly U.S. military aircraft.
- Jordan Thomas, whose legs were severed by boat propellers at age 15. Just weeks after the accident, he launched a fundraising foundation to provide life-changing prosthetics to children in need.
- The 40 passengers aboard Flight 93 on September 11, 2001. When Islamic terrorists highjacked the plane and were steering it toward either the White House or U.S. Capitol, these passengers stormed the cockpit and crashed the plane onto uninhabited

terrain. They lost their lives preventing what would have been a horrifying mass murder on the ground in Washington.

All of the inspirational acts just described serve as a model for action. Heroes move us, not just emotionally but also behaviorally. They set a high bar for us and then dare us all to join them. Heroes take us places that give us rich rewards. They lift our dreams and aspirations. We crave heroes and identify with them. We want to be with heroes, we want to be like them, and we want to bask in their successes. Psychologist Robert Cialdini has studied this very phenomenon, which he called *basking in reflected glory*.[8] We love to associate with successful, heroic people because they make us feel good about who we are.

The Shaping of Thoughts and Behavior

Next, we turn to the ways in which heroes affect our thinking. It is often the case that heroes challenge conventional thinking or traditional ways of viewing the world. Famous spiritual and religious leaders have most certainly defied their society's prevailing mindset. Confucius' moral philosophy 2,500 years ago challenged the prevailing views of Taoism and Legalism. According to Islamic theology, Muhammad received revelations from God, and these messages formed the basis of a new holy wisdom described in the Qur'an. According to Christian theology, Jesus of Nazareth was a revolutionary whose new moral doctrines challenged the existing moral landscape. The Dalai Lama, Desmond Tutu, Martin Luther King Jr., Gandhi, and other spiritual leaders have all challenged conventional thinking by advocating peaceful solutions to difficult (and often violent) intergroup conflicts.

Heroes offer a model for a new way of looking at an old situation. When we say a model, we mean a mental model, or schema. Heroes suggest new schemas or scripts for people to follow, and they inspire their followers to adopt these new ways of thinking and put them into action. In science, the set of assumptions that scientists draw from to do their science is called a *paradigm*, a term coined by Thomas Kuhn in 1962.[9] Any rapid change in assumptions that takes place within the scientific community is called a *paradigm shift*. One example of such a dramatic shift in thinking is Copernicus' idea that the earth rotates around the sun. This radical new way of thinking replaced the old notion that the earth was the center of the solar system. Other examples of paradigm shifts are Darwin's theory of natural selection, Einstein's theory of relativity, and Freud's psychoanalytic theory of unconscious motives. In all of these examples, a bold and heroic scientist dared to challenge the established and entrenched way of thinking by completely reframing the way the world works.

It may be cliché, but heroes do make us think outside the box. As a shining example, let's focus on Bill Gates, whom we picked on rather unfairly in studies we described in the previous chapter. Gates forever changed the way we work and play. With his childhood friend Paul Allen, Gates established in 1975 a small company called Microsoft, now one of the largest and most profitable companies in the world. Microsoft's Web site sums up Gates' heroic contributions nicely: "Guided by a belief that the computer would be a valuable tool on every office desktop and in every home, they [Gates and Allen] began developing software for personal computers. Gates' foresight and his vision for personal computing have been central to the success of Microsoft and the software industry."[10]

Sometimes our heroes make us rethink society's intergroup hierarchies. Lucretia Mott is a prominent example.[11] While Mott was alive in nineteenth-century America, women had very few rights and were clearly subordinate to men. Women were not legally permitted to vote. Once married, a woman's money and property became the property of her husband. Women rarely worked outside the home, and if they did so, they worked almost exclusively as maids, teachers, and nannies. The occasional woman who was allowed to work in a store or office had no chance for promotion and was paid considerably less than men. Moreover, women were never given the responsibility of handling money.

Lucretia Mott emerged as a champion of women's rights and is known as America's first feminist, but she didn't start out that way. As a young woman in the early nineteenth century, she first worked tirelessly to end slavery. Ironically, the anti-slavery organizations she wished to join would not admit women as members. In 1840, she was selected as a delegate to the World's Anti-Slavery Convention in

London, which she discovered was controlled by anti-slavery factions who were opposed to participation by women. She spoke at the convention, although other women attendees were forced to sit in segregated areas with no view of the speakers. To give women more of a voice in the anti-slavery movement, she founded the Philadelphia Female Anti-Slavery Society. She met with slave owners in Maryland and Virginia to discuss the morality of slavery, and she spoke with President John Tyler and members of Congress.

In 1848, Lucretia Mott and Elizabeth Cady Stanton organized a local women's rights convention in Seneca Falls. They composed the *Declaration of Sentiments*, which paralleled the American *Declaration of Independence*. In this declaration, Mott and Stanton wrote, "We hold these truths to be self-evident, that all men and women are created equal." After the Civil War, she was elected President of the American Equal Rights Convention. It was not until 1920, forty years after Mott's death, that women were granted the right to vote. This breakthrough for social equality was the result of almost a century of activism by early social reformers such as Mott.

The fight for racial equality also has its share of heroes. No individual better personifies the modern civil rights movement than Martin Luther King Jr. In his famous "I have a dream" speech delivered in 1963, King followed Lucretia Mott's lead by referencing the founding fathers' documents and noting their deficiencies.[12] "When the architects of our republic wrote the magnificent words of the Constitution and the Declaration of Independence, they were signing a promissory note to which every American was to fall heir," said King. "This note was a promise that all men—yes, black men as well as white men—would be guaranteed the unalienable rights of life, liberty and the pursuit of happiness. It is obvious today that America has defaulted on this promissory note, insofar as her citizens of color are concerned."

King was a remarkable orator, perhaps the most charismatic person and speaker America has ever seen. In his "I have a dream" speech, he effectively uses short phrases to maximize emotional impact. "We cannot walk alone," "We cannot turn back," "I have a dream today," and "free at last," are all brief bursts of phrasing, often repeated for emphasis. He also uses similes, analogies, and metaphors with great effectiveness. Examples include his saying that "the Negro lives on a lonely island of poverty in the midst of a vast ocean of material prosperity," and "Now is the time to lift our nation from the quicksand of racial injustice to the solid rock of brotherhood." The use of this imagery punctuates the emotional appeal of his message.

Not that King was all style over substance. The content of his speech resonated with a nation that was poised to make sweeping enhancements to civil rights for all Americans, regardless of color. He expressed gratitude to many white Americans for supporting the cause: "For many of our white brothers as evidenced by their presence here today have come to realize that their destiny is tied up with our destiny and they have come to realize that their freedom is inextricably bound to our freedom. We cannot walk alone." He drove home the idea that people of all colors should, and will, peacefully coexist: "I have a dream that one day on the red hills of Georgia the sons of former slaves and the sons of former slave owners will be able to sit down together at a table of brotherhood." The importance of the most iconic line in his speech is self-evident: "I have a dream that my four little children will one day live in a nation where they will not be judged by the color of their skin, but by the content of their character."

First and foremost, King is a hero to millions of people because he promoted good will and freedom for all people of all backgrounds. Again, his 1963 speech clearly communicated this idea: "Let freedom ring. And when this happens, and when we allow freedom to ring—when we let it ring from every village and every hamlet, from every state and every city, we will be able to speed up that day when all of God's children—black men and white men, Jews and Gentiles, Protestants and Catholics—will be able to join hands and sing in the words of the old Negro spiritual: Free at last! Free at last! Thank God Almighty, we are free at last!" With this last line, we see how potent and stirring a speech can be when the unsurpassed beauty of its message is combined with a passionate, charismatic delivery. With this last line, the crowd listening to King responded in a frenzy of support, love, and hope. There is no doubt that it is the speech of a legendary hero.

Like Oprah Winfrey, Martin Luther King Jr. wonderfully personified all eight of the Great Eight traits that characterize heroes. He was clearly smart, as evidenced by his doctoral degree and gifted oratory skills. He was strong, as he was compelled to stand up to discrimination and to those who opposed civil rights. He was caring and selfless, as shown by his commitment to improving the quality of life of black Americans. His charisma and ability to inspire were unprecedented in American history. He was also reliable, a man true to his cause and loyal to his vision. He was also resilient for spending years battling racist forces intent on stopping his cause. The only thing he couldn't overcome was the assassin's bullet that killed him in Memphis in April of 1968.

The civil rights work of these last two heroes—Lucretia Mott and Martin Luther King Jr.—made it possible for an African American woman like Oprah Winfrey to achieve her remarkable success. This tells us an important fact about heroes. They not only shape us; they shape other heroes as well. Tiger Woods has often attributed his success to Charlie Sifford and Lee Elder, two black golfers who broke the color barrier on the professional golf tour. Major league baseball players have often expressed their appreciation for Jackie Robinson, who in 1947 was the first black player to be allowed to participate in major league baseball. Larry Doby, the first black to play in baseball's American league, always referred to Robinson as "Mr. Robinson." Doby's and Robinson's courage and grit made it possible for thousands of non-white players to participate in professional baseball. After Robinson opened racial doors, heroic sluggers like Willie Mays, Henry Aaron, and Roberto Clemente transformed the racial landscape of professional baseball, not to mention the record books.

Pioneering heroes sew the seeds for future heroes. Sir Isaac Newton in the seventeenth century was well aware that his success was dependent on the accomplishments of his predecessors. He observed, "If I have seen further it is only by standing on the shoulders of giants." One of the giants who provided a foundation for Newton's work was Galileo Galilei, known as the father of modern physics. Albert Einstein could not have revolutionized physics without the influence of Marcel Grossman, who mentored Einstein in the areas of differential calculus and non-Euclidean geometry. Charles Darwin had many influences, including Thomas Malthus' work on the limits of population growth. Sigmund Freud was deeply inspired by Frederick Nietzsche's views of the unconscious mind and by Arthur Schopenhauer's theories of human motivation.

Heroes begetting heroes can also be seen in the world of art and music. Elvis Presley can be said to have initiated a paradigm shift in the music world, spawning a genre of music called rock and roll. Rock music wasn't just a new sound; it was also a new look that threatened established norms of appropriate appearance and conduct. Presley was seen as a bad influence on the moral well-being of young women. With his wildly gyrating hips onstage, Presley would evoke rowdy and erotic dancing from audiences offstage. He developed a reputation for encouraging sexual rebelliousness in young people. Presley was accused as having an "anti-parent outlook" and was the "personification of evil" because he was viewed as being the visual and auditory embodiment of sex.[13] After Elvis' first TV appearance in 1956, Jackie Gleason said, "The kid has no right behaving like a sex maniac on a national show."[14]

But it wasn't just Presley that had America's youth twisting and shouting. Other greats of the 1950s who helped establish this new sound include Chuck Berry, Fats Domino, The Everly Brothers, Little Richard, and Buddy Holly. In the 1960s the The Beatles built on this foundation and took rock music to a level of creativity not seen before or since. The Beatles' lead guitarist John Lennon admitted that "if there hadn't been Elvis, there would not have been the Beatles."[15] The Beatles' 1967 album, *Sergeant Pepper's Lonely Hearts Club Band*, is viewed by many to represent the pinnacle of their innovative influence. According to Beatles' producer George Martin, Sgt. Pepper was inspired by the Beach Boys' groundbreaking album *Pet Sounds*. "Without *Pet Sounds*," said Martin, "*Sgt. Pepper* wouldn't have happened. *Pepper* was an attempt to equal *Pet Sounds*."[16] Musicians are thus much like scientists, building on the pioneering work of their predecessors and contemporaries.

The Beatles' two major songwriters, John Lennon and Paul McCartney, played an especially pivotal role in reshaping the popular music we listen to today. Along with Bob Dylan, Lennon and

McCartney are largely credited with transforming rock and roll lyrics from vapid love stories to edgy political statements designed to change the world. Their song "Revolution" belies its title by advocating peaceful social change. Lennon's song "Imagine" is especially inspiring in calling for all humans to tear down barriers that prevent world peace. Fans hung on The Beatles' every word. Ironically, one of the twentieth century's greatest villains, Charles Manson, used a twisted interpretation of a Beatles song to justify his murders. But for the most part, The Beatles provided a tonic for a world thirsty for music heroes. Unlike any other band, The Beatles could deliver a message of hope and peace packaged in a song with an unforgettable melody. Sadly, John Lennon's life was cut short by an assassin's bullet in 1980.

The Beatles could be called the artistic heroes of the 1960s social movements. All heroes of social movements have a vision. Lucretia Mott envisioned equality for women, Martin Luther King Jr. envisioned equality for African Americans, and John Lennon envisioned peace on earth. But what good is a vision without followers who will help the hero fulfill it? The leader of a social movement needs followers to accept his or her vision and, in return for this gift, followers give the leader their support. If The Beatles received no positive fan mail, wrote songs that few raved about, and gave live performances that stirred no one, then their influence would have been limited indeed. The Beatles showed great leadership, but their followers also showed great "followership," giving the Fab Four the feedback and financing necessary to shine on the world's stage.

Psychologist David Messick has theorized that the relationship between leaders and followers is, in essence, an exchange of services.[17] According to Messick, leaders provide direction and, in exchange, followers give leaders their focus. Leaders offer security and protection and, in return, followers give leaders their gratitude and loyalty. Leaders give followers group achievements and, in exchange, followers provide commitment and effort. Leaders give followers a feeling of inclusion and belongingness and, in return, followers cooperate and sacrifice. Leaders instill a sense of group pride and, in return, followers give the leader respect and obedience. Messick's model, shown in Table 6.1, nicely illustrates the fact that heroes do not

Table 6.1 Messick's (2005) Exchange Model of Leaders and Followers

Leaders Give Followers...		...In Return, Followers Give Leaders...
Vision and Direction	← →	Focus and Self-Direction
Security and Protection	← →	Gratitude and Loyalty
Achievement and Effectiveness	← →	Commitment and Effort
Inclusion and Belongingness	← →	Cooperation and Sacrifice
Pride and Self-Respect	← →	Respect and Obedience

perform their heroic work in a social vacuum. Heroes of social movements need us as much as we need them.

Messick does not suggest that these exchanges are formally discussed and agreed upon like you might find in a business relationship. Instead, these exchanges are usually "uncalculated, spontaneous, and unpremeditated." They emerge naturally and implicitly. Messick also argues that the exchange is the *result*, not the *goal*, of leadership. Moreover, for the exchange relationship to work, leaders must show *benevolence* and *objectivity* in their dealings with their followers. Do all leaders who follow this exchange relationship successfully become heroes? Not necessarily. For the vision to be heroic it must be noble, courageous, creative, groundbreaking, and risky. Martin Luther King Jr.'s vision for a color-blind America is a more heroic vision than the psychology department chairperson's vision of a well-run psychology department. Still, given the right vision, Messick's model does provide a nice model of the dynamic social relationship between heroes of social movements and their followers.

James MacGregor Burns' concept of transformational leadership is relevant here.[18] Leaders who are transformational help their followers advance to a higher level of motivation and morality. Also central to transformational leadership is the idea that *good leaders help shape their followers into leaders*. This is one of the central themes of this chapter: great heroes beget other great heroes. All of us who have listened to popular music, flipped on a light switch, used a phone, or flown in a plane, have all stood on the shoulders of giants such as

The Beatles, Thomas Edison, Alexander Graham Bell, and the Wright Brothers. Some of us become transformed by these giants, and dare to reframe society ourselves.

HOW WE SHAPE HEROES

Heroes not only shape us; we shape them. How? First, all of us contribute to the formation and maintenance of the societies from which heroes arise. Heroes therefore represent the best parts of us all. Moreover, as Messick's model suggests, once heroes of social movements begin their heroic work, they need our commitment and support to fulfill their visions. Heroes are as influenced by us as we are by them. We propose that the most powerful shaping of heroes takes place in our heads. Specifically, we argue that people mentally construct and maintain heroic images through the use of schemas and scripts, and that these mental constructions play a pivotal role in how people think, feel, and act toward heroes.

In Chapter 2 we discussed how our mental constructions of heroes affect our expectations regarding how they should look, speak, and act. The heroic script typically contains a dramatic ending in which the hero saves the day. One variation of this script's ending has the hero dying selflessly for the good cause. Many great heroes such as Roberto Clemente and the passengers of Flight 93 follow this script to perfection. The perfect hero makes the ultimate sacrifice. Sometimes this sacrifice takes the form of assassination. The list of assassinated luminaries is depressingly long: Mahatma Gandhi, Abraham Lincoln, Anwar Sadat, John F. Kennedy, Robert Kennedy, Martin Luther King Jr., John Lennon, and many others. There is little doubt the assassins didn't approve of the way the heroes were shaping us. But how exactly do these assassinations shape the reputations of the victims?

Psychologist Dean Keith Simonton has conducted many thorough studies of the factors that determine the perceived greatness of U.S. Presidents.[19] His morbid finding is that getting assassinated truly helps a president gain stature as a great leader. Simonton concludes that "getting assassinated adds about as much to a former president's greatness rating as serving five years in office or leading the nation through four years of war." His data also show that for an assassination attempt to improve a president's reputation, it has to be successful. Failed assassination attempts do nothing.

The cause of death doesn't have to be assassination for the reputation benefit to be gleaned. As Clemente's story shows, accidental deaths also heighten one's heroic status. An especially intriguing case is that of Missouri governor Melvin Carnahan, who was elected to the U.S. Senate on November 7, 2000.[20] Ordinarily, there is nothing noteworthy about such an election, except in this instance it was well known on election day that Carnahan had died in a plane crash 3 weeks earlier. Even more extraordinary was the fact that Carnahan was trailing his opponent by several percentage points in opinion polls prior to the plane crash. Polls clearly showed that his popularity soared as a result of his death, enabling him to be elected posthumously. As Carnahan was obviously unable to serve, his wife was appointed to fill the position.

Death by natural causes also can help a person's reputation. In June of 2004, the death of former U.S. President Ronald Reagan triggered an outpouring of praise and admiration from former political allies and adversaries alike. These tributes caught many anti-Reagan liberals by surprise. Media coverage of Reagan became significantly more positive after his death than during his tenure as president. Shortly after Reagan's death, a Gallup poll ranked him as the second best U. S. President, trailing only Abraham Lincoln.[21] We suspect that Reagan's reputation was boosted not only from his death but also from the way he died. For many years prior to his death, Reagan's brave and heroic battle against Alzheimer's disease attracted much sympathy and admiration.

Heroes are not the only ones whose reputations benefit from death. It seems apparent that *anyone's* death leads us to value him or her more. Philosophers have long been keenly aware of this norm prescribing reverence for deceased individuals. For example, the great playwright Sophocles warned his audiences "not to insult the dead."[22] Athenian statesman and legislator Solon echoed this sentiment when he implored citizens to "speak no ill of the dead."[23] The eminent Greek historian Thucydides extended this thinking by observing that "all men are wont to praise him who is no more."[24] In more modern times, American poet John Whittier noted that "death softens all resentments, and the consciousness of a common inheritance of frailty and weakness modifies the severity of judgment."[25]

We recently conducted a series of studies to investigate the tendency to evaluate the dead more favorably than the living.[26] In one study, our participants learned about a man who had a family, worked in a bank for 30 years, and then retired. Participants were then asked how much they liked him, respected him, and were inspired by him. Some participants were told that the man was still alive and well, while others were told that he had died last year. Our results showed that participants liked, respected, and were inspired significantly more by the man when they believed he was dead than when they believed he was alive. We've called this tendency to evaluate the dead more positively than the living the *death positivity bias*.

The banker in this study was described as fairly competent. So we next wanted to know whether people show the death positivity bias for incompetent people. Some participants learned of a man who managed a company very well. This competent person hired good employees, made wise investment decisions, and earned the company a good profit. Other participants were told that the man managed the company very poorly; he hired bad employees, made foolish investment decisions, and ran the company into a deficit. Our findings showed that participants showed the death positivity bias for both the competent and incompetent manager. It apparently doesn't matter if a person is inept. He or she will still be liked more dead than alive.

But what about immoral people? Can a villain reap the reputational benefits of dying as much as an average person or a hero? To test this idea, we informed participants about a manager who consistently made ethical choices his entire career. He was careful in disposing of toxic waste. He gave his employees generous salaries and benefits. And he gave generously to charities. Other participants learned about an unethical manager who dumped toxic waste illegally, underpaid his employees, and actually stole from charitable organizations.

The results of our study are shown in Figure 6.1. For the moral manager, we replicated the death positivity bias. A dead moral manager was viewed as more likeable and inspiring than a living moral

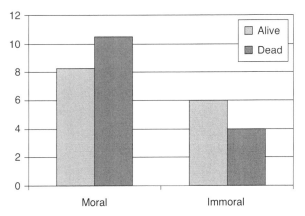

Figure 6.1 Liking for a moral or immoral person who is living or dead.

manager. But for immorality, we found the reverse pattern. A dead immoral manager was viewed as *less* likeable than a living immoral manager. Death appears to intensify whichever evaluative tendency we have of others based on what we know about their moral character. Upon death, a good person is seen as better, and a bad person is seen as worse.

It seems that people intuitively recognize that, when all is said and done, a person's basic goodness is more important than what particular skills he or she had. People appear to conclude that in the grand scheme of things, one's ability level is not all that important and, besides, one's ability is only partly under one's control. Thus, even an inept person is deserving of at least a pat on the back upon his or her death. A person's morality, however, is a different story. Morality is a choice, completely under one's control, and it appears to define a person's final legacy. Hence, death cannot salvage the reputation of a moral scoundrel. Death only reinforces our belief that morality, or lack of it, is the true measure of a man.

Our research findings support the idea that death can turn a merely good person into a great person or hero. The assassination of John F. Kennedy, which we discussed in Chapter 2, may offer a compelling example. Prior to his death in 1963, Kennedy was not considered an extraordinary president. He was loved by some, hated by some, and treated with the usual amount of indifference by most. He had barely defeated Richard Nixon in the 1960 presidential election, and while his presidency was going fairly well, he was nowhere near being the iconic legend that he is today. Only after his shocking assassination at such a young age did his image undergo a truly remarkable transformation. His death catapulted him into the rarified air of presidential myth and legend. People began viewing Kennedy as a fallen hero tragically unable to fulfill his vast potential.

People who die young are especially loved and revered. The list of mega-heroes who perished long before their time include Kennedy, Marilyn Monroe, Princess Diana, James Dean, Heath Ledger, Janis Joplin, John Belushi, Anne Frank, Bruce Lee, Jesus of Nazareth, Lou Gehrig, Martin Luther King Jr., and many others. We conducted a study to demonstrate the tendency of people to show a greater death positivity bias for young people than for old people. Participants learned of a man who drove a cab for a living. Some participants learned that he was 25 years old, while others learned that he was 65 years old. Then participants were informed that he had died. Our results showed that participants liked and admired the dead 25-year-old cabbie significantly more than they liked the dead 65-year-old cabbie. Perhaps Billy Joel was right after all when he sang that only the good die young.

When John F. Kennedy died in 1963, the Kennedy mystique was born. No other president, before or since, has had as many buildings, monuments, and schools named after him. Martin Luther King Jr., another hero who died young, has almost 800 streets in America that bear his name. Humans place those who die young on an especially high pedestal, and apparently there can never be enough physical reminders of them. But no matter at what age heroes die, in virtually all cultures one sees an abundance of tangible memorials honoring them. There are statues, monuments, and shrines. Cities, roads, buildings, and children are named after departed heroes. Epic stories and poems are composed. Images of dead heroes appear on stamps, coins, and paper currency.

Heroes who fight for a cause, and who die as a result of that fight, are often called *martyrs*. Martin Luther King Jr. is a classic example of a martyr, but there are others. Nathan Hale was hanged by the British during the American Revolutionary War and is known for uttering that famous line, "I only regret that I have but one life to give for my country." Once we label someone a martyr, that person can become an especially powerful symbol for a cause. Philosopher Soren Kierkegaard recognized this fact when he observed that "the tyrant dies and his rule is over; the martyr dies and his rule begins."[27]

Surprisingly, very little research has been conducted on martyrdom. The concept has its roots in ancient Greek and Roman cultural values. Socrates has been called the "saint and martyr of philosophy" by Anthony Gottlieb of *The Economist*.[28] Socrates willingly accepted his death sentence and took his own life to uphold his belief system. Psychologists Lynne Despelder and Albert Strickland have stated that the suicide of Socrates "has stood for 2,400 years as a symbol of dying for one's principles."[29] Greeks and Romans valued the idea of meeting death with both courage and acceptance. Romans revered both the bloody deaths in the gladiator arenas as well as intellectual suicides in the tradition of Socrates. Professor of Religion Margaret Cormack has argued that the Roman belief system contained the idea that life "was a treasure that gained value or power only when expended" and that martyrdom "transformed weakness into power."[30]

In modern times, martyrdom is probably most often considered in the context of religious extremism, but this religious context also has ancient origins. Two thousand years ago, Christianity was transformed from a peripheral offshoot of Judaism to a beleaguered underdog religious sect. Early Christians were put to death in great numbers for preaching their illegal faith to their fellow Roman citizens. This era of persecution spurred the growth of Christianity, as each publicly executed martyr attracted a new cult of converts. According to scholars who study death, such as Robert Kastenbaum, the suffering and death of Jesus held a "fatal attraction" for early Christians and was a strong advertisement for a threatened faith.[31] Like Socrates before him, Jesus willingly chose his suffering and death, according the Gospel of John (10:18): "No one takes my life, but I lay it down of my own accord." The redemptive value of suffering became part of the Christian heroic ideal. Martyrs did not just expect to be resurrected in the next life but also for their memories to be resurrected for all of time. The unshakeable determination of these early Christian martyrs shamed the Roman Empire's tactics of brutality, attracted sympathy for the Christian cause, and fueled the growth of Christianity.

Virtually all religions feature at least some history of martyrdom or suggestion of martyrdom in their belief systems. There are numerous scriptural accounts of Jewish martyrs resisting the Hellenizing of their Seleucid overlords, being executed for such crimes as observing the Sabbath, circumcising their children, or refusing to eat meat sacrificed to idols. In Hinduism, the term *sati* refers to a woman's act of immolating herself on the funeral pyre of her husband. Why would she do this? According to Margaret Cormack, remaining alive after one's husband's death carries with it the feared social sanction of being "an alluring or lustful widow who might tarnish the family reputation."[32] Satis are venerated as martyrs for embodying and affirming the truth. The Islamic view of martyrdom defines specific rewards for those who would die for their God. The Qur'an specifies that the Muslim martyr, or *shahid*, is spared the pain of death and receives immediate entry into paradise. Islam accepts a much broader view of what constitutes a martyr, including anyone who succumbs in territorial conflicts between Muslims and non-Muslims. Today there remains significant disagreement within the Muslim community about whether suicide bombers should be considered martyrs.

A dead martyr appears to derive sympathy and support from two different sources. First, we know from our research on the death positivity bias that a person's death leads to great liking and admiration for that person. Second, most martyrs embrace underdog causes and, as we know from Chapter 4, people tend to root for underdogs. Thus, it is easy to understand how and why we construct martyrs into powerfully heroic figures. To demonstrate the power of a martyr, we conducted a study in which participants learned of a person who died while engaged in a fierce political fight against poverty. Some participants learned that this individual was a financially disadvantaged person (the underdog condition), while others learned that this individual was a financially advantaged person (the top dog condition). In addition, some participants learned that this person took his own life for the cause he championed (the suicide condition), while others learned that this person was killed by opponents of his cause (the assassination condition).

Our findings showed that the martyr who attracted the highest degree of sympathy and support was the underdog martyr who was assassinated by the opponents to his cause. Martyrs who took their own lives—whether underdog or top dog in status—were viewed the least sympathetically and received the weakest emotional support. These findings suggest that martyrs can inspire others, but they also underscore the stigma associated with suicide regardless of underdog or top dog status. For a martyr to have maximum positive impact, his or her death must not be self-inflicted. This finding, of course, may be culturally specific. Palestinian suicide bombers have been treated like celebrities, their legacies cemented by community-wide celebrations, and their personal items coveted as objects of worshipful devotion.

SHAPING IN PERSPECTIVE

How do heroes shape us? They give us exactly what we need. There is an underlying human need for heroes to show us the best side of human nature. A century ago Carl Jung proposed that humans are born with an archetypal "readiness" to encounter heroes, to want them, to seek them, to recognize them, and to deal with them. The need for heroes is an unconscious need that feels good when it is satisfied. Heroes fulfill us emotionally just as food and water fulfill us physically. Heroes model exemplary behavior and challenge us to rise to their level. Heroes inspire us to aim higher. They make us feel good to be a member of the group or society in which they do their heroic work.

Heroes improve the quality of our lives. Scientific heroes usher in technological advances that transform our lifestyles and enhance living conditions. Spiritual heroes give us greater meaning in our lives. Athletic and artistic heroes entertain us. Heroes of social movements ensure equal rights for the oppressed. Sometimes heroes are everyday people who find themselves in an extraordinary circumstance and somehow rise to the occasion. These everyday people may be the most inspiring because they aren't intellectual, athletic, or spiritual geniuses. They are just like us. And so their heroic actions are a reminder that each and every one of us has the potential to be a hero.

How do we shape heroes? We do so in three ways. First, our mental constructions of heroes help us identify them when their appearance and behavior match our schema or archetype of heroes. Sometimes, the overenthusiastic use of a hero schema can lead to mistakes. That is, a person who looks like a hero on the outside can convince us that he or she is a hero on the inside, when in fact the person does not have the right stuff. A classic example of this misidentification is the case of Warren G. Harding, described in Chapter 2. We will, of course, never know about all the potential heroes who had the right stuff on the inside but were denied leadership opportunities because they lacked the correct "look."

A central part of our hero schema is that heroes make selfless sacrifices to accomplish their noble goals. The ultimate sacrifice is, of course, death, and we have shown how this feature of the hero schema can skew our evaluations of people. A dead person is evaluated more favorably than an equivalent living person, and a dead person who dies performing a laudable act is viewed as especially heroic. Most of all, we cherish heroes who die at a young age while championing their worthy causes.

The second way we shape heroes is seen in the way that we maintain our beliefs about their heroic status even in the face of evidence that runs contrary to the hero script. Schemas resist disconfirmation, and hero schemas are no exception. Consider reactions to the Tiger Woods sex scandal in 2009. When it became known that Woods had extramarital affairs with several women, a number of fans went to great lengths to discount any information that threatened their heroic image of Woods. One pediatric nurse from Florida said, "I think all the fame, all the money he has, all the women took advantage of it. He and his wife love each other. I think they do, and Tiger will do what's right."[33] On the other hand, many other fans, including several of his sponsors, succumbed to *schadenfreude* and turned against Woods. Perhaps more Tiger victories on the golf course will help restore these fans' heroic schema of him.

We have conducted studies showing that the most surefire way for a hero's image to be protected and preserved is for the hero to die.[34] Shortly after movie critic Gene Siskel died in 1999, we gave some participants new information about Siskel "that had just recently surfaced."

Others were given new information about Ebert, whom participants knew was still alive. For some participants, the new information was evidence that Siskel had been the creative genius behind the *Siskel and Ebert* television show and that Roger Ebert had merely ridden Siskel's coattails. For other participants, the new information was the reverse, namely, that Ebert was the creative genius behind the *Siskel and Ebert* show and that Siskel had ridden Ebert's coattails.

Our findings showed that in response to the new information, participants were significantly more likely to change their opinions of Ebert, whom they knew to be alive, than they were to change their views of Siskel, whom they knew to be dead. When new information had surfaced about Ebert that was flattering to him (i.e., he was the brains behind *Siskel and Ebert*), participants evaluated Ebert more favorably. Moreover, when evidence surfaced about Ebert that was unflattering about him (i.e., he had been riding Siskel's coattails), participants evaluated him less favorably. But when this same information was provided about the late Gene Siskel, our participants did not change their initial evaluations of him. It appears that once someone dies, our impressions of that person become fiercely resistant to change. In death, people become frozen in time.

The third way we shape heroes is seen in the many ways that we give heroes what they need in order to achieve their heroic vision. Heroes are leaders, and leaders cannot lead without the support of followers. For heroes to fulfill their noble visions, they need our commitment, effort, focus, loyalty, cooperation, sacrifice, respect, and obedience. Heroes need social support. This idea is supported by the numerous heroes who rely on sidekicks to achieve their goals. Batman has Robin. The Lone Ranger has Tonto. Han Solo has Chewbacca. Ralph Kramden has Ed Norton. Sherlock Holmes has Dr. Watson. Johnny Carson had Ed McMahon. Heroes do not spring from a social vacuum, nor do they operate in one. We are all part of the social fabric from which heroism is weaved.

The same is true, ironically, about evil. Evil does not come out of nowhere. It is also shaped by social forces. When a Birmingham church was bombed by racists in 1963, Martin Luther King Jr., opined that all of society made it possible for the bombers to do their evil work that day. Villains have their sidekicks, too. Captain Hook has

Mr. Smee. Dr. Frankenstein has Igor. Dr. Evil has mini-me. Hitler had Goebbels. Lex Luthor has Otis. Evil is shaped by social forces, but in many of our tales evil is reformed by social forces, too. It is not unusual for the villain's sidekick to recognize his or her wrongdoings and undergo a conversion to the good side. An impassioned speech delivered by the hero, or an act of kindness from the hero, can trigger the conversion. And we feel good knowing that although evil can be shaped, it can be unshaped, too.

An episode of *Star Trek* offers an example of the shaping and unshaping of evil. The episode, *Plato's Stepchildren*, features an evil race of beings, called the Platonians, nearly all of whom possess telekinetic powers. These powers are used to humiliate and torture the hero, Captain Kirk, and his officers. The one Platonian lacking these powers, Alexander, plays a small role in tormenting Kirk and his crew, but eventually Alexander becomes appalled at the cruelty of the Platonians. To save Kirk, he boldly attempts to kill the leader of the Platonians. Later, after the Platonians are defeated, Alexander's conversion to the good side is recognized and he is allowed to go free.

Sometimes what inspires us most about our leaders isn't their leadership per se; it is the way we mentally construct events that took place *before* and *after* their leadership. With regard to Barack Obama, many Americans are inspired by their belief that he overcame centuries of institutional racism to become the first African American president. Obama is viewed as an underdog who triumphed over the many social forces working against his successful run to the White House. In short, what happened *before* Obama took office inspires us the most about him. With regard to John F. Kennedy, it was what happened *after* his presidency that inspires us most. His assassination at such a young age moved us deeply and triggered the construction of an iconic hero. Thus, we see that a leader's most transforming actions may precede his or her leadership, or they may be constructed after the leader's tenure. To be effective sources of inspiration, these actions must be emotionally powerful to followers, engendering sympathy, respect, and veneration for the leader.

Another prominent example is the leadership of Nelson Mandela, who endured 27 years of imprisonment before assuming the presidency of South Africa.[35] While imprisoned, he and other inmates performed hard labor in a lime quarry. Prison conditions were harsh; prisoners were segregated by race, with black prisoners receiving the least rations. Political prisoners such as Mandela were kept separate from ordinary criminals and received fewer privileges. Mandela has described how, as a D-group prisoner (the lowest classification), he was allowed one visitor and one letter every 6 months. Mandela's ability to prevail after such long-term suffering made him an inspirational hero. His remarkable triumph over adversity, occurring before his presidency, propelled him to international fame and admiration.

What do all of our mental constructions of heroes have in common? Central to all of them is the idea that we are sympathetic to those who suffer to achieve laudable goals. Underdogs suffer the stigma of disadvantage, and when they prevail we are inspired and grant them heroic stature. The dead suffer by being snuffed out of existence, and the only way we can help them is to elevate them to the status of hero. The self-sacrificing actions of heroes cement their positive legacies to such a degree that their values, the things that they stand for, become firmly imbedded into our society's social identity. Suffering is the essential ingredient in hero construction. As Helen Keller once observed, "Character cannot be developed in ease and quiet. Only through experience of trial and suffering can the soul be strengthened, vision cleared, ambition inspired, and success achieved."[36]

Conclusion

The challenger seemed so crazed, they almost called off the fight. It was early 1964. The United States was getting ready for The Beatles' first visit to America. Lyndon Johnson was president, and the Vietnam War was beginning to cause unrest. But a heavyweight title fight between the champion Sonny Liston and the young challenger, Cassius Clay, also captured the nation's attention. The odds makers were betting heavily against Clay. Some sports writers felt that the lamb was being led to slaughter. They couldn't imagine Clay winning. When Clay's pulse hit 120 just before the weigh in, people thought he was scared to death, or had become completely unhinged. And there was good reason for him to become unhinged.

Sonny Liston, the Heavyweight Champion of the World, was a fearsome figure. He had won the belt 2 years earlier by knocking out Floyd Patterson in the first round. Then he easily won their rematch, with another first-round knockout over Patterson. Liston was rumored to be associated with organized crime, and his glare scared most people. He wasn't well liked, but he was respected, and he was feared. He seemed invincible. Cassius Clay was a 22-year-old former light-heavyweight Olympic Champion from Louisville, Kentucky, who had somehow maneuvered to meet Liston. Other fighters were avoiding what seemed like an almost suicidal match-up. And Clay seemed too young, too inexperienced, and too small. He was fast, but Patterson had been fast. There seemed no way for him to win.

Even though Liston was generally loathed, few people liked Clay much either. He was regarded as a loudmouth who couldn't back up his boasts. Although he had written poems that accurately predicted when he would stop some of his earlier opponents, when he bragged about beating Liston he seemed like so much hot air. He was dubbed the "Louisville Lip" and "Gaseous Cassius." In addition, there were rumors about Clay being associated with "Black Muslims," a terrifying thought to most white Americans in early 1964. He was nobody's hero. Many people would have been happy if both men lost.

But, as Clay trumpeted after the fight, "I shook up the world." He easily beat Liston in a stunning upset, using blinding foot speed, and cutting combinations. He made good on his promise to "float like a butterfly, sting like a bee." After that, his career first captivated the sports world, and then the whole world. His talent and charisma began to win people over. But nothing went smoothly. After winning the championship Clay changed his name to Muhammad Ali and openly joined the Nation of Islam. Many cities wouldn't let him fight. But he defeated one challenger after another, almost effortlessly it seemed. He said he always moved fast enough to prevent getting hit, so that he wouldn't mess up his pretty face.[1] But the establishment, or what Chief Bromden from Chapter 2 would have called "the Combine," caught up with him. After initially failing the army mental test, the standards were lowered so that Ali was eligible for the draft. He asked for a deferment from military service on the grounds that he was a minister in the Muslim faith. At first few people believed he was sincere. But rather than joining the armed forces, Ali tolerated a 3-1/2 year ban from boxing during the prime years of his career while his lawyers appealed his draft eligibility. He proved to most of the country's satisfaction that his religious beliefs were genuine, and that they came before his career or even his freedom.

Ali eventually won his legal argument in a unanimous U.S. Supreme Court decision. He was allowed to fight again, and most people welcomed him back to the ring. But Ali soon suffered his first defeat to then champion Joe Frazier. He then set out on a quest to regain the championship, and 3 years later he succeeded, winning the heavyweight title back in a classic matchup with George Foreman in Zaire, Africa. He called it "the rumble in the jungle." In that fight, he was as much an underdog as he had been 10 years earlier, against Sonny Liston. Like Liston, Foreman seemed invincible. And now, Ali was viewed as too old, not too young. Once again, he confounded the pundits, covering his head with his arms while leaning back along the ropes until Foreman punched himself out. Ali called this strategy "the rope-a-dope." In Round 8, it left Foreman vulnerable to an Ali knockout punch.

After regaining the title, Ali continued fighting and speaking. He became one of the most recognized figures in the entire world. His philosophy emphasized black people determining their own identities and taking care of their own problems. He had always insisted that he was going to be his own person, even if the majority of the country disliked his attitudes about race, religion, or the Vietnam War. Over the years, many, many people in the United States changed their mind about the "uppity" black man they hated in the 1960s. They respected his commitment to help people of his own race and other oppressed groups, and the firmness of his religious principles. And he won them over with his skill, wit, and charisma. When the Olympic Games were held in Atlanta, Georgia, in 1996, there was no question as to which former American medal winner would light the Olympic torch. By that time Ali was suffering from Parkinson's disease, but he rose to the occasion and ignited the flame.

In an interview long after his boxing days were over, Ali said he would like to be remembered as a man who fought for his people, and for freedom, justice, and equality. But he added, with typical Ali wit, "I guess I'd settle for being remembered only as a great boxing champion who became a preacher and a champion of his people. And I wouldn't even mind if folks forgot how pretty I was."[2]

MATCHING AND MAGNETISM: PERCEIVING AND NEEDING HEROES

Muhammad Ali's transformation from obnoxious boxer to iconic hero took place over a long period of time, about 30 years, and illustrates many of the most important themes of our book. We have emphasized two pieces to the heroism puzzle. First, heroes typically have certain characteristics and do certain things. There is a template for perceived heroes, but it is not rigid. It flexes to accommodate a range of different heroic individuals. Nor is it completely elastic, because there are several defining attributes of heroes. For example, heroes almost always work hard for good causes. Second, we have argued that perceivers ultimately decide who is and who is not a hero.

Some people, such as Martin Luther King Jr., are widely regarded as heroes by the general public. Others, like Irena Sendler, are seen as heroes once people learn about them. Still others are regarded as heroes by some people, but not everyone. They may actually be seen as villains, or maybe just nonentities. This raises the question of how we, as authors, define heroism, and how we decide who is and who is not a hero. The answer is that we don't define who's a hero. You do.

We think that whom people regard as heroes depends on a matching of a mental image of a hero with a mental image of a specific person. When the image of the person matches the image of a hero, that individual is deemed a hero. But the match is a two-way street. Both our schema or template for "a hero" and our schema or opinion of the specific person we potentially see as a hero are flexible. When they sufficiently mesh or match, the person becomes a hero. As always, we add the qualification, the person becomes a hero *to the perceiver*. Heroism exists in the eyes of beholders.

We can illustrate this matching process by considering people's perceptions of Muhammad Ali. We noted that many white Americans were initially offended by Ali's bragging and his association with the Muslim religion. He was typically seen as an obnoxious loudmouth and he certainly didn't fit the reigning cultural image of a black boxing champion. That image had been defined by great fighters such as Joe Louis, who was (and still is) revered as perhaps the greatest fighter in history and also "a credit to his race." As champ during the 1940s, Louis adopted a modest, even humble persona that was comfortable for most white Americans. His demeanor was decidedly deferential, despite his undeniable personal power. When Floyd Patterson became the next prominent black champ in 1956, he adopted the same persona and fit the same schema. Cassius Clay didn't fit it at all. And he fit it even less after he became Muhammad Ali. He simply didn't behave as most people believed a heavyweight champ should behave, especially a black one. From this perspective, the schema of a hero and the image of Ali were miles apart. But over the years, this mismatch changed for many people. How did that happen?

For one thing, over the years people's image of Ali became a little more complicated. Yes, he was a braggart, and he could be pretty obnoxious about it, but he was clever. There was always some wit and tongue-in-cheek humor in his rants: "I'm young, I'm handsome, I'm fast, I'm pretty, and can't possibly be beaten."[3] This was clearly part of the show. And then people sort of liked his doggerel. For example, he drew smiles when he predicted that he would defeat Sonny Liston in their first title fight: "Yes the crowd did not dream when they put down their money, that they would see a total eclipse of the Sonny." He deflected critics, such as those who believed that he deliberately failed the Army mental test: "I never said I was the smartest. I said I was the greatest." And then slowly, his serious side came to be acknowledged and respected for the depth of its commitments. Though people didn't agree with Ali's opposition to the Vietnam War ("I ain't got no quarrel with them Vietcong"), they realized that he meant it, and if he had to go to jail because of his refusal to be drafted, he would do it. He was a man of conviction about issues much larger than himself. So the initial image of a dangerous ego-maniac bled over to a more complicated image of a witty, intelligent, talented, and committed athlete who could back up his braggadocio.

If the image of Ali changed, and became more complicated, a changing image of the hero met him halfway. Our Great Eight outline of the hero schema includes the traits Smart, Strong, Selfless, Caring, Charismatic, Resilient, Reliable, and Inspiring. Ali began to be perceived as Caring, Selfless, and Inspiring as well as Smart, Strong, Charismatic, and Resilient. But he was also perceived as someone who challenged deeply rooted cultural assumptions about race, religion, and personal style. Could the hero image accommodate those elements? The answer was yes. Ali was a loudmouth, but a clever one. And many people had come to think that as part of being Strong, heroes could be pushy and outspoken. Martin Luther King Jr. and Malcolm X along with Ali led people to expand their images of heroes to include people who forcefully spoke up for minority rights and equality in America. It became not only "OK" to push the white establishment for change, it became increasingly "the right thing" and ultimately heroic.

By 1998 Ali was admired widely enough to appear on Wheaties cereal boxes. The label named him "the world's most recognized and beloved sports icon" and described him as "confident, graceful, [and] strong-willed." And even his political side was endorsed by General

Mills, the manufacturer of Wheaties, as follows: "Throughout his career, Ali was a courageous man who fought for his beliefs. He became an even larger force outside the ring with numerous humanitarian efforts . . ."[4] Such praise would have been unthinkable 30 years earlier.

There are other important examples of the meshing of schemas with images of specific people. For example, our schema for "leader" very much includes the attribute of assertiveness. But many people's schema about women has been that they are not assertive. They are typically just assumed to be cooperative and deferential. The discrepancy between the image of a leader and the perception of most women creates "role incongruity" such that it has been hard to perceive women as leaders. Now, however, there has been change in both directions.[5] First, many women are now recognized as assertive. In fact, the changing image of women as a whole has freed an increasing number of individual women to behave more assertively than they might have before. And the schema for leaders is changing just as much as the schema for women. The ideal leader isn't seen so much as a "command and control" CEO who issues orders like the captain of a naval vessel. He or she is seen as someone who listens, treats individuals fairly, and recognizes the contributions of followers. It's as though the image of women has become more traditionally masculine, and the image of leaders has become more traditionally feminine. So that now the image of many individual women meshes with the image of the leader.

The meshing of hero images with perceptions of individuals occurs on a small scale as well as more broadly. Our study of people's heroes showed that about one-third of those listed are family members. Mothers were frequently mentioned. For their sons and daughters, the image of a hero includes a warm and self-sacrificing woman who gives all for her children, and their image of their mothers downplays how controlling or demanding she might be. Whether heroes are real or fictional, personal or national, or for large populations or small groups, there must be a matching of the hero schema with the characteristics of the hero.

In this regard, one of the most striking things about our study of people's heroes is how easily heroes come to mind. Few people looked stumped when we asked them to list their heroes. Jung's idea of the hero archetype suggests our readiness to perceive heroes. We are prepared to see them. And the archetype idea suggests more than readiness to perceive heroes. It also suggests that we are willing, even eager, to perceive them. An archetype is more than a schema. It is a schema with an emotional charge. When we perceive a hero, we like the feeling. We have discussed the significant overlap between heroes and leaders, and the notion that we might need heroes has a counterpart in Sigmund Freud's theories of leadership. Freud wrote about how people often "place themselves instinctively under the authority of a chief." We have a need to be led, and we ascribe to leaders great prestige, which Freud described as a "mysterious or irresistible power" that acts as "a sort of domination exercised by an individual, a work or an idea." We crave a person or idea that "fills us with wonderment and respect,"[6] and when we encounter such a person or idea we bind ourselves strongly to it. Similarly, we crave heroic images and heroic stories, or in a word, heroes.

It's useful to think of heroes as magnets and perceivers of heroes as the metal that is drawn to the magnet. But what qualities make potential heroes magnetic? Obviously, charisma is one key. In fact, we recall that magnetism is part of the definition of charisma. Like heroism and leadership, charisma is always in the eye of the beholder. But whatever it is, some people have it more than others. Martin Luther King Jr. and John F. Kennedy had it, and Oprah Winfrey has oodles of it. And Muhammad Ali, with the combination of his athletic artistry and his way with words, had as much as anyone. The fact that we are so easily enchanted by charismatic figures speaks again to our readiness to perceive heroes and our need to have them. The hero archetype is a powerful one.

CONSCIENCE AND COMPETENCE: HEROISM'S DEFINING QUALITIES

At the start of our book we noted that *Casablanca*'s Rick Blaine had charisma derived from great competence and a complicated conscience. It was clear that he was an able person, but whether he was a moral one was tantalizingly uncertain. In his first scene he showed that he wouldn't be pushed around by obnoxious Nazis—"you're lucky the bar's open to you"—but then his repeated statements that "I stick my neck out for nobody" raised questions about whether he really only cared about himself. The dramatic tension of the film is always whether Rick has the moral core to be a hero. We are deeply moved when he proves that he does. His example underlines the dual dimensions of heroism, conscience, or morality, and competence.

Although heroism can be based in either conscience or competence alone, most of the examples we've considered here combine both qualities. At great risk to herself, Irena Sendler used her interpersonal competence to smuggle Jewish children out of the Warsaw ghetto. R. P. McMurphy channeled his charisma and competence into a highly moral challenge to arbitrary authority and crushing conformity. Muhammad Ali became a hero for many because of his extraordinary skill as a fighter and his deep commitment to social justice, as he understood it. It took time for some people to acknowledge the depth of his moral principles, but once they recognized their importance for him, they granted Ali hero status.

But just as important are heroes whose stature is based on consummate competence alone, or on unusual moral purity alone. For many people, the Wright Brothers, Wilbur and Orville, are heroes for doggedly and skillfully pursuing the dream of manned flight, and for finally succeeding in designing, building, and flying the first motor-driven airplane. Sherlock Holmes is a fictional detective hero due to his deductive powers. Many of his personal idiosyncrasies, such as his discomfort with women and his critical remarks about Dr. Watson's stories, have become endearing to Holmes lovers. But such qualities are enduring because he is a hero, and is forgiven his eccentricities. They certainly don't make him a hero in the first place. Also because of extraordinary ability, Beverly Sills is a hero to opera lovers, and Meryl Streep is a hero to overwhelming numbers of actors, both men and women. People admire all of these individuals for their achievements. Their morality is largely irrelevant. On the other side of the coin, people who make self-sacrificing choices for the common good are viewed as heroes without much regard to their competence. In the Czech Republic, a young man who burned himself to death in 1969, to protest the hardening of Communist rule after the overthrow of the liberating 1968 "Prague Spring," is honored as a Czech hero. He gave his life to express a moral position, but there was no element of competence in his sacrifice. Similarly, Nathan Hale is regarded as an American Revolutionary War hero for bravely risking his life, and losing it, without demonstrating much competence. His moral commitment, as stated in his final words—"I only regret that I have but one life to lose for my country"—makes him a hero, despite the fact that he wasn't a very effective patriot spy. In short, heroism is based on perceptions of competence and morality, in different combinations for different individuals.

UPHILL BATTLES: OVERCOMING OBSTACLES AND TOPPLING TEMPTATIONS

Struggle and sacrifice are hallmarks of heroism. Sir Ernest Shackleton's success in leading his crew to safety after a year and a half of intense struggle is one of our most riveting accounts of human triumph over natural obstacles. Shackleton had to maintain his men's health and morale through months of darkness, deprivation, and cold. Once the *Endurance* was crushed in the floe he had to get his men in and out of sleds, tents, and small boats until they finally set themselves afloat in the ice pack. Then in their struggle to get to Elephant Island, he had to keep his three small boats together under dauntingly dangerous conditions. Shackleton and his crew had to avoid being crushed in the ice, upset by whales, capsized by waves, and separated by darkness. Almost miraculously, powered by sail and oar, they made landfall. Almost immediately after reaching Elephant Island, Shackleton realized that while there was enough food and shelter for several months, the crew would eventually freeze or starve or both unless they were rescued. Then came the most perilous portion of the saga. Shackleton sailed with five other men in a small boat through freezing hurricanes and mountainous waves to reach South Georgia Island. Finally, Shackleton and two of his five companions crossed the island to a whaling station. In a few days, the other three sailors were rescued by boat, and in several more months Shackleton was finally able to sail a ship to Elephant Island to rescue all of the men left there. Shackleton's heroism derives from his success in overcoming seemingly insurmountable obstacles, and never wavering on his commitment to save his crew.

Muhammad Ali faced the obstacle of an implacable white sports establishment that strove mightily to thwart his career and all that his independence and outspokenness stood for. His success in challenging and ultimately changing that establishment made him both a hero and a widely respected leader. Many who initially feared, resented, or impeded him came to respect and follow his commitments to openness and social justice. Of course, Ali gained credibility in large part because he overcame the most daunting obstacles of all, his Heavyweight Champion opponents, Sonny Liston and George Foreman.

Our study of heroes also reminds us of internal obstacles. In many cases those internal obstacles are closely related to external obstacles. They generally take the form of temptations to give up or give in. We want to give up when faced with seemingly insurmountable obstacles. In one of the most famous championship fights in boxing history, Panamanian welterweight Roberto Duran quit in the seventh round, saying "No mas" or, in English, "No more." He had had enough of the former champ, Sugar Ray Leonard. While there is controversy about what Duran actually said, it was clear he quit. He was unable to overcome the temptation to give up. That rarely happens in sports, but the Duran example underlines how tempting giving up can become. In the last year of the Civil War, Abraham Lincoln was tempted to reverse his commitment to emancipation, by the possibility of achieving a quick end to the war, on the South's terms. It appeared that if he would only agree not to free slaves, the rebel states would return to the Union. It is not clear whether Lincoln could actually have restored the Union by backtracking on emancipation, but he thought about trying. Ultimately, he was unmovable in his commitment to ending slavery, but the appeal of ending the horrible bloodshed of the war was powerful.

When external obstacles overwhelm people's abilities, as they have with many athletes, artists, soldiers, musicians, or scholars, the world loses a potential hero. But when internal temptations overwhelm an individual's morality, the world may not only lose a hero but gain a villain. We can see this clearly with Brutus in Shakespeare's *Julius Caesar*. Goaded and flattered by the villain Cassius, Brutus began to believe anonymous letters that both praised him and urged him to confront Caesar. Of course, Cassius had orchestrated the letters. Brutus's own ego, combined with the somewhat plausible concern that Caesar would become a dictator, led him to murder his friend. If he had had the judgment and self-control to ignore the flattery and the temptations of power, he would never have let himself be manipulated into the assassination. Shakespeare's stories of pride and ambition (recall Macbeth as well as Brutus and Caesar) resonate to the ancient myths of Lucifer, or Satan. The themes of many such myths are combined in English poet John Milton's *Paradise Lost*, written roughly a half century after Shakespeare's plays. Milton's Lucifer had been cast out of Heaven because his pride would not let him accept the fact that he was an inferior being to God. He led an unsuccessful rebellion and was cast into Hell, where he devoted himself to evil. The temptations of pride clouded his judgment, overwhelmed his self-control, and led him down the paths of darkness.

SHAPING AND BEING SHAPED: THE CREATION OF VIRTUE AND VICE

We noted earlier that during the Civil War Abraham Lincoln refused to take full credit for formulating his emancipation policy, a policy which proved militarily effective as well as morally correct. He wrote of his decision to adopt it, "I attempt no compliment to my own sagacity. I claim not to have controlled events, but confess plainly that events have controlled me."[7] While Lincoln was being too modest about both his wisdom and his power, his words confirm one of the themes of this book. People are obviously shaped by events in their lives and in the world around them. Sometimes those events lead them to become heroes, and sometimes they lead them to become villains.

We can see such shaping on both sides of the coin. Consider villains, fictional and real. Brutus was shaped by the events of Rome in the last century BCE. Caesar had achieved great military success and stirred fears of monarchy. Cassius fanned the flames of Brutus' fears, and the embers of his egotism. While his choice to murder Caesar was his own, external circumstances affected his thinking and decision making. They led him to what his Roman countrymen ultimately construed as villainy. Adolph Hitler was also shaped by the events of his life. The harsh punishment of Germany by the Allies following World War I stirred resentment among many Germans, especially those, like Hitler, who had fought in the war. In addition, Hitler's aspirations to develop a career as an artist failed, breeding further resentment. The failure of the post-war German government provided a focus for his resentments and his aspirations. Hitler raised villainy to almost unfathomable levels, and he must be held responsible, but his choices were substantially shaped, as are our own, by events.

If Hitler was a villain, one of the principal heroes of the world war against him was his counterpart and contemporary, Franklin D. Roosevelt. Roosevelt's life was also shaped by the events of his life and times. In 1932 the global economic depression destroyed the credibility of the Republican Party in the United States and gave Roosevelt a landslide election victory. That victory gave him much more latitude to act and initiate change than most presidents are given. But more than political events, personal circumstances shaped FDR. In 1920 he was the young, rising star of the Democratic Party. He became its nominee for vice president. Though the Democrats were defeated, Roosevelt was the heir apparent to party leadership. But then the next year, Roosevelt contracted polio, and he was paralyzed, for the rest of his life, from the waist down. His strenuous efforts at personal rehabilitation left him a different man. He was no longer a shallow, glad-handing politician. He became a person who understood personal pain and cared deeply about people who were in trouble. He became perhaps the most empathetic president in American history. And his empathy combined with energy and optimism, enabling him to reassure an anxious nation that "the only thing we have to fear is fear itself." His bold actions, emerging from the well-springs of that energy, empathy, and optimism, made him a hero for millions. In a famous 1984 Democratic Party convention speech, former New York Governor Mario Cuomo eloquently framed FDR's heroism: "He lifted himself from his wheelchair to lift this nation from its knees."

One of the most vivid recent examples of events shaping heroes is that of US Airways pilot Chesley "Sully" Sullenberger, who successfully landed an Airbus A320 on the freezing Hudson River in January, 2009, saving the lives of all passengers and crew aboard Flight 1549. But shaping works the other way, too. Heroes shape as much as they in turn are shaped. We have emphasized that heroes are almost always leaders, by their example, by their persuasiveness, or by their works. They show us or tell us how to lead exemplary lives. We need heroes and leaders to inspire and direct, to energize and steer, to serve, in effect, as both the propeller and the rudder for our personal ships. Ernest Shackleton showed us what can be accomplished through leadership, determination, and commitment. Oprah Winfrey showed us how celebrity can be turned toward encouraging reading and serious intellectual and moral engagement. A hero to many, comedian Bill Cosby showed how a television comedy can be used to model love, caring, and understanding in a typical family. And he did it by portraying an African American family with both African American and white friends and neighbors. In this way he powerfully illustrated the lesson that love, caring, and understanding can also reach beyond the family.

We have also seen that villains can be leaders who wreak havoc. Shakespeare's Iago played on Othello's insecurity and jealousy in order to destroy him. Adolph Hitler played on a nation's insecurities and jealousies. In doing so, he led his regime to murder most of the Jews of Europe, and he eventually led his country to total ruin. James MacGregor Burns argues that transforming leaders engage their followers in ways that raise them to higher levels of motivation and morality.[8] But villainous leaders can move followers by appealing to their basest motives and their capacities for evil.

In the end we discover it's a fine line between whether an individual chooses a moral path, grounded in the love of humanity, or an immoral path, wallowing in self-pity and loathing. On the one hand, with the help of her family, Betty Ford was encouraged to make the life-affirming choice to battle alcohol and drug dependence. She had almost sunk beyond hope into an abyss of permanent addiction. Fortunately, once she helped herself, she spent the rest of her adult life helping others, through the Betty Ford Center. Others have opted for the dark side. And sometimes they pay a steep price. Romanian leader Nicolae Ceausescu became more and more obsessed with personal power and control during his three decades as his country's dictator. By late in the fall of 1989, when many Eastern European countries were throwing off the yoke of Communism, Ceausescu and his wife had lost all political legitimacy with their people and were executed by their own army. He led his country into an economic abyss, and he paid the price along with his countrymen.

There is also a fine line between whether followers are or are not engaged by the uplifting visions of heroic leaders or the destroying delusions of villains. Most American soldiers during the Revolutionary War cast their lot with the selfless hero George Washington and followed him through to ultimate victory. But a few such as Benedict Arnold were more concerned about themselves than the patriot cause and betrayed both their leader and their country. Similarly, while many, many Germans willingly followed Hitler in all of his policies, some, particularly in the German military, knew that he was a villain in a hero's clothes. There were at least a dozen attempts to assassinate Hitler, but all failed. Eventually Hitler took his own life, but not before killing millions and destroying most of Europe. Some followers face a different kind of choice. Rather than deciding whether to follow or to sit on the sidelines, as in Hitler's Germany, they have to choose between the path of a hero or the path of a villain. Sailors on the *Endurance* crew had to decide whether to be loyal to Shackleton or join a mutiny led by the carpenter Frank McNeish. For the good of all, they followed Shackleton. A different choice by a few more discontented followers would almost surely have doomed all hands.

Ultimately, heroes inspire us to work toward great accomplishments or to perform selfless acts that improve the human condition. They may be seen as heroes for their competence and achievement in a specific domain such as science, art, or sport, or for their commitment to and sacrifice for the welfare of others. Either way, they appeal to what Abraham Lincoln called "the better angels of our nature" and beckon us toward attaining our highest possible levels of competence and morality. We need them, and we are lucky to have them.

HEROISM AND THE HUMAN CONDITION

In the final analysis, human beings create heroes and villains to both energize and guide their thinking and behavior. The human condition constantly presents us with challenges, choices, and obstacles. Each of us rises to those challenges and faces those obstacles in different ways. Most of us achieve our goals only some of the time. And most of us make bad moral choices as well as good ones. We need all the help we can get to act effectively and morally. Heroes blaze the trail toward competence and morality, and villains remind us of the dark side. Randle Patrick McMurphy and Oprah Winfrey give us inspirational and motivating examples of charisma, competence, and helpfulness. Like other heroes, they point the way toward doing the right things and doing them well. In contrast, Adolph Hitler and Shakespeare's Iago remind us of dangerous and disturbing human potential. Why people achieve or fail and why they choose good or evil is probably unknowable. But we do know that people create heroes and villains to help them understand and navigate their daunting worlds. Mostly for the better, we think.

Notes

Introduction

[1] All quotes from *Casablanca* are from the screenplay by Julius J. Epstein, Philip G. Epstein, and Howard Koch, retrieved from http://digittool-demo.exlibrisgroup.com. Film released by Warner Brothers, 1942, Michael Curtis, Director.

[2] Fiske, S. T., & Taylor, S. E. (1991). *Social cognition*. New York: McGraw Hill.

[3] Collins, G. (2000). Public interests: A New York moment. *The New York Times*, March 3, 2000, A21.

[4] Acuff, D., & Acuff, R. (1961). Big Bad John. Performed by Jimmy Dean. Released by Columbia Records.

[5] Ellis, J. J. (2004). *His Excellency George Washington*. New York: Knopf.

[6] Coppola, F. F., & North, E. H. (1970). *Patton*. Film released by 20th Century Fox, Franklin J. Shaffner, Director.

[7] Hillenbrand, L. (2001). *Seabiscuit: An American Legend*. New York: Random House. Ross, G. (2003) *Seabiscuit*. Film released by Universal Studios, Gary Ross, Director.

[8] Morison, S. E. (1965). *Oxford History of the American People*. New York: Oxford University Press.

[9] Lieber, J., & Stoller, M. (1959). Along came Jones. Performed by The Coasters. Released by Atlantic Records.

[10] Johnson, L. B. (1965) Presidential address on voting rights. Delivered to Congress, March 15, 1965.

[11] Kellerman, B. (2004). *Bad leadership: What it is, how it happens, why it matters*. Boston: Harvard Business School Press.

Chapter 1: Heroes

[1] For more information about the remarkable Irena Sendler, see http://www.auschwitz.dk/Sendler.htm or http://info-poland.buffalo.edu/classroom/sendler/index.html.

[2] The 2010 Time 100 (2010). Retrieved from http://www.yachtingnet.com/time/time100/heroes/

[3] Mayer, C. (2010). 60 years of heroes. Retrieved from http://www.time.com/time/europe/hero2006/opener.html

[4]American Film Institute (2010). The AFI's heroes and villains. Retrieved from http://www.afi.com/tvevents/100years/handv.aspx

[5]Pollard-Gott, L. (2010). The Fictional 100: A Tour of the Top 10. Retrieved from http://www.fictional100.com/top10.html

[6]Chicago Tribune (2008). Retrieved from http://archives.chicagotribune.com/2008/oct/22/news/chi-obama-grandmother22-weboct22

[7]Associated Press (2008). Barack Obama's grandmother dies. Retrieved from http://www.msnbc.msn.com/id/27522679/ns/politics-decision_08/

[8]Ferguson, D. (2006). Earl Woods, father of Tiger Woods, dies. Retrieved from http://www.highbeam.com/doc/1P1-122980166.html

[9]Armstrong, L. (2001). *It's not about the bike: My journey back to life.* New York: Berkeley Books. p. 77.

[10]Smith, J. M. (1964). Group selection and kin selection. *Nature,* 201, 1145–1147.

[11]Wikipedia (2011). Virginia Tech massacre. Retrieved from http://en.wikipedia.org/wiki/Virginia_Tech_massacre

[12]Biography.com (2011). Britney Spears' biography. Retrieved from http://www.biography.com/articles/Britney-Spears-9542229

[13]Thomas, E. (2008). The myth of objectivity. Retrieved from http://www.newsweek.com/id/117850

[14]Campbell, J. (1949). *The hero with a thousand faces.* New York: Pantheon Press.

[15]Associated Press (1982). A hero-passenger aids others, then dies. *The Washington Post,* January 14, 1982.

[16]Crowthertrust.org (2011). Welles Remy Crowther. Retrieved from http://www.crowthertrust.org/welles_story.htm

[17]Booth, N. (2005). Be confident like Tiger Woods – it pays. Retrieved from http://ezinearticles.com/?Be-Confident-Like-Tiger-Woods---It-Pays&id=2368088

[18]Hauser, M. (2006). *Moral minds: How nature designed our universal sense of right and wrong.* New York: HarperCollins.

[19]Gladwell, M. (2008). *Outliers.* Boston: Little, Brown, and Company.

[20]Mischel, W. (1968). *Personality and assessment.* New York: Wiley.

[21]Gardner, H. (1995). *Leading minds: An anatomy of leadership.* New York: Basic Books.

[22]Petty, R. E., & Cacioppo, J. T. (1981). *Attitudes and persuasion: Classic and contemporary approaches.* Dubuque, Iowa: Wm. C. Brown Company.

Chapter 2: Exemplars

[1]This and subsequent quotes from *One Flew Over the Cuckoo's Nest* are from Kesey, K. (1962) *One flew over the cuckoo's nest.* New York: Viking.

[2]Hauben, L., & Goldman, B. (1975). *One flew over the cuckoo's nest.* United Artists Film, Directed by Milos Forman. Screenplay by Lawrence Hauben & Bo Goldman.

[3]Forsyth, D. R. (2008). Seeing and being a leader. In C. L. Hoyt, G. R. Goethals, & D. R. Forsyth (eds.), *Leadership at the crossroads, Vol. 1, Leadership and psychology* (pp. 116–131). Westport, CT: Praeger.

4 Hoyt, C. L., & Chemers, M. M. (2008) Social stigma and leadership: A long climb up a slippery ladder. In C. L. Hoyt, G. R. Goethals, & D. R. Forsyth (eds.), *Leadership at the crossroads, Vol. 1, Leadership and psychology* (pp. 165–180). Westport, CT: Praeger.

5 Fiske, S. T. (1998) Stereotyping, prejudice, and discrimination. *The handbook of social psychology* (4th ed.), Vol. 2 (pp. 357–411). Boston: McGraw Hill.

6 Darley, J. M., & Gross, P. H. (1983). A hypothesis-confirming bias in labeling effects. *Journal of Personality and Social Psychology, 44,* 20–33.

7 James, B. (1988). *The Bill James Historical Baseball Abstract.* New York: Villard, p. 377.

8 Rosenthal, R., & Jacobson, L. (1968). *Pygmalion in the classroom: Teacher expectation and pupil's intellectual development.* New York: Holt, Rinehart & Winston.

9 Gladwell, M. (2005). *Blink.* Boston: Little, Brown, and Company.

10 Osgood, C. E., Suci, G. J., & Tannenbaum, P. (1957). *The measurement of meaning.* Urbana: University of Illinois Press.

11 *American Heritage Dictionary of the English Language* (3rd ed.). Boston: Houghton Mifflin, p. 322; Merriam-Webster OnLine Dictionary (2009). Retrieved from http://www.merriam-webser.com/dictionary/charisma.

12 Weber, M. (1921) The sociology of charismatic authority. In H. H. Gerth & C. W. Mills (eds., 1946), *From Max Weber: Essays in sociology.* New York: Oxford University Press.

13 King, M. L. (1963). "I have a dream" speech, August 28, 1963. Retrieved from http://www.americanrhetoric.com/speeches/mlkihaveadream.htm.

14 Bass, B. M., & Avolio, B. J. (1993). Transformational leadership: A response to critics. In Chemers, M. M., & Ayman, R. (eds.), *Leadership theory and research* (Chapter 3, pp. 49–80). San Diego, CA: Academic Press.

15 Hollander, E. P. (1993). Legitimacy, power and influence: A perspective on relational features of leadership. In Chemers, M. M., & Ayman, R. (eds.). *Leadership theory and research* (Chapter 2, pp. 29–48). San Diego, CA: Academic Press.

16 Freud, S. (1921). Group psychology and the analysis of the ego. In J. Strachey (ed.) *The standard edition of the complete works of Sigmund Freud, V. 28. Beyond the pleasure principle, group psychology, and other works.* London: Hogarth Press, Pp. 65–143. P. 81.

17 Foote, S. (1958). *The Civil War: A narrative, Fort Sumter to Perryville.* New York: Random House, p. 802.

18 Foote, S. (1958). *The Civil War: A narrative, Fort Sumter to Perryville.* New York: Random House, p. 803.

19 Lincoln, A. (1861). First inaugural address, March 4, 1861. Lincoln, A. Annual message to Congress, December 1, 1862. Lincoln, A. Second inaugural address, March 4, 1865. All in D. Fehrenbacher (ed.), *Abraham Lincoln: Speeches and writings, 1859–1865.* New York: The Library of America. Pp. 224, 415, 687, respectively.

20 Emrich, C. G. (1990). Context effects in leadership perception. *Personality and Social Psychology Bulletin, 25,* 991–1006.

[21]Keegan, J. (1987). *The mask of command.* New York: Viking.

[22]Abelson, R. P. (1981). The psychological status of the script concept. *American Psychologist*, 36, 715–729.

[23]Campbell, J. (1949). *The hero with a thousand faces.* Bollingen Series 17. Princeton, NJ: Princeton University Press.

[24]For an introduction to Jung's work, see Hall, C. S., & Nordby, V. J. (1973). *A primer of Jungian psychology.* New York: Signet.

[25]Jung, C. J. (1969). *Collected works of C. G. Jung. Vol. 9 (Part 1): Archetypes and the collective unconscious.* Princeton, NJ: Princeton University Press, p. 48.

[26]Hall, C. S., & Nordby, V. J. (1973) *A primer of Jungian psychology.* New York: Signet, p. 42.

[27]del Toro, G., & Hogan, C. (2009). Why vampires never die. *The New York Times*, July 31, 2009.

[28]Freedman, D. G. (1971). Behavioral assessment in infancy. In G. B. A. Stoelinga, & J. J. Van Der Werff Ten Bosch (eds.), *Normal and abnormal development of brain and behavior.* Leiden, The Netherlands: Leiden University Press. Fantz, R. L. (1961). The origin of form perception. *Scientific American*, 204, 66–72. Fantz, R. L. (1963). Pattern vision in newborn infants. *Science*, 140, 296–297. Klinnert, M, Campos, J. J., Sorce, J., Emde, R. N., & Svedja, M. (1983). Emotions as behavior regulators: Social referencing in infancy. In R. Plutchik & H. Kellerman (eds.), *Emotions in early development, Vol. 2, The emotions.* New York: Academic Press.

[29]Melville, H. (1851). *Moby Dick.* Indianapolis: Bobbs-Merrill, 1964, pp. 23 and 25.

[30]C-SPAN. (2009). Historians' presidential leadership survey. Retrieved from http://www.c-span.org/PresidentialSurvey/Overall-Ranking.

[31]Rasmussen Reports (2007). Presidential favorables. Retrieved from http://www.rasmussenreports.com/public content/politics.favorables/presidential favorables.

[32]Simonton, D. K. (1987). *Why presidents succeed: A political psychology of leadership.* New Haven, CT: Yale University Press.

[33]Simonton, D. K. (1987). *Why presidents succeed: A political psychology of leadership.* New Haven, CT: Yale University Press, pp. 238–240.

[34]Abelson, R. P. (1968). Computers, polls, and public opinion—Some puzzles and paradoxes. *Transaction*, 5, September 1968, 20–27.

[35]Hovland, C. I. (1959). Reconciling conflicting results derived from experimental and survey studies of attitude change. *American Psychologist*, 14, 8–17.

[36]Dunning, D., & Sherman, D. A. (1997). *Journal of Personality and Social Psychology*, 73, 459–471.

Chapter 3: Redemption

[1]Morton, A. (1997). *Diana: Her true story, commemorative edition.* London: Simon & Schuster.

[2]Bradford, S. (2007). *Diana.* London: Penguin.

[3]Bradford, S. (2007). *Diana.* London: Penguin, p. 293.

[4]Chua-Eoan, H. (2007). The saddest fairy tale. *Time*, August 16, 2007.

[5]Greene, J. R. (2004). *Betty Ford: Candor and courage in the White House.* Lawrence, KS: University of Kansas Press.

[6]Ford, B. (1987). *Betty: A glad awakening.* Garden City, NY: Doubleday.

[7]Tucker, N. (2006). Betty Ford, again putting on a brave face. *The Washington Post,* December 29, 2006.

[8]Rafferty, K. (2008). *Harvard beats Yale 29-29.* A film by Kevin Rafferty. Kevin Rafferty Productions.

[9]Schenk, N. (2008). *Gran Torino.* Film by Warner Brothers. Directed by Clint Eastwood. Screenplay by Nick Schenk. Quotes from International Movie Database (retrieved from http://www.imdb.com), Memorable quotes from Gran Torino.

[10]Gardner, W. L., Avolio, B. J., Luthans, F., May, D. R., & Walumbwa, F. O. (2005) "Can you see the real me?" A self-based model of authentic leader and follower development. *The Leadership Quarterly,* 16, 343–372.

[11]McClelland, D. C., Atkinson, J. W., Clark, R. A., & Lowell, E. L. (1953) *The achievement motive.* New York: Appleton-Century-Crofts. McClelland, D. C. (1971). *Motivational trends in society.* Morristown, NJ: General Learning Press.

[12]Maslow, A. H. (1970). *Motivation and personality.* New York: Harper.

[13]Erikson, E. (1968). *Identity: Youth and crisis.* New York: Norton, p. 123.

[14]Brown, R. (1965). *Social psychology.* New York: Free Press.

[15]Higgins, E. T. (1987). Self-discrepancy: A theory relating self and affect. *Psychological Review,* 94, 319–340. Higgins, E. T. (1998). Promotion and prevention: Regulatory focus as a motivational principle. In M. P. Zanna (ed.), *Advances in Experimental Social Psychology,* 30, 1–46. Higgins, E. T., Kruglanski, A. W., & Pierro, A. (2003). Regulatory mode: Locomotion and assessment as distinct orientations. In M. P. Zanna (ed.), *Advances in Experimental Social Psychology, Volume* 35, 293–344.

[16]McCullough, D. (1977). *The path between the seas: The creation of the Panama Canal, 1870–1914.* New York: Simon & Schuster, p. 469.

[17]Barber, J. D. (1992). *The presidential character: Predicting performance in the White House.* Englewood Cliffs, NJ: Prentice Hall.

[18]Smith, J. E. (2007). *FDR..* New York: Random House. Brands, H. W. *Traitor to his class: The privileged life and radical presidency of Franklin Delano Roosevelt.* New York: Doubleday.

[19]Canellos, P. S. (ed.) (2009). *Last lion: The fall and rise of Ted Kennedy.* New York: Simon & Schuster.

[20]Kennedy, E. M. (2009). *True compass: A memoir.* New York: Twelve.

[21]Lincoln, A. (1864). Letter to Albert G. Hodges, April 4, 1864. In Fehrenbacher, D. E. (ed.), *Abraham Lincoln: Speeches and writings, 1859–1865.* New York: The Library of America, p. 586.

[22]Lincoln, A. (1861). First inaugural address, March 4, 1861. In Fehrenbacher, D. E. (ed.), *Abraham Lincoln: Speeches and writings, 1859–1865.* New York: The Library of America, 215–224.

[23]Lincoln, A. (1864). Letter to Orville H. Browning, September 22, 1861. In Fehrenbacher, D. E. (ed.), *Abraham Lincoln: Speeches and writings, 1859–1865.* New York: The Library of America, 268–270.

[24]Lincoln, A. (1861). Remark attributed to Abraham Lincoln. Lincoln and Kentucky's secession crisis. Retrieved from http://www.kylincoln.org/lincoln/secession.htm

[25]Lincoln, A. (1864). Letter to Horace Greeley, August 22, 1862. In Fehrenbacher, D. E. (ed.), *Abraham Lincoln: Speeches and writings, 1859–1865.* New York: The Library of America, 357–358.

[26]Lincoln, A. (1864) Letter to Albert G. Hodges, April 4, 1864. In Fehrenbacher, D. E. (ed.), *Abraham Lincoln: Speeches and writings, 1859–1865.* New York: The Library of America, 585–586.

[27]Lincoln, A. (1863). Quoted in D. K. Goodwin (2005), *Team of rivals: The political genius of Abraham Lincoln.* New York: Simon & Schuster, p. 499.

[28]Lincoln, A. (1864). Letter to James C. Conkling, August 26, 1863. In Fehrenbacher, D. E. (ed.), *Abraham Lincoln: Speeches and writings, 1859–1865.* New York: The Library of America, 495–499.

[29]Thorndike, E. L. (1898). Animal intelligence: An experimental study of the associative processes in animals. *Psychological Review Monograph Supplement, 2* (4, Whole No. 8).

[30]For a thorough discussion of these issues, see Skinner, B. F. (1959) *Contingencies of reinforcement: A theoretical analysis.* New York: Appleton-Century-Crofts.

[31]Bandura, A. (1973). *Aggression: A social learning analysis.* Englewood Cliffs, NJ: Prentice-Hall.

[32]Bandura, A. (1977). *Social learning theory.* Englewood Cliffs, NJ: Prentice-Hall.

[33]Brown, R. (1965). *Social psychology.* New York: Free Press.

[34]Freud, S. Group psychology and the analysis of ego. In J. Strachey (ed.), *The standard edition of the complete works of Sigmund Freud, Volume* 28 (pp. 65–143). London: Hogarth Press. See also Erikson, E. (1968). *Identity: Youth and crisis.* New York: Norton.

[35]Kohlberg, L. (1969). Stage and sequence: The cognitive-developmental approach to socialization. In D. A. Goslin (ed.), *Handbook of socialization: Theory and research.* Boston: Houghton Mifflin, p. 379.

[36]Sorensen, T. C. (1988). *"Let the word go forth": The speeches, statements and writings of John F. Kennedy, 1947–1963.* pp. 192–197. New York: Delacorte.

[37]Krebs, D. L. (2008). Morality: An evolutionary account. *Perspectives on Psychological Science, 3,* 149–172.

[38]Baumeister, R. F., Vohs, K. D., & Tice, D. M. (2007). The strength model of self-control. *Current Directions in Psychological Science, 16,* 351–355.

Chapter 4: Obstacles

[1]For more information about the extraordinary life of Babe Zaharias, see Susan Cayleff's excellent book, *The Life and Legend of Babe Didrikson Zaharias,* published in 1996 by the University of Illinois Press.

[2]Johnson, W., & Williamson, N. (1977). *Whatta-Gal: The Babe Didrikson story.* Boston: Little, Brown, and Company.

[3]Barra, A. (1999). Hit or myth. Retrieved from http://www.villagevoice.com/1999-12-28/news/hit-or-myth/

[4]*Guinness Book of World Records* (1981). New York: Sterling Publishing Co., Inc. New York City.

[5]Washington, B. T. (1901). *Up from slavery: An autobiography.* New York: Doubleday.

[6]Barczewski, S. (2007). *Antarctic destiny: Scott, Shackleton and the changing face of heroism.* London: Hambledon Continuum.

[7]Kelley, H. H. (1973). The process of causal attribution. *American Psychologist, 28,* 107–128.

[8]Jones, E. E., & Berglas, S. (1978). Control of attributions about the self through self-handicapping strategies: The appeal of alcohol and the role of under achievement. *Personality and Social Psychology Bulletin, 4,* 200–206.

[9]For more information about the courageous life of Nick Vujicic, see http://www.youtube.com/watch?v=4LtCrlXdd2E and http://www.attitudeisaltitude.com/

[10]Youtube (2011). Life without limbs. Retrieved from http://www.youtube.com/watch?v=4LtCrlXdd2E

[11]The Daily Telegraph (2008). Double arm transplant man Karl Merk speaks out. Retrieved from http://www.dailytelegraph.com.au/news/world/double-arm-transplant-man-karl-merk-speaks-out/story-e6frevo0-1111117703259

[12]Youtube (2011). German doing well after double arm transplant. Retrieved from http://www.youtube.com/watch?v=GATCiaeuK0E&feature=fvw

[13]Wittman, V. (2009). Karl Merk's transplant. Retrieved from http://www.bild.de/BILD/ratgeber/gesund-fit/2009/07/23/bauer-karl-merk/transplantationen-ablauf-moeglichkeiten-operation.html

[14]Wubbels, L. (2001). *September 11, 2001: A time for heroes.* Destiny Image Publishers. Shippensburg, PA.

[15]Bush, G. W. (2001). Today our nation saw evil. Retrieved from http://www.cnbcfix.com/bush-speech-ovaloffice-911.html

[16]John 3:16, *New International Version Bible.* New York: Thomas Nelson Publishers. Nashville, TN.

[17]For some compelling examples, see http://attacked911.tripod.com/, http://www.our911tribute.com/, and http://www.worldtradetribute.com/yellow7/usa/.

[18]Asch, S. E. (1951). Effects of group pressure upon the modification and distortion of judgment. In H. Guetzkow (ed.), *Groups, leadership and men.* Pittsburgh, PA: Carnegie Press.

[19]CBS News (2008). Hit and run crime victim. Retrieved from http://cbs2.com/national/hit.and.run.2.745505.html

[20]Eyewitness News (2008). We no longer have a moral compass. Retrieved from http://www.wfsb.com/news/16497579/detail.html

[21]Darley, J. M., & Latané, B. (1968). Bystander intervention in emergencies: Diffusion of responsibility. *Journal of Personality and Social Psychology, 8,* 377–383.

[22]Milgram, S. (1974). *Obedience to authority: An experimental view.* New York: Harper and Row.

[23]Brenner, M. (1996). The man who knew too much. *Vanity Fair*. May 1996 issue.

[24]Alexander, P. (2002). *Man of the people: The life of John McCain*. Hoboken, NJ: John Wiley & Sons.

[25]Goethals, G. R. (2008). Imagining Ulysses S. Grant: Sifting through the shifting sands of conventional wisdom. *The Leadership Quarterly*, 19, 488–500.

[26]First Samuel 17, *New International Version Bible*. New York: Thomas Nelson Publishers. Nashville, TN.

[27]Kim, J., Allison, S. T., Eylon, D., Goethals, G., Markus, M., McGuire, H., & Hindle, S. (2008). Rooting for (and then abandoning) the underdog. *Journal of Applied Social Psychology*, 38, 2550–2573.

Chapter 5: Evil

[1]Shakespeare, W. (1599/1999). *Julius Caesar*. New York: Signet Classics.

[2]Bradley, A. C. (1904, 1974). *Shakespearean tragedy*. Basingstoke, England: Macmillan Press.

[3]Foakes, R. A. (1987). *Colderidge, Samuel Taylor lectures 1808–1819 on literature*. Princeton, NJ: Princeton University Press.

[4]Nietzsche, F. (1887). *On the genealogy of morals*. Translated into English by Ian Johnston of Malaspina University-College, Nanaimo, BC.

[5]Hobbes, T. (1651/1994). *Leviathan*. Cambridge, MA: Hackett Publishing.

[6]Milgram, S. (1974). *Obedience to authority: An experimental view*. New York: Harper and Row.

[7]Zimbardo, P. O. (1972). *Stanford prison experiment: A simulation study of the psychology of imprisonment*. Stanford, CA: Philip G. Zimbardo, Inc.

[8]Dalberg-Acton, J. E. E. (1949). *Essays on freedom and power*. Boston: The Beacon Press.

[9]Du Pre Jones. *The New York Times*, October 28, 1973.

[10]White, T. H. (1978). *In search of history: A personal adventure*. New York: Harper & Row.

[11]American Film Institute (2010). AFI's 100 years of heroes and villains. Retrieved from http://www.afi.com/tvevents/100years/handv.aspx

[12]Cashill, J. (2009). *Why George Tiller is on trial in Wichita*. WorldNetDaily, March 19.

[13]Apell, J. (2009). Letter to the editor. *Los Angeles Times*, March 22.

[14]Graham, J., Haidt, J., & Nosek, B. (2009). Liberals and conservatives use different sets of moral foundations. *Journal of Personality and Social Psychology*, 96, 1029–1046.

[15]Allison, S. T., Goethals, G. R., & Eylon, D. (2010). *Double standards in evaluations of underdogs and top dogs*. Unpublished manuscript. University of Richmond.

[16]Aronson, E., Willerman, B., and Floyd, J. (1966). The effect of a pratfall on increasing interpersonal attractiveness. *Psychonomic Science*, 4, 227–228.

[17]Pentler, A. (2006). Burger King helped me beat addiction. Retrieved from http://www.nydailynews.com/gossip/2008/06/09/2008-06-09_burger_king_helped_me_beat_addiction_rob.html

[18]Warner, R. (1963). *The confessions of St. Augustine*. New York: Penguin Books.

[19]Nicklaus, J. with Bowden, K. (2007). *Jack Nicklaus: My story*. New York: Simon & Schuster.

[20]*Discover* magazine's excellent article on Marc Hauser's work was authored by Josie Glausiusz in the May 2007 issue. Hauser's groundbreaking book *Moral minds: How nature designed our universal sense of right and wrong* was published in 2006 by Harper Collins/Ecco.

[21]Chomsky, N. (1959). On certain formal properties of grammars. *Information and Control*, 2, 137–167.

Chapter 6: Shaping

[1]Kelley, K. (2010). Oprah: A Biography. New York: Crown. Page 28.

[2]Additional information on the extraordinary life of Oprah Winfrey can be found in biographies written by Helen Garson, Ilene Cooper, Kitty Kelley, Katherine Krohn, Wil Mara, Robin Westin, Ken Lawrence, Merrell Noden, and others. Her Web site provides her official biography at http://www.oprah.com/pressroom/Oprah-Winfreys-Official-Biography.

[3]Associated Press (2009). Time to start missing Oprah. Retrieved from http://www.cbsnews.com/stories/2009/11/20/entertainment/main5726958.shtml

[4]Garthwaite, C., & Moore, T. (2009). The role of celebrity endorsements in politics: Oprah, Obama, and the 2008 Democratic primary. Retrieved from http://econweb.umd.edu/~garthwaite/celebrityendorsements_garthwaitemoore.pdf

[5]Lake, T. (2009). The way it should be. *Sports Illustrated*. June 29.

[6]Denenber, D., & Roscoe, L. (2005). Fifty American Heroes Every Kid Should Meet. New York: Lerner Publications. Page 35.

[7]Toyn, G. W. (2006). *The quiet hero: The untold medal of honor story of George E. Wahlen at the battle for Iwo Jima*. Clearfield, UT: American Legacy Media Publishers.

[8]Cialdini, R. B., Borden, R. J., Thorne, A., Walker, M., Freeman, S., & Sloan, L. (1976). Basking in reflected glory: Three (football) field studies. *Journal of Personality and Social Psychology*, 34, 366–375.

[9]Kuhn, T. S. (1962). *The structure of scientific revolutions*. Chicago: University of Chicago Press.

[10]Microsoft News Center (2011). Bill Gates. Retrieved from http://www.microsoft.com/presspass/exec/billg/bio.mspx

[11]Bryant, J. (1995). *Lucretia Mott: A guiding light, Women of Spirit series*. Grand Rapids, MU: Eerdmans.

[12]King, M. L. (1963). "I have a dream" speech, August 28, 1963. Retrieved from http://www.americanrhetoric.com/speeches/mlkihaveadream.htm

[13]Brown, P. H., & Broeske, P. H. (1998). *Down at the end of lonely street: The life and death of Elvis Presley*. New York: Signet Books.

[14]Elvis Presley history (2011). The history of Evlis. Retrieved from http://www.elvis-presley-biography.com/ElvisFacts-75ElvisFacts.htm

[15]Australia, E. (2011). Elvis meets the Beatles. Retrieved from http://www.elvis.com. au/presley/elvis_meets_the_beatles.shtml

[16]Brianwilson.com (2011). Musicians on Brian Wilson. Retrieved from http://www. brianwilson.com/brian/musicians.html

[17]Messick, D. M. (2005). On the psychological exchange between leaders and followers. In D. Messick and R. Kramer (Eds), *The psychology of leadership*. Mahwah, NJ: Lawrence Erlbaum Associates.

[18]Burns, J. M. (1978). *Leadership*. New York: Harper & Row.

[19]Simonton, D. K. (1994). *Greatness: Who makes history and why*. New York: Guilford Press.

[20]PBS.com (2000). Carnahan wins. Retrieved from http://www.pbs.org/newshour/ election2000/races/mo-senate.html

[21]Pollingreport.com (2009). Presidents and history. Retrieved from http://www. pollingreport.com/wh-hstry.htm

[22]Lines, P. (1999). Antigone's flaw. Retrieved from http://www.nhinet.org/lines.htm

[23]Duhaime.org (2011). Solon's laws. Retrieved from http://duhaime.org/LawMuseum/ LawArticle-306/530-BC--Solons-Laws-Greece.aspx

[24]Edinger, H. G. (2002). *Thucydide: Speeches of Pericles*. New York: Frederick Ungar Publisher.

[25]Representative Poetry Online (2011). Ichabod. Retrieved from http://rpo.library. utoronto.ca/poem/2298.html

[26]Allison, S. T., Eylon, D., Beggan, J. K., & Bachelder, J. (2009). The demise of leadership: Positivity and negativity in evaluations of dead leaders. *The Leadership Quarterly*, 20, 115–129.

[27]Knowles, E. (Editor, 2009). *Oxford dictionary of quotations*. Oxford, England: Oxford University Press.

[28]Gottlieb, A. (2000). *The dream of reason*. New York: W.W. Norton.

[29]DeSpelder, L. A., & Strickland, A. L. (1996). *The last dance: Encountering death and dying*. Mountainview, CA: Mayfield Publishing.

[30]Cormack, M. (2001). *Sacrificing the self: Perspectives on martyrdom and religion*. Oxford, England: Oxford University Press.

[31]Kastenbaum, R. (2004). *On our way: The final passage through life and death*. Berkeley: University of California Press.

[32]Cormack, M. (2001). *Sacrificing the self: Perspectives on martyrdom and religion*. Oxford, England: Oxford University Press.

[33]Associated Press. Like everyone else, Tiger's colleagues wait and wonder. *USA Today*, December 13, 2009.

[34]Eylon, D., & Allison, S. T. (2005). The frozen in time effect in evaluations of the dead. *Personality and Social Psychology Bulletin*, 31, 1708–1717.

[35]Mandela, N. (1995). *Long walk to freedom: The autobiography of Nelson Mandela*. Boston: Back Bay Books.

[36]Knowles, E. (Editor, 2009). *Oxford dictionary of quotations*. Oxford, England: Oxford University Press.

Conclusion

[1]Ali, M. (1975). *The greatest: My own story.* New York: Random House.

[2]Remnick, D. (1998). *King of the world: Muhammad Ali and the rise of an American hero.* New York: Random House.

[3]Gast, L., & Hackford, T. (1996). *When we were kings.* A David Sonenberg Production. Gramercy Films.

[4]General Mills. (1999). Wheaties cereal box.

[5]Eagly, A. H., & Carli, L. L. (2004). Women and men as leaders. In Antonakis, J., Cianciolo, A. T., & Sternberg, R.J., *The nature of leadership.*

[6]Freud, S. Group psychology and the analysis of ego. In J. Strachey (ed.), *The standard edition of the complete works of Sigmund Freud, Vol.* 28 (pp. 65–143). London: Hogarth Press.

[7]Lincoln, A. (1864) Letter to Albert G. Hodges, April 4, 1864. In Fehrenbacher, D. E. (ed.), *Abraham Lincoln: Speeches and writings,* 1859–1865. New York: The Library of America.

[8]Burns, J. M. (1978). *Leadership.* New York: Harper & Row.

Index

Printed in the USA/Agawam, MA
January 9, 2015

606006.044